Supper Club

KERSTIN RODGERS

MENU

Supper Club

KERSTIN RODGERS

To all the single parents,

you are superheroes!

Contents

Part One – The Notes

Part Two – The Recipes

Introduction

We think of the restaurant as an ancient institution but in fact it dates back only a couple of hundred years to the French Revolution. Chefs emerging from the households of a destroyed aristocratic class no longer had jobs. The very idea of a restaurant at this time was revolutionary: a place where anybody who had the money could pay to eat. Suddenly, traders were sitting cheek by jowl with aristos; housewives next to duchesses. They were being waited on, not by their own private staff but by *serveurs*, people who would serve anyone with the financial means.

That was the first revolution in eating out. 2009 was the year of the supper club. A new revolution.

L ondon is a newcomer to the supper-club scene, although in the 1930s an experimental dining club 'The Half Hundred', held in the modernist Isokon building in Hampstead, was attended by the artists and intellectuals of the day, such as Agatha Christie and Henry Moore.

In fact, the very idea of food being important to British culture is quite a recent phenomenon. Britain leads the world in protesting against GM foods and declining fish stocks, while also promoting vegetarianism, animal rights and the growing of your own vegetables. At the same time, Britain, especially London, is a powerhouse of youth and alternative culture. Underground restaurants were just waiting to happen...

Home restaurants have been popular in Latin America since the Cuban revolution, where *paladares* (Spanish for 'roof of the mouth' or 'palate') were set up in response to government restrictions and the American embargo.

The pioneers of this phenomenon in London were Horton Jupiter, musician and host of supper club The Secret Ingredient, and me, under my blogging pseudonym of MsMarmiteLover. We both sprang from an alternative sub-culture in London where people lived cheaply, ate at donation-only squat cafés and 'skipped' food from supermarket bins ('dumpster diving'), partly in response to sheer poverty, but also as a protest against consumer waste.

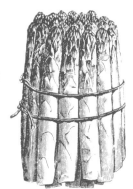

In January 2009, Horton opened his living room to strangers. Two weeks later I did the same thing. Now a new home restaurant or pop-up is starting every week in London, and is gradually rippling out to the rest of Britain. I get daily e-mails from all over the country, asking me advice on how to set up a home restaurant. In this book I set out a 'how to', a manual.

When I started The Underground Restaurant in January 2009, I announced it on my blog and was shocked when a hidden readership emerged out of the digital woodwork and left comments, asking if they could attend the first dinner. Things continued from there. It was difficult to handle the onslaught of interest from the world's media at the same time as working out how to run a restaurant in my living room.

I called my living-room diner 'The Underground Restaurant', which has become a generic name for this type of restaurant. It's not really a restaurant, more a table d'hôte with a fixed menu. It's not literally 'underground' either (I have been asked this!), but conceptually, in the 60s counter-culture sense. The legality of supper clubs is not yet clear and the risks will be explored later in this book (see pages 68–9).

MY FOOD

I try to avoid classic restaurant dishes. I'll make things that restaurants don't have the time or business model to make, like Stargazy Pie (see pages 198–9) or a Croquembouche. Another difference from the average restaurant: I don't cook or eat meat, I'm a pescatarian. Things like paté, liver, kidneys, faggots and gristle in my favourite spaghetti sauce always revolted me. I feel uncomfortable with eating animals. I have to suspend my imagination even to eat fish, but I do like the taste. I'm not a proselytising vegetarian, I've had relationships with meat-eaters, snogged them and everything. But you won't find any meat recipes from me in this book. Fear not, there are guest meat recipes from other supper clubs.

As the chef/patronne of my supper club, I don't feel obliged to serve meat. I can cook whatever I feel like. I often make themed meals based on the season, the date (eg Feast of the Assumption), popular culture (film night, Elvis, Patrick O'Brian) a type of food, (umami night) or a nationality (Arabian night).

At first, I charged very little and made a loss; I could not continue like that. I now charge a price comparable with a restaurant, but at least you know you are getting everything, the whole experience – from aperitif to coffee – included. It's not cheaper, but why should it be? To dine at The Underground Restaurant is a unique experience. I don't 'turn tables': you have a table for the night. It's economic because you can bring your own wine, and you come secure in the knowledge that you have paid for every aspect of the meal. In restaurants people often share a dessert or decide to save money by having coffee at home.

At a home restaurant, people have to come with realistic expectations; it's not a normal restaurant. For instance, I had an Italian family come for a brunch: one asked for a latte, the other an espresso. I laughed. I don't have a big expensive coffee machine. You eat what I give you. It's more like going to your mum's house (if your mum was stylish and an original cook).

If going to a supper club was initially a novelty, people are getting used to the fact that home restaurants now form part of the eating-out landscape. Culturally, home restaurants are a boon for tourists: you can eat in English homes and learn about the British in this way.

THE HOME RESTAURANT

There are different types of underground restaurant. The 'home restaurant' is, for me, the most interesting, intimate and authentic of the supper-club genre.

The notion of the home as a private space is quite recent, only since Victorian times. The home restaurant is blurring the lines between public, work and family space. You are welcoming complete strangers into your home. Your taste in décor, your books, your music taste, your crockery, your bathroom toiletries, even your underwear (if, like me, you sometimes forget to tidy it from the drying line) is open to inspection.

The home restaurant appeals to the foodie and the voyeur. It is as if the TV programme *Come Dine With Me* (in which strangers eat at someone's house and award them points) has mated with *Masterchef* (the TV cookery competition for amateur chefs hoping to become professional) and *Through the Keyhole* (in which the camera films inside a private home and a panel has to guess the celebrity to whom it belongs).

At a home restaurant, the food is usually cooked by a talented amateur or a wannabe professional. It can be a rehearsal for opening a commercial restaurant. In the case of Nuno Mendez, chef of former restaurant Bacchus, his home restaurant (supper club The Loft) was a way of testing out menus in preparation for opening his subsequent restaurant Viajante. His restaurant now open, Nuno retained The Loft as a showcase for talented young chefs.

For David Clasen, who has been running the supper club First Weekend since 2003, his home restaurant is 'a slow burn. I'm building up skills, menus and a clientele for the part-time restaurant I hope to open in a few years'.

Even pop stars' wives are getting in on the act: Ronnie Wood's ex-wife Jo Wood has opened up her mansion and gardens to the public for 'Mrs Paisley's Lashings'. Does Jo, who has cooked nutritional food for The Rolling Stones on tour, stand sweating behind the stove? No, she has hired in a pro, Arthur Potts Dawson, from Kings Cross restaurant Acorn House. The price is equally starry...£160 per person. Doubtless, guests are hoping to be sat next to diners like Mick Jagger, who happens to be Arthur Potts Dawson's uncle.

THE 'POP-UP' RESTAURANT

Occurring in unusual places – an abandoned shop, a boathouse, a garden or a hired location – it's 'pop-up' because it is temporary, either in terms of the space or the amount of time it will remain open. Frequently the chefs are professionals and the waiting staff experienced. Prices tend to be higher. But it is a great opportunity for young chefs without their own restaurants to showcase their food.

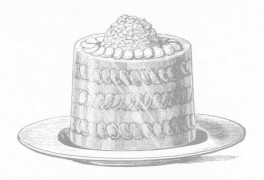

Another type of 'pop-up' is Latitudinal Cuisine, organised by architect Alex Haw. Nobody pays; it's based on participation. Every week a supper is held at a different house and the guests bring a dish based on the latitude or longitude announced in a lengthy e-mail essay by Alex. The week I went, this included an eclectic menu based on places ranging from Graz in Austria, the Congo and Svalbard, to Bari in Italy, Sweden and Libya (see page 238).

For Sam Bompas, of food event artists Bompas & Carr, a pop-up restaurant is an installation, a mix of art and food. He's held events experimenting with glow-in-the-dark jelly, the history of food, a breathable cocktail and a 'parliamentary' pop-up that served cocktails and food and held debates around the time of the election. Each event is innovative and researched. Sam obviously has his ear to the ground in the food world, as he attended my very first dinner, bringing along jellies for the guests.

Pop-up restaurants also include legitimate outdoor pop-ups in marquees, such as The Griffin, which opens to the public for six weeks every summer round the back of Grays Inn, London. This pop-up is more legal than most; its clients are usually barristers and judges.

VARIETY

There is a huge variety of styles of underground restaurant. Some operate weekly, some monthly, some just when they feel like it. The locations can vary from a council flat, a suburban semi, a bedsit, a château, a shed, a boat, a warehouse. Some underground restaurants can feed 50 people at a time; others are more intimate affairs of 6–10 people. I've even held private dinners for two in my garden shed!

The phenomenon is very site specific. Each underground restaurant is as individual as its host…and you have the freedom to fit it around your lifestyle. The style will depend on your space, even the amount of knives and forks you own…

David Clasen serves only 12 people because he happens to own just 12 place settings, three tables and a tiny kitchen. I have a large Victorian garden flat, so can fit up to 30 people at a time in my living room. When the weather is good, we can spill out into my garden and balcony. I host my evenings on a Saturday because my daughter is at school during the week and I felt it might be a little distracting for her to arrive home from school on a weekday faced with a horde of strangers in the living room.

Horton Jupiter can fit 10 people comfortably in his council-flat living room. Horton is in a band, 'They came from the stars, I saw them…' and therefore needs weekends off for gigs.

Artist Tony Hornecker's extraordinary studio space, a little crooked house in the back streets of the East End (soon host to the 2012 Olympics, let's really show the world how we entertain, eh?), displays his talents as a set designer. The food, although good, is almost secondary to the setting. He sits diners all over his house; couples can even book his bedroom!

WHY START A SUPPER CLUB?

D o you make money from a home restaurant? Not much. The home chef hasn't got access to trade discounts and suppliers because they order in only small amounts. Even so, as the banking system collapsed and parliamentary democracy trembled in the wake of financial scandal, were supper clubs a response to the recession?

Many of the home-restaurant chefs certainly started up because of financial necessity. I'm a single mother, raising a child on a low income. This is a way of starting my own business from my home. Working away from home is always an issue for parents, particularly mothers, so a home restaurant is a perfect entrepreneurial match.

But it has its problems too: the rest of your family must become accustomed to sharing their private space with strangers. There are sacrifices. These I will elaborate on later in the book.

Tony Hornecker, on why he started his home restaurant, The Pale Blue Door, in his studio, says that 'because of the recession, I wasn't getting any work. I was literally living on onions. Now at least I can pay my rent.'

While it is probably no coincidence that the ubiquity of supper clubs in Buenos Aires increased in the wake of their financial crisis in 2003, more important, I believe, than the 'recession story' is the opportunity to socialise. Most home restaurants are based in big cities, where, despite the crowds, it's hard to get to know other people. One of the things that surprised me at first was the social-networking aspect of my underground restaurant. As the weeks went on, I realised that larger mixed tables worked better than many small tables. Part of the attraction was meeting other people face to face, people that you may so far have 'met' only on the Internet. Even though you are with people you don't know, there is an instant connection, you are all strangers in a strange land, and there are common subjects – the food, the house, and the cook – to talk about.

It's also great for lone diners. Women in particular may feel uncomfortable going alone to a restaurant on a Saturday night. Large mixed tables remove the stigma, the embarrassment of dining alone publicly. You won't feel like a saddo!

The first home-restaurant marriage surely is not far away. (Although once, a couple who had got together six weeks previously at Horton Jupiter's restaurant split up while at my restaurant. As the hostess, I was left with the responsibility of making sure the abandoned, drunk and scantily dressed ex-girlfriend got home safely.)

I must admit, in the back of my mind, I thought I could meet someone through my supper club. The reality is that I'm too busy in the kitchen, perspiring the welcome cocktail, staggering around in heels and a smeared apron, and shouting at people, for this to have been a successful romantic venture.

In a sense, a home restaurant, which celebrates the oldest communal activity in the world – eating dinner together – has been made possible by the Internet, by new media. It's turning the virtual into the real.

I had been blogging about food for a couple of years before starting The Underground Restaurant. I mentioned in a post that it was about to open and was delighted that some readers immediately requested an invitation.

From the beginning, The Underground Restaurant has been open to complete strangers, people I have never met. Other supper clubs trod more warily, with a long period entertaining friends and acquaintances before opening up to the public. I remember Horton announcing, slightly nervously, on Facebook, two months after opening, 'This is the first evening that nobody I know will be coming!'

Some supper-club hosts vet their guests carefully. I had problems getting a reservation at one when I booked in my real name, sending at least ten e-mails without reply. When I booked under MsMarmiteLover, I immediately got a reply: 'You should have said who you were,' he announced, 'You would have got in straight away!' This supper-club host doesn't want lone diners who 'make everybody feel uncomfortable sitting there on their own,' or anybody that he considers would not 'fit in'. This host is as exclusive as I am inclusive. As I said, everybody has their own style.

Is all this a rejection of overpriced formal restaurants? I liken the home restaurant phenomenon to the punk revolution of 1976. At that time, young people had become frustrated with mega-rich pop stars escaping to America to become tax exiles, hanging out with Princess Margaret on the island of Mustique, and creating concept albums filled with meandering songs. (Pop is, after all, a grassroots movement in which talented people from humble beginnings can ascend the social ladder.) Young people wanted three-minute pop tunes and bands playing local venues for which they could afford tickets. Punk was born.

Most celebrated chefs today are media creatures, for the most part male, and rarely behind the stove of the restaurant that bears their name. Cooking professionally is hard work and long hours, for little pay. Bullying is rife

in the industry, both physical and psychological. Even the names, the rankings – chef de rang, chef de partie – have their roots in the army. The glory of cooking in a professional restaurant lies only in repeat bookings and murmurs of 'My compliments to the chef.'

Like dinosaur prog rockers from the 70s, 'sleb' chefs have sometimes turned their backs on the audience. Chefs can make more money from TV shows, cookbooks and endorsed cookware than from their restaurants. Like haute-couture fashion houses, the money is not in the clothes but in the merchandising, the perfume. Like women's magazines, the gloss and the perfect lifestyle of today's cookbooks can both inspire aspiration and depression.

For me, my Underground Restaurant is a chance to put into practice some of my political ideals: do-it-yourself culture, making good food available to everyone at a reasonable price, improving the image of vegetarian food. I am probably the only restaurant in the world that reserves cheaper seats for the unemployed, people on benefits, those who may not be able to afford to eat out.

Unlike France, Italy and Spain, there exists a culinary apartheid in Britain. Poorer people are confined to ethnic restaurants, fast food and chains when eating out. London is one of the most expensive cities in the world in which to eat out and most people simply can't afford to eat at good restaurants. Our food markets, while improving, do not offer the freshness, affordability and diversity of European street markets. A home restaurant in every neighbourhood could be a route to change, raising the status of home-cooked food.

Trust is also important. Many commercial restaurants simply cannot be trusted to provide cooked-from-scratch fresh food or meals for special diets. I cheffed in a 'vegetarian' café at festivals that served bacon sandwiches in the morning because they were such a money spinner. The bacon and the vegetarian food were regularly cut up on the same chopping boards, prepared with the same knife. But the fashion for food intolerances can drive the home chef up the wall, too.

Some customers like the idea of exclusivity. Food blogger Krista of Londonelicious describes the appeal for her:

'I went to Bacchus, but chef Nuno Mendez did not come to the table to personally describe each dish as he did at The Loft. This is way more special.'

This exclusivity comes at a price, though... £120 per head.

Other guests love the idea of illegality, the notion that they could get busted. It's not so much extreme sport, but the thrill of extreme dining. I have to admit, I do play up this aspect. Guests are asked to memorise a password before they can enter. I tell them that if we get raided by the police, start singing Happy Birthday! (In reality I've had policemen come as guests and they don't have a problem with it!) It evokes memories of the 1920s prohibition era, as does the Argentinean term for underground restaurants, *puertas cerradas* – 'closed door restaurants'.

A SUPPER CLUB IS A CHANCE TO CATAPULT YOURSELF INSTANTLY TO THE POSITION OF CHEF/PATRON:

...if you are too old or have too many family commitments to work your way through the ranks.

...if it is too late to go to catering college, to train via the accepted route.

...if you just want to cook part time, want a practice run before you open a mainstream restaurant.

...if you lack the finances to rent a premises, hire staff, enter into contracts with suppliers.

...if you have discovered, like me, rather late in the day, that this is where your heart lies.

Open an underground restaurant. I double-dare you...

THE STORY OF MSMARMITE LOVER

I've always cooked. I remember the first dish: I was at nursery school and we baked chocolate butterfly cakes. Even all these years later, I remember how incredibly pleased I was with myself. It seemed a magical process. The trick of removing the top of the cake and cutting it in half to make wings was unbelievably cool. I became obsessed with cakes for a while after that. I'd get up early before my parents awoke and get busy cake-mixing. One day I decided to go a step further and turn the oven on. At 6 a.m. my parents awoke to the smell of burning plastic – I'd decided to bake my cake in a red plastic bowl. My mum came downstairs and opened her brand new oven; the red plastic

was dripping through the bars of the rack. 'You can't heat up plastic!' she cried. And for a while, that was the end of my baking career.

At the age of eight I was given a copy of *Good Housekeeping's Children's Cookbook,* which gave step-by-step instructions in black-and-white photographs of how to make a cup of tea or toast a slice of bread. Many of the instructions started with 'First comb your hair...' From this I learnt how to make macaroni cheese, fudge, peppermint creams and coconut ice.

When I was 15, I got a Saturday job at WHSmith. A new series of magazines had come out: *Supercook*. As staff, I got a ten per cent discount. Every week, a copy of *Supercook* was set aside for me, illustrated with typically 70s food photography showing wood-varnished chickens and earthenware pots. The colour brown was big in the 70s. Three months into the subscription, I made a Sunday lunch for the family, from *Supercook* recipes. As the series was in alphabetic order – a letter a month – I'd only got up to 'C', which limited the menu to...Cabbage, Chestnut stuffing, Chicken, Chocolate mousse.

Eventually I got the sack from WHSmith. Not for my punky spiked green and blue hair (to match the uniform, I was pushing the brand!) but for lateness. This meant that my *Supercook* issues stopped at 'R'. I could not cook dishes starting with the letter 'S'.

This didn't deter me. I hosted a dinner party for a guy I thought fancied me. My menu was sophisticated: grilled grapefruit halves with glacé cherries, spaghetti bolognese (the only thing beginning with 'S' that I knew how to cook) and baked apples with custard. I had 12 guests, a ridiculously large amount for a 15-year-old. Grilling the grapefruits took forever and the main course didn't get served until 11 p.m., by which time I was exhausted and drunk. Then my friend Clare kissed the object of my affection, a cocky guy with a mullet, whose millionaire father owned a plastic-bag factory. Story of my life: I'm sweating in the kitchen, imagining that my beautiful food would

attract soul mates, while my friends are outside, wearing platforms, face glitter and flicked-up fringes, getting some action. What idiot came up with that phrase, 'The way to a man's heart is through his stomach'? It's so not true.

When I left school, however, I decided to become a photographer, not a cook. Becoming a chef didn't seem within the realm of possibilities. TV schedules were not full of cookery game shows as they are now. I loved the Galloping Gourmet and Fanny Cradock, but that was about it. My mum had a boxed set of Elizabeth David books, but there were no photos and I wouldn't cook something unless it had a photo

with it. She also had Robert Carrier cooking cards. These were in a cardboard box, like a file, and each one had a photograph of the dish.

My parents had sophisticated tastes in food. They had a house in France, a wrecked stone cottage with twelfth-century walls that were three-feet thick and a fireplace you could sit in. It was outside a small town named Condom, 100km south of Bordeaux in the Aquitaine region. Every school holiday it took us two days to drive there from

London. The route to Condom was devised around recommendations in a red, plastic-bound volume, *Le Guide des Relais Routiers de France*. It was our job as kids in the back seat to spot the Routier logo. Usually they were proper restaurants, cheap, with a set menu and a parking lot full of

lorries. Sometimes, however, you would go into a private house listed in the guide and eat in a woman's kitchen, just one table covered with a chequered oilcloth. The woman would be wearing her flowery apron and cooking in front of you, turning around from her gas stove to plonk platters down on the table. Once for hors d'oeuvres we were given a dish of long red radishes with their green tops still on, a basket of fresh baguette with a sourdough tang, a small hunk of unsalted butter and a pile of salt. We all looked at it, including my parents, not quite knowing what we were supposed to do with this array of ingredients. The son of the woman, noticing our hesitation, laughed and showed us what to do: he cut a little cross in the end of the radish, smeared on a scrape of butter, then dipped it in salt, crunching the radish with torn-off chunks of bread. So simple, just fresh produce, but so delicious.

Wine was always included and everybody, even children, had a little carafe of rough red table wine. This impressed us kids enormously, we felt so grown-up.

In those days I ate meat. My favourite meal, when we were allowed to order à la carte, was steak and chips. One night near Rouen, we stopped at a hotel-restaurant. We kids, as usual, ordered steak frites. There were strange mutterings from the proprietor; there seemed to be a problem. But then no, it was fine, steak frites it was.

When the steak arrived, I bit into it.

'What do you think?' asked my dad.

'It's yummy. Sort of sweet.'

'But you like it?' he asked, in a rare display of interest in my opinion.

'Yeah, it's great,' I enthused.

 At the end of the meal my dad told us that it was horse meat.

So I've been brought up to eat well, to eat adventurously. My parents loved to travel even before they had kids; my dad, in an attempt to woo my mum, suggested that they go on a cheap tour of Europe. They hitched everywhere. Their budget was the equivalent of 50p a day. When they arrived in Cologne, my mum perused the menu at a restaurant and chose the cheapest thing. The menu being in German, she had no idea what she would be getting.

The waiter, with a silver-domed platter held high, weaved his way through the crowded restaurant. He placed the heavy silver dish on their table and, with a dramatic flourish, lifted off the lid. There, squatting angrily on the platter, an apple between its teeth, was an entire pig's head. That was what my mother had ordered.

She gasped.

'I'm not eating that!' she exclaimed.

The whole restaurant, having followed the progress of the waiter, burst into laughter.

When things had calmed down, my dad whispered:

'Don't worry. I'll eat it.'

As he commenced tucking in, a smile playing around his lips, my mother breathed out heavily:

'I think you should know that I'm pregnant.'

It turns out that I was conceived in Minori, Italy, earlier in the trip. My dad, unperturbed, gestured with his fork towards the pig's head and said:

'I suppose we are going to have to marry you, then.'

So, as I was growing up, my family travelled through France, Italy and Spain every summer, stopping at Relais Routiers and family-run restaurants en route. Every winter we went skiing, eating fondue, raclette and drinking glühwein in Austria and Switzerland.

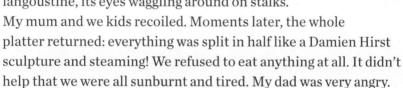

Once, my father insisted on taking us to a very expensive and reputable restaurant in Spain, near Malaga. We drove through winding mountain roads for hours to get there. My father ordered the best Rioja wine and taught us to savour its aroma from specially designed glasses. The speciality of the house was the seafood platter, which the waiter displayed in its raw state: it was dominated by a two-foot long sprawling langoustine, its eyes waggling around on stalks. My mum and we kids recoiled. Moments later, the whole platter returned: everything was split in half like a Damien Hirst sculpture and steaming! We refused to eat anything at all. It didn't help that we were all sunburnt and tired. My dad was very angry.

My father will eat anything. It's probably a reaction to war-time rationing. He'll suck the bone marrow out of bones...not just from his plate, from yours too. He was intolerant of any fussiness at the table; we were pushed to eat frog's legs and snails.

The snail incident was traumatic; we stayed in a farmhouse in France that belonged to family friends. The back room was dedicated to keeping snails, mostly kept in buckets; their digestive systems were 'cleaned' by being fed on bread for three days. Some of the snails escaped, they were everywhere, shiny trails on the chalky walls and stone floor. We went to a nearby restaurant that served snails stuffed with garlic, butter and parsley. My dad exhorted us to try.

'Go on, just one.'

We three kids spent the next couple of days in bed with terrible diarrhoea. Our bedroom was upstairs in this farmhouse, thankfully far from the snail room, but there was no inside toilet. We spent two days shitting in a communal bucket as we were too ill to make it to the outside toilet. I never tried snails again.

On this same trip, same farmhouse, my dad woke us early.

'We are going mushroom hunting,' he whispered.

Sleepy-eyed, we stepped out into the dark and walked what seemed like forever, down the poplar-lined French country roads to the forest. On this holiday, my dad read us a chapter every night, with all the voices, from *The Lord of the Rings*, by the huge fireplace. The forest, when we arrived, seemed to me to be populated by elves, trolls and hobbits. After hours of searching, dawn came, and all we had found were three orange chanterelle mushrooms and a few ceps. We carried them back to the farmhouse, where they were fried in butter and garlic. Nothing has tasted better since, although we found the texture of the ceps a little slimy. I still love to forage for mushrooms in the autumn.

In London, special occasions were marked with dinner at Robert Carrier's restaurant in Islington. I remember my first meal there: every course was tiny and perfectly arranged on the plate. Sights that are now common in haute cuisine, like French beans all lined up in a neat pile, exactly the same size, were objects of wonder back then. You felt you wouldn't get enough to eat, but of course you did.

One night my dad brought home an entire octopus. He laid out this huge tentacled creature, with its large body full of ink, on the kitchen table. We kids came down to stare at this monster. My dad was excited; my mum left the room, muttering, 'I'll leave you to it.'

In those days Google didn't exist. My mother's cookbooks didn't explain how to deal with octopus either. So my dad, a journalist, dealt with this crisis just as he would a story: call an expert, a good 'source', and ask them. He phoned Robert Carrier, whom he didn't know and who was at that time probably the most famous chef in Britain, at his restaurant. In the middle of service. Robert Carrier, a very helpful gentleman, came to the phone and patiently explained to my father how to remove the ink sac, prepare and cook this octopus. He followed the instructions, amazed, despite his habitual cheek (something I seem to have inherited) at getting this help.

Of course, none of us would touch it.

My background is part Italian, part Irish and entrepreneurial to the core. My great-grandmother Nanny Savino had a shop in her Holloway council flat. I loved visiting her; the hallways were lined with bottles of Tizer and R. White's lemonade, the bathtub with pickled pig's trotters, the kitchen provided toffee apples and apple fritters and, most excitingly, under her enormous cast-iron bed were rustling brown boxes with the illicit earthy smell of tobacco – Woodbines, Player's Weights cigarettes and matches. People would come to the door and ask to buy cheap fags from 'Mary'. Her real name was Assunta but no-one could pronounce it. She came to Britain at the age of 16, before the First World War, from the small town of Minori, south of Naples. During the Second World War, the Italians were our enemies and her radio was confiscated. She wasn't put in a camp, as several of her sons were in the British army. I never met my great-grandad,

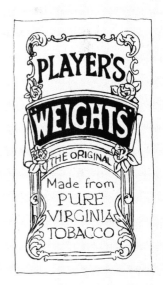

but from family stories he seems to have been a skinny man, under the iron fist of my enormous, rectangular, black-clad Nan. They started small businesses: a cart selling home-made ice-cream in the streets of Islington, then an Italian café. Even at the age of 80, infirm with arthritis, Nan was doing business from her house. It's the Neapolitan way; even today there are independent street-sellers in Naples.

One of my most memorable meals was when I was eight years old, and we drove to Minori to see the Italian side of the family, many of whom lived in caves (the front looked like an apartment but the back was a rocky cave). My father's godfather turned out to be the mayor of the village. He took us to a darkened restaurant, the best in the locality. The godfather wore a crisp white shirt, a tailored dark suit and gold glinted about his cuffs. The small finger on his right hand had a long, curly, yellowing nail. This was an Italian peasant's way of saying 'I don't have to work the land.' The waiters lined up as if it were a royal visit. Nobody kissed the godfather's ring, but that wouldn't have been out of place.

As we left, my brother piped up:

'Dad, I like this restaurant, we don't even have to pay!'

My parents hushed him. A few days later, we were invited to the godfather's house. We had to climb a small mountain of lemon groves; the lemons were half a foot long, with thick knobbly skins, so sweet you could eat them straight off the plant. I remember being so thirsty as we made our way up the dusty lemon grove. The crickets were deafening and the sun beat down. At the top we were welcomed by the widowed godfather's two 16-year-old daughters – twins I think – who had made us dinner. This time the godfather was wearing a white vest and blue work trousers. This dinner lasted for hours; they had pulled out all the stops: antipasti, pasta, a seafood course, a fish course, a red-meat course, a white-meat course, salads, vegetables, cheeses, puddings. It was the first time I had cannelloni, large stuffed rolls home-made by the young girls. It was a tremendous feat, this banquet, especially for such young cooks. We didn't speak Italian (they spoke in dialect) and they didn't speak English. After a few courses, we were struggling; my brother saved the day by groaning and clutching his stomach. At first the girls found this funny and offered him camomile tea but eventually his cries grew so loud and insistent that we had an excuse to leave.

Looking back, meals like this were the inspiration behind The Underground Restaurant, an attempt to recreate the languorous feasts of the continent. You see, the buzz for me, the shiver up my spine, the 'Oh wow, this is all worth it' moment, lies in these words: 'community', 'sharing', 'experimentation', 'dismantling boundaries'. My instrument is food, that which binds us all (sounds a bit *Lord of the Rings*, doesn't it?). We all need to eat. Many of us love to cook.

Feeding is how mothers show their love for their families. It's how countries and communities and religions and families can identify with each other. Meals are memories, milestones in our lives; the first date, the lover that proposed, the husband that did not return for dinner (in retrospect, the first signs of divorce), the tentative feeding of your baby, the family discussions and rows around the table as the children grow up. Sunday lunch, one of the few remaining meals requiring mandatory attendance for family members, is where you might bring a prospective mate to meet

the relatives. When I travel, new tastes and smells are intrinsic in recalling that country. Food divides us too: religions are distinguished via what they will not eat or drink.

My philosophy stems from a punk, do-it-yourself ethic. You don't need a degree in music to start a band, you don't need permission from the authorities or a catering-college diploma to start a restaurant. Some of the best chefs are self-taught: Raymond Blanc and Heston Blumenthal are two well-known examples. Sometimes, not having a formal education can help you think differently, laterally.

I had an unusual route into food. I did not go to catering college, I did not do a 'stage' at a top restaurant, I have not worked in 'normal' restaurants at all. Of course, I got the usual grounding that many receive from their mothers and grandmothers and from the societal expectation that being in possession of mammaries and ovaries should lead inevitably to being in charge of cooking dinner.

I've wondered, 'Why am I doing this?' Why am I sacrificing my social life (I never go out from Thursday to Sunday nowadays), my living room (life is lived in my bedroom, the living parts of the flat have shrunk to bedsit proportions), my mental health (my daughter says my personality totally changes every weekend; I turn into a stressed-out monster).

But then something like this happens...

One evening, from the kitchen, I heard a glass being clinked in the living room, then quiet. Somebody was speaking seemingly to the entire room. Agog, I sneaked out to have a look. A young woman was standing up, introducing herself and saying, 'It's such a nice atmosphere here and I'd like to know more about the other tables so, if you like, perhaps you could say who you are, what brought you here...'

There was a little silence, then one by one, people started to stand

up and say their names, where they came from, how they had heard about The Underground Restaurant.

This display of 'show and tell' was fantastic. It was also a little weird, like an intervention or a 12-step programme entitled 'Supper-club addicts anonymous'. People were participating, contributing and using the space and the occasion in an unusual way. There was a lot of love in the room.

I've cooked at anti-G8 camps, catering for 'barrios' of 250 activists using local ingredients and whatever 'The Anarchist Teapot' catering company got delivered. Our materials were dumpster-dived; once, needing an enormous spoon to stir a large pot, we used a cricket bat instead. I've cooked in Belgrade for the People's Global Action conference. Ever fed 450 hungry Serbian trade unionists, German punks and French philosophers? I have.

I cooked at a co-operative vegan cafe in Hackney, whose principles are as strong as their customers are random. It is in Crackney after all. I cooked weekly at the appropriately acronymed R.A.G., the Radical Anthropology Group, an evening class of anthropologists who mostly discuss the moon, Stonehenge, periods and Marxist sex strikes in hunter-gatherer societies. I've cooked at festivals, in fields, while the rest of the staff were high on E and K. I've cooked in squats, one of which was in a swimming pool, where I lived with my boyfriend in a changing room. I've cooked cans of soup on my car engine, on the way to camping. I pulled mussels from the freezing Antarctic sea, having backpacked to a national park in Tierra Del Fuego carrying white wine and garlic in my pockets to make moules marinières. I've dug clams at low tide on the Ile de Ré to make a campfire Spaghetti Vongole. I've cooked from a tiny cramped 'vis à vis' apartment in Paris, on a two-ring camping gaz stove, watching my neighbour's every movement, the routine of 'metro, boulot, dodo'(train/work/sleep). I cooked for the fortieth birthday of a man that had just dumped me. Heartbroken, humiliated, I made sure that there was a great spread, for him and his new girlfriend. Cooking is therapy.

In the last two years, since I started The Underground Restaurant, so many things have happened. I've had problems with trademarks, my freeholder, and Warner Brothers (the latter because I hosted a Harry Potter-themed dinner serving Butterbeer).

All along, I have encouraged others to start up their own supper clubs, via a social-networking site (http://supperclubfangroup.ning. com/) where supper-club hosts can publicise their meals, chat to each other about problems, successes and suppliers. I've also recently started up a bakery from my house. There is a dearth of bakeries in the UK; every high street should have a good organic baker. The idea to start selling bread from my house came, again, from Latin America, when I stayed with a Chilean family after randomly meeting them at a countryside bus stop when I was travelling there. One morning, the man of the house started to bake bread, and I watched as he put a notice in his window, 'Hay pan' (There is bread). Gradually neighbours dropped by and bought hot buns from him.

'I always make a larger batch when I bake, everybody does in the village, to sell to others,' he told me.

It makes sense: your oven is heated, it doesn't take much work to double or triple your recipe, plus you can earn a little money. In the old days in Britain, each street had a communal oven; people didn't necessarily have their own. I have an Aga, a large and expensive bit of kit, which produces beautiful bread. My first attempt was nerve-wracking but very successful, although the notice in my window didn't suffice – I had to go out on the street to collar passersby. I sold most of my bread, wrapped in brown paper, and met my neighbours. I'm assigning a regular day of the week to sell the bread now.

In 2010, I launched The Underground Farmers' & Craft Market in my home and garden, a huge success with 40 stalls and 200 punters. The idea was to promote small businesses and local, urban and home-cooked food. As well as stalls, there were live cooking demonstrations: I showed how to bake focaccia, a porridge expert who had won a prize at The Golden Spurtle Championship showed how to make the perfect porridge, and an urban cheese maker from Peckham demonstrated how to make South-London Halloumi (see page 156). We also had a cocktail bar on an ironing board and live music.

On another occasion, Marmite, manufacturers of my favourite spread, asked me to create recipes for Marmite cupcakes. They put my face on a jar of Marmite, a career highlight for me, the equivalent of winning a foodie Oscar! I was also asked to talk at the Women's Institute and the Real Food Festival.

One question at the Women's Institute did trip me up, however. A lady asked:

'Do you mind it when other people use your toilet?'

For some reason I replied:

'No. I'm not anal.'

I'm pretty sure this is the first time the word 'anal' has been used at a Women's Institute lecture.

And it's true, I don't mind when 200 strange bottoms use my loo. After all, I've been to India and Tibet.

A question people never ask: Why are you doing this?

Because I love to cook. Because I love to mother. Because I'm a feeder. Because I love to share. Because I like to be in control. Because I enjoy the potential for chaos. Because I'm lonely. Because I like to stir things up. Because I like causing trouble. Because I find it funny and it makes me laugh. Because I want to change things. Because it's now my job, it's my living. Because it makes me cook things I wouldn't be bothered to try for just me and my daughter. Because I don't have a big family. Because I love community. Because it's fun to come up with an idea and make it happen. Because, although I love words, I like action even better.

HOW TO
START YOUR
OWN
UNDERGROUND
RESTAURANT

If you are a keen cook, a foodie or a traveller, you will probably, at some point, have dreamed about opening your own restaurant or café. People put their life savings into setting up a restaurant, but the reality is that around a third of all restaurants close within the first year. The long hours and small profit margins are tougher than you could ever imagine.

On the other hand, you may never have wanted a professional restaurant but simply adore cooking.

Or perhaps you are sick of inviting people to dinner, always being the host, spending a small fortune and never being invited back?

This chapter is for all of you...

So before you spend your money on buying a lease, hiring staff and equipping a professional kitchen, why not rehearse by starting a supper club? The main qualities you will need are friendliness, trust in others, faith, hospitality and a certain amount of bravery.

First of all, just do it. Go on, play restaurants. Take the plunge. It may even cure you of any urge to open a restaurant. I'm not going to hide the fact that it is a lot of work, you won't make much money, you may even make a loss, but hell, it's great fun. And believe me, you will never again go to a conventional restaurant with the same attitude. Suddenly all will become apparent: the mistakes, the cover-ups, the pressure and the sheer bloody slog of making food for large amounts of strangers.

Starting a supper club requires different rules to opening a restaurant. As a new phenomenon, the parameters are changing all the time. I will give you the benefit both of my experience and of the expertise of other underground restaurateurs.

So here is the 12-step programme:

1 LETTING PEOPLE KNOW...............

Most guides on how to start your own restaurant focus on things like making sure your restaurant is in a good location and is obvious from the street, with effective 'signage'. You don't have that problem. The harder it is to find your supper club, the more obscure the location, the better. You will have no business from the street. Your clientele will come from word of mouth or word of mouse!

First of all, announce it. Tell your friends and family, and their friends and families. But you also want strangers, don't you? Otherwise it's just a dinner party with your mates. So you need to know how to pull in strangers. (Sounds like L'Auberge Rouge, a kind of hoteliers' Sweeney Todd, doesn't it?)

New media is your friend. Facebook, Twitter, blogging, Craigslist, Gumtree, Ning, these are all great methods for spreading the word. Start a Facebook group, set up a Twitter account, write a blog. By the time this book comes out there is bound to be some new fashionable social-media method, so find out what it is and use it. Age is no barrier to this: most of these media are user-friendly. Lynn Hill, who started the My Secret Tea Room near Leeds, is in her 60s and adept at making connections with new media.

But don't forget old media: once you've found your feet, let your local newspaper know. You could even put ads up in newsagents and shops. (Sheen supper club did this, got a few snooty remarks but soon filled up with locals.) If you have a particular theme – say, organic seasonal food – then put up a little notice in your nearest organic produce shop.

Get cards printed; I get mine from MOO.com via Flickr. Easy-to-design, small and attractive. Personal marketing: every time you go out, take your cards with you, hand them out, explain your new venture. You could also get brochures done. Flypost, as if for a gig. All this is basic marketing and PR. You want to fill your places. Bums on seats.

Choose a name that is emblematic of your living-room restaurant. Most supper clubs use words like hidden, secret, underground or midnight in their name. This gives an indication of the clandestine and guerilla nature of the operation. Sometimes they call it after the location, such as The Shed or Ahoy there! (on a boat), or the menu served, like The Bruncheon club.

Best not to call the press until you've set foot in the kitchen. Go for a soft opening and practise your mistakes in private. (As one of

the first, I did not have this advantage. The *Guardian* and several
food bloggers insisted on coming for the first night even though I had
explained that I probably wasn't ready. It really added to the pressure.
I had not foreseen the level of interest that my home restaurant would
trigger.) However, it has not been PR expertise that got me publicity
and renown: I've been making it all up as I go along, but I was excited
about it, and that enthusiasm conveys itself to others...

It's also a good idea to do some research. Go and visit other
supper clubs. Read up on them if you are too far away to visit.
Volunteer to help out for a night or two. I get e-mails all the time
asking to work. Lady Grey of the Hidden Tea Room in London
offered to take me to lunch to pick my brains. Feeding a cook is a
perfect method of extracting information. You will soon work out
what tricks and techniques you want to retain and which do not
suit you. When I started, there were no others to check out. Now
there are...so use them!

2 TAKING BOOKINGS...............

Once you have people booking, you will need to
work out a method for handling their enquiries.
Do be courteous and answer all their e-mails within,
say, a 24-hour period. If they have paid all or a
portion up-front, remember that they don't know you.
If you don't reply, they will get anxious, especially if you
haven't given them the address yet. I went to a supper club
in Brighton that didn't give me the address until the morning of the
dinner. Anything could have happened, my e-mail could have gone
down, I could have been staying the night elsewhere.

Another underground restaurateur didn't give the address, only literary clues. It turned out she had a blue plaque of a well-known poet on the wall of her house. You could do a treasure hunt of clues, but while a little mystery is quite a good thing, don't go over the top and exhaust your guests before they arrive!

So, bearing in mind that answering all these e-mails takes up a lot of time that you could be spending in the kitchen practising dishes, get yourself a system. Write a stock response, copy and paste it into each email. Have several replies ready:

1) I'm afraid we do not have space for that date blah blah but will put your name on a waiting list.

2) This is where to pay (bank details) or where to book tickets (web address).

3) Here is the address and time to come. How to get there, a map perhaps or transport directions. You may want to give them a phone number. But be wary of this unless you have someone to answer the phone for you. There's nothing more annoying than last-minute phone calls from people who think nothing of pestering you endlessly with questions and requests for step-by-step directions to your doorstep. I've actually lost friends at my own parties by snarling at them when they called wanting to discuss their love lives, what they should wear etc., just as you are trying to organise everything and get your own make-up on.

4) Any house rules or information you might want to give.

5) Menus. I change them every week and post it up on my blog or on my Facebook

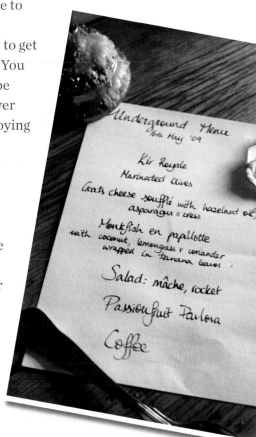

group. But they are subject to change; the lack of choice is part of the appeal. You will eat what Mummy tells you!

At the beginning I would have, say, a group of four people booking and each of them would e-mail me twice. That's eight e-mails for one group. Your head starts to explode and it can be a struggle to stay polite. Early on I had one guest who called me when I was in the bath. I tried to sound professional but he could hear the splashing. Eventually I confessed, 'Well, this is a home restaurant, it's not every day you get the chef taking reservations from his bath!'

If you have done a few dinners and want to continue, consider signing up with a ticket agency who will take the pressure off you and answer those e-mails. You will still get e-mails...from, say, people informing you of food allergies or birthdays, but not as many.

I forgot to give my address to one couple. My dinners start at 7.30 p.m. I was cooking all afternoon, but at 8 p.m. I just happened to check my e-mails. There were several desperate messages saying, 'We've booked babysitting and we don't know where you are! Please please call.' I felt terrible. They did get here in the end and were rightly given a free bottle of wine.

So a website handling all that is rather a good idea. Unless you've got a huge amount of elves working for you for free.

3 PAYMENT...

Are you going to allow people to pay on the night? In cash? I knocked that idea on the head after the first week.

I had sold 15 places, the last two places booked only that afternoon. I was turning other people away. The last two people did not turn up! They had got drunk and could not be bothered. A supper club has no walk-in traffic. You need everybody to attend and pay. Profit margins, especially at the beginning, are so tight that you will, as I did, make a loss.

I had already spent the money on ingredients and increased the amount that I was cooking. Straight away I realised I needed a system of prepayment, or I would be losing money every week. One week, Horton Jupiter had ten no-shows. You can't afford that. Nor do you want to live on the same leftovers for the rest of the week.

It's not only the money: empty tables and spaces look bad, especially if it's supposed to be a large mixed table and some people haven't turned up.

Now in the confirmation e-mail I say: 'Treat this like an invitation to a friend's dinner party. If you can't come, at least let the hostess know.'

So my advice is to at least take a deposit, if not to get them to pay the full amount beforehand. You can go two routes with this: they can pay directly into your bank account, in which case you are revealing your name and address. If you do not want to do that, they can pay via Paypal or a ticket seller. I started with Paypal, but I still had to respond to e-mails and their customer service is abroad.

Also, let's face it, it is a multi-national company, and part of the underground-restaurant movement's ethos is that you are sticking it to The Man. Why sign up with a globalised corporation? It's everything we are against.

I went with a British ticket seller: wegottickets.com. They charge ten per cent on top, to the customer not to you. There are other ticket sellers too, like brownpaper tickets, but I haven't tried them.

You have to remember that this is still a new thing

for many people. They can be quite nervous about coming and need reassurance. A ticket agency is, hopefully, reputable and gives the added guarantee that should something go wrong, the customers have a third party to complain to, get their money back from.

A good ticket agency will quickly deal with e-mails, bookings, and have English-speaking customer service. The only disadvantage is that, under British law, they will be the ones who have the mailing list, not you, and it's an opt-in list. You need to build your mailing list for future events, so I suggest that you get a visitors' book where people can write their comments, e-mail addresses and Twitter IDs. Or come to an arrangement with the ticket seller.

DECIDE YOUR PRICE...

Find out what local conventional restaurants are charging. That's a good guideline.

While many people expect to pay less at a home restaurant – after all, you are not paying business rates and rents – at the same time you are not getting the bulk discounts and trade prices that conventional restaurants benefit from. Also, if they don't sell a dish one night, they can sometimes sell it the next.

But remember that you are offering a unique experience that restaurants cannot offer. Don't undersell yourself. It's a tough balance.

Work out what you are comfortable with and stick to it. The rule is a third of your income should get used for expenditure on ingredients; a third on staff, laundry, equipment, utilities, bills, everything else; and the remaining third is profit. You probably won't make a profit at first. In your anxiety to please, you may overspend on ingredients, buy new furniture and all sorts of equipment.

Decide on your policy about free places. I don't give any free places except to my mother. My friends pay. The press pays. I can't afford to give away free seats. I run a tiny little operation.

You could give discounts to friends if you like, or people could volunteer to work in exchange for dinner. I save places at cheaper rates for the unemployed. I do this for a couple of reasons: I've been a single mother for many years, living on very little money. I have a great deal of understanding of what it feels like to be left out of something because you simply can't afford it. Plus I'm political, idealistic. I want the world to be a better place. That may sound mawkish but it's true.

4 LOCATION...............

As I said before, you have an advantage over a conventional restaurant. It doesn't really matter where you are located. People are, in effect, 'invited guests' and you are not depending on footfall in the vicinity. In some ways, just like at the peak of the rave culture, the more obscure the location, the more exciting it is for the guests.

Are you going to have it in your home or a pop-up location? It's easier logistically to have it at home, especially if the pop-up location doesn't have a kitchen. You don't have to transport all the cooking utensils, plates, silverware and ingredients to the new place.

There are plenty of locations to host pop-up restaurants: ask for the use of a café that is open only at lunchtimes and would be happy to get a little rent for the evenings, or one that is normally closed at weekends. Do a deal with a pub, ask to use their function room while they provide the drink. This would avoid licensing problems. Other ideas for locations: an art gallery, a squat, a loft, a boat, a factory, a garden or allotment if the weather is good.

Personally I prefer it in the home. Part of the excitement is the voyeurism of going into someone's private space. I love looking at people's houses.

It's true however that this takes a certain amount of bravery; where you live, how you live, your cooking, perhaps even your family life, is exposed to public view and possibly public criticism. But, people are aware of that and are always – so far, in any case – very polite. To your face at least. Who knows what they say on the car ride home? But they don't expect restaurant-level cooking and a spotless, luxury location. The kind of people who book will be adventurous, curious and flexible. They just want something authentic and some proper home cooking.

So, banishing any insecurities, think about your space, where you live, where people are going to eat. Play to its strengths…do you have a big balcony or garden? Have the drinks on the balcony, or use it for barbecue cooking. Is there something quirky or unusual about the design of your place? Do you have a large or particularly nice kitchen? Make sure you invite people to have a look.

Where are people going to eat? The likelihood is that your living room is the largest room. I had to move first one, then the other sofa into my bedroom, then the TV, then everything else. My bedroom, formerly a luxury boudoir, designed to ensnare men, now looks like a junkshop.

The look: part of the charm of a supper club is your personal style...whatever it may be. I lived for six years in Paris and one year in Provence (a cliché, but true) and I've been collecting vintage crockery and French kitchenalia for years, so that is part of my style, shabby chic Francophilia.

You may prefer a more modern and clean look. A friend of mine, originally from Zimbabwe, has only wooden crockery and bowls, much of it African. Her flat is like going into a little forest, full of birds' nests and chunks of tree trunk.

If you haven't got much money, you might go to Ikea, or your local second-hand and charity shops. Freecycle and eBay are also options for free/cheap furniture and crockery. I've been to squats where you drink out of jam jars rather than glasses, it was fun!

It's about vaunting your style...you may love heavy, hand-made pottery, slate platters, silver cloches or Toby Jugs. Even if you have no style or very bad taste, that too can be part of the experience. If you are in a large city and there are several supper clubs, you will find that people will do the circuit, come around to see you all, and they want each one to be different.

The individuality of the place and the table settings is part of the appeal. The quirkiness, the individuality, the absence of corporate tableware, all this is key to the success of a home restaurant.

There are some supper clubs that imitate restaurants. You book a table for two, you don't talk to other tables. You have imitation restaurant food. The portions are tiny, nouvelle-cuisine restaurant stylee. You aren't invited into the kitchen and all signs of slovenly family life have been tucked away. The service is formal, even obsequious. The china matches, and has been bought especially for the occasion.

I don't get it. This is our chance to muck about with the format. Frankly, if I feel like serving a dozen starters and no pud, or vice versa, well why not? Let's play. Yes, one has to give some food, there has to be some kind of chef/dinner/guest equation, but let's push it around a little. 'Guests' can help out, come into the kitchen, get their own water. They keep their cutlery between courses, just like in France. 'Staff' can sit down and chat. The hierarchy is horizontal. It's anarchy, but in the true sense of the word: 'an' (Greek for 'without') 'archy' (a ruler). Not chaos.

Remember: you are not a proper restaurant; you don't have to pretend to be one. At first you will probably try to ape a restaurant – after all, this is the model that we know. But afterwards, as you gain confidence, tear up the rulebook!

Work out how many tables and chairs you have. Borrow from neighbours and relatives. (I went to one supper club that was allowed to borrow neighbour's chairs only until midnight! Like Cinderella we had to sit on the floor afterwards!) You could also buy some cheap fold-down ones, depending on the look you want. You can always paint them, add nice cushions. Chairs, crockery, glasses and cutlery do not have to match: mismatching is great if everything 'shouts' at the same volume.

If you don't have enough chairs, and the guests live nearby or have a car, let them bring their own. (Two girls once brought their own chairs to my place, then went out partying later, carrying them to a nightclub. They told me it was very handy for sitting down in the club later, not to mention a great conversation starter.) I have also used piano stools, drum stools, boxes, dressing-table stools.

The tables you buy, borrow or retrieve from the garden will guide whether you put your guests on small tables with separate parties or large mixed tables.

As for the bathroom, label it and signpost it so that people know where to go. Make sure it's clean. Always have enough loo paper. A clean towel to dry their hands is good. After several weeks during which I kept having to buy more ear buds, I realised they were being used by the guests! I think conventional restaurants are missing a trick by not providing them! You could really go to town and provide eau de cologne, hairspray and lipstick as they do in the bathrooms of New York nightclubs.

5 FOOD....................................

Obviously this is the most important element. The menu is at the heart of what you are creating.

WHAT ARE YOU GOING TO COOK?.......................

The first few times, I'd stick to the dishes you are most comfortable with cooking. You will be nervous enough, you don't want to cock up the cooking! Later on, you can let rip with the molecular experiments!

Leave enough time to prep, and for mistakes. In your anxious state, it's amazing how dishes you've cooked perfectly a hundred times can go wrong. If you do decide to experiment, practise it first. Also remember that a dish that works wonderfully for 2–6 people is very different when you are doing it for double or more than that amount of people.

The secret of good food is: spend less time cooking and more time shopping! Unusual and seasonal ingredients, even just to garnish, can add that extra flair. This is what I do, but how you do it is up to you.

~ Cocktail with olives, pretzels or nuts ~
~ Starter ~
~ Home-made bread ~
~ Main course ~
~ Salad ~
~ Cheeseboard ~
~ Dessert ~
~ Coffee ~
(sometimes fresh mint tea, depending on the meal)

For £40 that's not bad value. The point is, you can afford the whole experience. In conventional restaurants, a lot of mental arithmetic is involved, trying to figure out if you should share a starter, miss out pudding, have coffee at home. Those little bits really add up and that is how normal restaurants make their money, with the drink, the desserts and the coffees...in short, the extras. It can make dining a frustrating experience. Even when restaurants do fixed menus, frequently there are 'supplements' that are added on, generally for the dish you really want.

Other times I have done tapas or meze, up to 12 small courses.

SUPPLIERS AND INGREDIENTS.....................................

So you've made a shopping list. But how much to buy? Another
difficulty. In a conventional restaurant, what you don't sell one
night, you can sell the next. For an occasional supper club
you have to get it right. Only experience can tell you that.

And where are you going to buy, say, 30 artichokes
for your starters? They cost a fortune in the supermarket.
Suppliers are the bane of most restaurants. Reliable
suppliers are the most important element of any
business. If you do have connections to professional chefs
or kitchens, ask them who their suppliers are...and whether
they mind adding on an order for you. You will get better deals
and normally they deliver to your doorstep. That's a huge relief when
prepping can take up so much time, and you don't want to be popping
out to the shops every 5 minutes.

My local organic vegetable box scheme guy came to a dinner. He
loved the concept and will now do me bulk prices. It does take a while
to build these relationships but they are invaluable. Repay favours in
kind, invite them to a dinner!

I do a mix of shopping between the local organic veg supplier and my local street markets. Going to a street market can be very inspirational when you are feeling a bit flat, a bit 'What the hell shall I cook this week?'

Use good ingredients. Don't skimp on quality. If your ingredients are good, you can't go too far wrong. One supper club I read about didn't cook anything. They just ordered great cheeses, hams, salamis, bread, salads, chutneys, smoked fish and set it out picnic-style.

If you or your friends have gardens or allotments, ask them to sell you their excess.

I do buy from large multi-national supermarkets sometimes. It's convenient and they deliver, saving time for you. But I try not to do so. I feel this whole 'movement' is about circumventing large-scale corporations.

PLAN YOUR MENU..

Decide what kind of food, how many courses. When you know how many people you have coming, multiply whatever recipe you are doing to make that number of servings. Make a little extra. Many home restaurants do serve seconds, just like your mum would. Better to have more than less.

Think about your equipment in the context of your menu. Remember you have only a domestic kitchen. Plan your menu around your oven/cooker/ fridge capacity. If you are doing three courses, have your menu balanced around hot and cold dishes. This relieves the pressure on your oven.

So think it through. Maybe you want to start with a soup that can be made on the hob, a main that can be baked in the oven and a cold pudding.

A soup can also be prepared in advance and set aside; the salad won't use up precious oven or hob space. Dessert can also be pre-prepped, made the day before.

Then prep. For your first meals, depending on how many people you have, give yourself two days. Make a 'countdown' of timings, what needs to be done first until last, and tick off tasks as you complete them. Obviously prep the stuff that stays less fresh last. Maybe part-cook some dishes and finish them off on the night.

Word of advice: don't do pasta, unless it is baked, for more than eight people. It's too hard to make it al dente for any more than that.

Yes, the food is important, but if they just want good food they can go to a conventional restaurant. What is essential is attention to detail, character, personality, intimacy, personal touches and...humour! You are really going to need that.

PORTION CONTROL............................

This can be really hard to work out.
Serve some dishes family-style. That is:
a big plate in the middle for people to share.
People love that, it encourages conversation.

Dishes that are plated-up obviously need to be more or less equal portions. I normally do this by eye, but you can also weigh them. Use one of those nifty digital scales on the counter and weigh each portion before putting it on a plate. This does slow things down but can be useful.

I always overestimate how much people want to eat. I have a morbid fear of people going home hungry, feeling ripped off. Once, a helper sent out very small portions of a starter. I took over and the rest of the starters were more generous. I didn't know how to handle the situation with the poor diners that only had tiny portions, I was too embarrassed to take the plates back and put more food on them.

Now I would go up to the diners and say that was a mistake, give me your plates back and I'll put on some more! An underground restaurant doesn't have to be a seamless operation. Mistakes are ok, they are even funny.

For plating up, you need a lot of counter space. If you haven't got much space, use an ironing board, which is a nice long stretch to add to your counter length (make sure it's steady), or even the floor if necessary. I've kept dishes needed for later covered on the floor in a corner.

Warm the plates if you can. I use an Aga and so I have the simmering oven for this, but you can also use the bottom of a conventional oven. This will keep the food warmer for longer, which is important if you have several tables. You don't want the last few tables to get cold food.

Another trick about plating up is to have the plates that are ready to go out nearest to the door. It's obvious I know, but it took me weeks to work that one out! In the panic, I often ended up doing it the wrong way around and the front-of-house would have to go around me to grab the plates.

SLOW FOOD..

I don't 'turn tables'. I believe in taking time over your food.
I like a restaurant where you feel you could stay all night if
you wanted. The table is yours for the night, as long as you
want (within reason, although I have had people stay the
night when they are too drunk to make their way home).

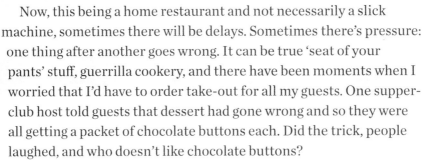

    Send food out with short intervals, say 20–30
minutes between courses. In a normal restaurant
it's usually 15 minutes between courses, but there
they want the table back. On the one hand you
don't want to rush people, on the other, you don't
want them sitting there twiddling their thumbs.
The front-of-house should be able to gauge and
tell the cook when people are ready for their next
course, when their plates are empty and they are
starting to get restless.

    Now, this being a home restaurant and not necessarily a slick
machine, sometimes there will be delays. Sometimes there's pressure:
one thing after another goes wrong. It can be true 'seat of your
pants' stuff, guerrilla cookery, and there have been moments when I
worried that I'd have to order take-out for all my guests. One supper-
club host told guests that dessert had gone wrong and so they were
all getting a packet of chocolate buttons each. Did the trick, people
laughed, and who doesn't like chocolate buttons?

    If the delay becomes obvious, then 'fess up, go out there and say
'Sorry, waiting for the food to cook.' Most people are understanding.
If the delay is really bad, you could swap courses, serve something
that's ready, the salad, say. As a last resort you could get your
front-of-house to go around with a bottle of wine, fill their glasses.
Be open and humble about your mistakes, and all will be forgiven.

6 FRONT-OF-HOUSE............................

If you haven't got a partner in crime, then get help, ask for volunteers. Crazy it might sound, but people want to work for you for free! People love to join in and if you are a good cook, it's like a free cooking lesson for your volunteer. It is also more companionable to have someone to bounce your ideas/mistakes off!

Typical conversation:

'Not quite sure about this sauce/bread/dish. Think I'll get away with it?'

Volunteer tastes.

'Yeah. I like it. Maybe cut off the crack/funny colour/burnt bit, or cover with cream/bit of parsley/sauce.'

I also tell my 'staff', 'Don't take any shit from the guests. Be nice of course, but you are not a servant, you are not at their beck and call.'

In a home restaurant, the customer is not always right: I am.

Don't have too many people in the kitchen. It confuses matters, takes up space, and can sometimes turn into a backstage party. Which might sound fun, but the focus is the diners, their enjoyment of the evening. In my experience, four people, including me, is enough: two for front-of-house and an assistant in the kitchen is perfect.

In an emergency, if your front-of-house can't cope, is ill, or doesn't turn up, get a guest from each table to come and serve their own table. This has happened to me. The guests really didn't mind; in fact, they enjoyed it. So don't be afraid to get the customers to pitch in. This informality, communality, is part of what distinguishes a home restaurant from a conventional restaurant. If they need water and you are too busy, let them get it themselves.

7 DRINK..

My advice is to give your guests a free drink when they enter. It breaks the ice if you have guests that don't know each other. People are a little shy on arrival. It often takes a couple of drinks before you start hearing laughter. Generally by the main course, the room is buzzing. People have forgotten that they are in a stranger's house.

A drink will relax them, encourage them to socialise, ease them into the experience.

But you, however, cannot drink. Oh maybe just one. NO MORE. Take it from me: you don't want to be half-cut as you try organising a meal for upwards of ten people. You need to be alert, on the ball, and watching all your timings like a hawk. A slip up, too long a chat with a guest, and your mains are burnt. You can start drinking once the main course is out.

Now to the sticky subject of licensing laws: out of all the possibly illegal things you are doing with a home restaurant, the most illegal is the booze. You are supposed to have a personal licence and a premises licence. I've got a personal licence. I haven't got a premises licence. It's practically impossible to get a premises licence for a residence. So you are stuck.

This is what I've been told by a licensing officer: you can give drink away for free but you can't include it in the price of the meal. You can't sell it. If caught, you can go to prison for six months or be fined £20,000.

BYO (bring your own) is legal. You could charge a corkage fee. After all, it's you that has to provide glasses and wash them, replace them when they break, and all that work and expense adds up. However, guests often don't bring enough drink and you don't want them coming and going to buy more. That would piss off your neighbours and create more work for you, endlessly answering the door bell. So emphasise that guests should bring enough drink, and have the address of a local off-licence.

At first, I sold wine via lottery ticket. This turned out to be illegal, as you need permission from your local council to hold a raffle. I've also linked up with a small wine supplier. People pay online for the wine beforehand, with a small mark-up going to me, and it's delivered to The Underground Restaurant. That's what rules are for, finding a way around them!

Another pop-up restaurant, 'The Surreal Dinner Party', gave away a free bottle of wine in exchange for an artwork...not sure if that makes it any more legal but it was fun, especially as the guests did their own artwork and swapped.

It goes without saying that I wouldn't serve a minor, nor would I continue to serve somebody that has clearly had far too much to drink. But it's risky. I may end up in prison.

Then I'll start a supper club in prison 'Goodfellas' style. Dress code: stripy pyjamas. Menu: porridge.

 ON THE NIGHT...........................

Have someone to welcome the guests. You can't be in two places at once. After guests have had their initial drink and have sat down, I do a little announcement or introduction at the beginning of the meal.

I'm naturally a backstage person, as are most chefs. Quickly I learnt, after a few weeks at The Underground Restaurant, that it was essential to make my presence known front-of-house. Now I do a talk at the start of every meal. It makes sense. People are in your home, they want to meet the host. Going to somebody's house to eat and never meeting the host/chef is as strange as getting in the back of a friend's car, while they drive alone up front, feeling like a taxi driver. So describe the meal, the inspiration behind it, maybe give some information about the ingredients and a few house rules. This seems to start off the little ceremony somehow. Gets the ball rolling.

MUSIC

The iPod, which doesn't require too much attention, is great for continual playlists. This is a task I outsource to my teenager. If it's a lunch, my teen makes a sunny '60s playlist; for dinner she uses instrumental, 'chillaxed' music. For themed nights she has created specialist playlists: Midnight Feast (see pages 262–73) had only songs with the word 'black' in the lyrics (which tended to be heavy metal!), for 'Night of the Senses' my teen actually composed a song on her laptop to represent the seascape. She also has playlists that are guided by the weather. It's probably best to have fairly mellow music without lyrics so that people can talk to each other. I've also had living-room concerts by up-and-coming artists in exchange for food and drink. Mostly I don't pay musicians, but I did hire an accordion player for Bastille Night to add to the French atmosphere of the evening.

TABLE SETTINGS...

Lay the tables. I always feel more relaxed once
the tables are laid. Choosing the flowers, candles,
tablecloths and napkins, vintage glasses and pretty
salt and pepper is one of my favourite parts.

Write or print out menus for the guests, perhaps
one per table, or write it on a blackboard (one pop-up restaurant used
their children's blackboard) or on a wall mirror with liquid chalk.

Chill the white wine or beer and soft drinks. If people want their
own wine chilled, I'm afraid I say no. I have only one teensy under-
the-counter domestic fridge. I have enough problems fitting in my
drink and food, I can't chill their stuff too. At times, I've had to resort
to asking neighbours if I can use their fridges. If you have the fridge
space, great, but if not, be tough.

Just as people arrive: light the candles, pour out the initial
cocktails, put on the music.

9 THE HOST...

One of the biggest assets of an Underground
chef is personality. It really helps to be willing to
share yourself. Be warm. Be funny. Be cheeky. Boss
them about. Sometimes the guests need chivvying along.
Remember, it's your house. As I said before, sometimes you,
as the host/ess, need to break the ice. Your guests are waiting
for a lead from you. If the vibe is a bit chilly at first, pop out
of the kitchen, make a joke. The atmosphere will change
in the blink of an eye. It's called hospitality for a reason.

So do go out and talk to people after the main course, when you can relax to a certain extent. If you are the chef, you can't do that while you are cooking. Guests like to feel special. People love that personal touch. How often do they get to talk to the chef in a normal restaurant?

If you are feeling generous, go around with some cognac or dessert wine. This is a good opportunity to find out who has come to your house for the night. The kind of guests you have will probably be very interesting. Boring people don't go to underground restaurants.

Part of being a host is expressing and sharing your interests with your guests. It might be great art or photography on your walls. As my training is a background in photography and travel, my living room has 40 large black-and-white photographs of my travels.

A tip: I'm sure you've had dinner parties where you've spent so long concentrating on the food that you end up opening the door to your guests in your dressing gown with no make-up and scraggy hair. So...get ready in the morning. I put on make-up, shower and wear something nice covered with an apron, so that if I run out of time, I still look ok. Then you can always just touch up your lipstick and spray on a bit of perfume to hide the cooking smells if you run out of time.

10 GUESTS..............................

My guests come from the internet, they are mostly strangers. Some hosts set rules, such as you must write in with a little biography, give some indication of what you are about, who you are. Other hosts allow only friends and friends of friends to attend. You can do what you feel comfortable with. I've never yet had a problem with any of my guests. It can be a little startling for them to sit at a table of strangers, but usually the food and drink and strangeness of being in someone's living room binds them together. As I've mentioned, I also do themes: quizzes, a Marmite menu, an umami menu, an Elvis night. This gives guests something to talk about.

It does help if guests 'get it' and are willing to throw themselves into the unconventional spirit of underground restaurants. It's difficult when they behave as if they are in a normal restaurant and expect staff to be at their beck and call.

One difficulty you need to be prepared for is guests and their 'allergies'. Allergies are on the rise and, frankly, are the bane of every cook's life, especially if, as in my case, you do a fixed menu. Of course, anybody in hospitality would want to cater for a genuine food allergy, but you'd be amazed at how many people 'upgrade' an aversion to a full-blown allergy in restaurants. Short of demanding that your guest has a blood test on the spot to determine a positive IgE antibody reading, the cook is in a helpless position to rebut these claims.

So have some rules or strategies. At first, I catered for everybody as long as they ordered in advance. If they turn up and halfway through the meal announce an allergy to, say, olive oil, you are a bit stuck. Yes, this has happened to me. So it's good to have a pack of tofu in the cupboard for those last-minute vegans.

Another problem: people who book online and then go through the whole meal before confessing that they wrote to you a week ago saying they were strictly vegetarian. For some reason they think you know what they look like, even though it's not like they send in a photo with their reservation. I've had this even when the front-of-house staff have asked every guest if they have a special diet. I would be lying if I didn't say this can cause minor moments of despair and rather a lot of swearing in the kitchen.

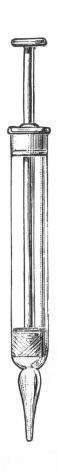

11 HEALTH AND SAFETY......................

If you want to continue doing this, invest in Food Hygiene training. You can do it online or you can go to a local college. It's a one-day course costing around £45 and it's invaluable, especially if you are cooking meat.

Get your kitchen checked out by your local environmental health officer.

You can also get public liability insurance for around £90 a year. Strictly speaking, your helpers should be insured too.

Get in a couple of fire extinguishers and a fire blanket. You can get them from Argos. Paper napkins or cloth? If you are using candles, do be aware of the fire risk of paper napkins: I have learnt from experience that they are not a great combination, especially if people are drinking.

A bit of admin too. Keep temperature records of your fridge. Keep all your receipts. If you do start to make money, you may have to pay taxes.

12 CLEARING UP AND NEXT TIME..........

It's good to get as much of the clearing up out of the way on the night, while your adrenaline is still pumping. Otherwise you will be amazed to find in two days time that your kitchen still looks like a bombsite, with flies hovering over the piles of washing up.

So you've successfully done one night. Still want to do it? Loved the buzz and not frightened by the stress and the work?

Get the laundry and ironing done early each week. I lay the tables as early as possible before the next dining event. But then I don't have a living room anymore. Sacrifices have been made to turn my home into a restaurant.

Every so often, if you are doing this regularly, do give your whole kitchen a thorough deep clean. Bleach floors, under cupboards, behind the fridge. Defrost the freezer. If you can, keep foodstuffs in storage above floor level. Most restaurant kitchens have mice. You don't want to be one of them. If you do get an infestation, call in pest control.

I must warn the potential supper-club host of one thing: it's highly probable you will get fat. All that tasting, all that cooking. I will also admit that I was always, shall we say, on the comely side, but two years of supper-club hosting will ruin anyone's figure.

But above all, enjoy it; the pros outweigh the cons. You get to pretend to be a restaurant at little financial risk. You get to improve your cooking. You will meet lots of interesting, exciting people, some of whom will become friends. You may even get a little attention from the press. But this is mainly about hospitality. You have to want to feed people and interact with them. Bon appetit!

Welcome to the Underground Restaurant!

Cooking Notes

I've organised the recipes in the order you'd get them if you were coming to dinner at The Underground Restaurant. Although I've also served teas and brunches, there wasn't enough room in the book for those recipes!

Here are a few more specific notes about the way I cook and useful advice for following my recipes.

A WORD ABOUT SALT

My advice throughout this book: 'check the seasoning' or 'salt to taste' means do actually taste. You can't cook well if you don't taste your food regularly. Salt and spices change intensity as they cook and seasoning is a skill in itself. So keep tasting, add a little salt if needs be. Go slowly. It's easier to add salt than to reduce it. However, I'm a great believer in good sea salt. All salt in my book is sea salt. The message should be: use good-quality salt rather than don't salt. Good salt has minerals in it that are healthy.

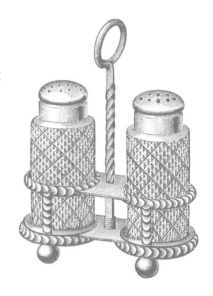

PEPPER

All the pepper mentioned in the recipes should be freshly ground. Unless specified, the type or colour of the pepper is up to you.

CHILLIES

Should chillies be seeded? Unless the recipe specifically says so, it's a matter of taste. And apparently it's actually the white pitch that is the hot bit, not the seed.

OLIVE OIL

When I say 'good-quality' olive oil, I don't necessarily mean extra-virgin olive oil. Not all extra-virgin is good.

CHEESE

Cheese isn't always vegetarian. Rennet, used in cheese production, is an animal product. However, most cheeses are available as a vegetarian version, so please always assume that is the type you need. Parmesan, Gorgonzola and Grana Padano, in order to be labelled under their names, have to be made by traditional methods and, as such, are always made using animal rennet. You can still get vegetarian versions of these, but they tend to have different labelling, such as 'Parmesan-style hard cheese'. Where these cheeses are used in my recipes, the recipe is labelled 'vegetarian if vegetarian cheese is used' to make sure you don't miss this.

AGA COOKING

An Aga is not just an oven, it's a whole relationship! It would take an entire book in itself to properly explain how to cook with an Aga, so I'm assuming that anyone who has one will have already got to know their own oven.

Most Agas have two separate ovens – a roasting oven and a simmering oven – but mine also has a third, a baking oven. Some even have a fourth, a 'warming' oven. An Aga is on all the time, so there's no need for preheating, and each oven only has one setting, one temperature. The different ovens generally have different levels of heat, as indicated below. Different people's ovens can vary, so you should test the temperature of your Aga with a thermometer and make a record of the readings to help guide your cooking. Another complicating factor, however, is that the Aga temperature drops the more you use it, so keep this in mind and adjust the cooking time to compensate.

Because I'm usually cooking for 30 people, I've had an Aga engineer whack up the heat to maximum and I turn my Aga up to full the day before a restaurant day. I also have to be careful to not cook everything on the restaurant day, as the oven would lose heat throughout the day and there wouldn't be enough heat left by the evening.

OVEN TEMPERATURES IN A FOUR-OVEN AGA

Roasting Oven
(Top-right on all models; this is the hottest oven and is good for grilling and browning, gratins, etc.)

Runners resting on oven bottom:	220°C (425°F),	Gas Mark 6
Runners second from top:	235°C (460°F),	Gas Mark 7
Runners at the very top:	240°C (475°F),	Gas Mark 8 or higher

Baking Oven

Runners resting on oven bottom:	180°C (350°F),	Gas Mark 4
Runners at top of oven:	200°C (400°F),	Gas Mark 5

Simmering Oven

Runners on bottom of oven:	120°C (240°F),	Gas Mark ¾

Warming Oven 60°C (130°F)

DEEP-FRYING

I tend to use an electric deep-fat fryer, as my Aga is not ideal for deep-fat frying for large amounts of people. If you don't have a fryer, you can use a deep heavy-based saucepan on a conventional hob. The easiest and safest way to lower food in and out of the hot oil is with a chip basket that fits inside the saucepan.

Make sure you have at least a couple of inches space above the oil as a safety margin. Deep-frying is something you have to do really carefully and be very alert about health and safety. Perhaps even lock kids in another room.

Never walk away from the fryer or pan. Don't let any water near it.

For deep-frying, the oil should be 190°C (375°F). A deep-fryer normally has a temperature setting, but in a saucepan you can use a thermometer or use the potato technique: cut a small wedge of potato and drop it into the pan as the oil warms. It will sit at the bottom of the pan until the oil reaches the perfect temperature, at which point it will rise to the top.

Make sure the food you deep-fry is dry, by patting it with kitchen paper. Then coat it in flour, breadcrumbs or batter. Don't put too much in the pan at once. The temperature will drop and the food will soak up more fat rather than sealing instantly.

Don't re-use the oil. Let it cool, then chuck it.

Cocktails
&
Nibbles

I always serve a free drink as people come through the door. Guests been through the rigours of public transport and they are probably thirsty. Plus it's an ice breaker, especially important in a supper club where guests do not necessarily know each other. My standard welcome cocktail consists of a Kir Royale, which is easy to make in the last ten minutes before guests arrive, and not too expensive especially if you use Cava or Prosecco rather than champagne. The bubbles give an instant lift to the evening. On other occasions, depending on the theme of the meal, I'll serve more complicated cocktails.

I'm a big fan of nibbles. One of the things I like best in pubs is the crisps that go with the beer. Some gastropubs do fancy nibbles like salted almonds and nice olives. I will often buy olives in brine, decant them into olive oil, and add lemon and garlic, leaving them to marinate for a few days. It is worth buying decent olives, however, such as Kalamata. I can't stand those tasteless slices of olive in tins. Giving people something savoury or salty to go with their drink means they drink more. Which means the atmosphere at your supper club will warm up quickly and you will avoid those initial awkward moments.

DAIQUIRI

My friend Angie, who sometimes helps out at The Underground Restaurant, makes a mean daiquiri. Getting it right is about measurements, shaking and straining, though I think most of it's in the shaking. She once hand-shook daiquiri cocktails for 42 guests; no bingo wings there! I must admit we indulged in a few after the guests had gone home, until I fell off the chair: a signal to go to bed. Here's Angie's recipe.

INGREDIENTS

Makes 1 gorgeous daiquiri

25ml (1fl oz) freshly squeezed lime juice

2 tsp caster sugar

50ml (1¾fl oz) Bacardi Superior white rum

Ice cubes and crushed ice

1 Put the lime juice and sugar in a cocktail shaker and stir so that the sugar dissolves.

2 Add the white rum and fill the shaker to the top with ice. (Ideally half the ice should be crushed and half should be ice cubes. If you don't have crushed ice, break up cubes into smaller pieces. It is really important to have smaller pieces of ice so that when you shake the cocktail some of the ice melts, chilling the drink and making it a little less potent.)

3 Shake! Shake with long, even movements, using both arms and your hips. As my mixologist teacher says, 'You need to shake from the hips with rhythm!!' It's best to hold the shaker with a tea towel – you want to shake until it gets so icy that the outside of the shaker is iced up. At that stage, unless you have a tea towel, you can't hold it anymore, as it is too cold.

4 Strain the drink from the shaker into a martini glass, leaving any bits in the strainer so that you end up with just lovely, clear, citrusy liquid.

5 Sip and enjoy the gorgeous sour, sweet, fresh, chilled goodness of a freshly shaken daiquiri.

KIR ROYALE

This is a blackcurrant champagne cocktail. You can vary it with other liqueurs, such as crème de mures (blackberry) or chestnut liqueur. I sometimes use violet liqueur for instance, which tastes a little like those Parma Violet sweets. Another glamorous variation is to put a hibiscus flower (which you can buy in syrup) at the bottom of the glass, along with a little of the syrup for flavour, and the flower opens out. You can also add other edible flowers (see page 106) or a few pomegranate seeds.

Makes 1

About 15ml (½fl oz) crème de cassis (blackcurrant liqueur)

125ml (4½fl oz) chilled champagne, Cava or Prosecco (Brut, not sweet)

1 Pour the crème de cassis into a champagne flute or your glass of choice – it should fill it about 1cm (½in), so add a little more if the glass is bigger. You don't need too much, or it will taste sickly, and do remember that crème de cassis is alcoholic.

2 Fill the rest of the glass with your fizz of choice.

BUTTERBEER

For my Harry Notter night (coughs, copyright) I made Butterbeer, which, as you will know, is featured in JK Rowling's Harry Potter books. It turns out this is actually a Tudor recipe. I've changed it from the original medieval recipe to funk it up a bit, making it stronger with my home-made butterscotch liqueur.

Serves 1–2

---

1 x 500ml bottle of Hobgoblin ale

Several cloves

5 whole allspice

60g (2oz) brown sugar

1 egg yolk

50g (1¾oz) unsalted butter

Swig of butterscotch schnapps (store-bought or see recipe below)

1 Pour the ale into a large saucepan with the spices and sugar. Stir over a medium heat until the sugar has dissolved.

2 Whisk the egg yolk in a separate bowl. Take the pan of ale off the heat and whisk the egg yolk into the mixture. Add the butter and stir until the surface becomes frothy, a bit like a 'top' on beer.

3 Lastly, add the butterscotch schnapps, being as generous as you wish, depending on the strength that you would like your Butterbeer. Mix together and serve straight away in a pint glass (or a couple of half-pints), as the Butterbeer is best drunk warm.

INGREDIENTS

Makes 700ml (24fl oz)

---

1 x 700ml bottle of cheap vodka

3 Dime bars or any butterscotch sweet, cut into slices

BUTTERSCOTCH SCHNAPPS

You can, of course, buy butterscotch schnapps but this is more fun!

1 Open the bottle of vodka and put your Dime bar slices into the bottle. Seal the top tightly with gaffer tape and place the bottle in the top drawer of your dishwasher. Turn on the dishwasher, without powder, for a couple of short cycles. When all the Dime bar slices have melted, your butterscotch schnapps is ready.

2 The schnapps will keep for up to 1 year stored in a bottle in your cupboard. Use as required, such as in the Butterbeer recipe, or perhaps smuggle a bit into your Horlicks!

POPCORN WITH LIME & CHIPOTLE SAUCE

Popcorn comes in more flavours than just salted or sweet. I first had this utterly moreish popcorn in Mexico. I must say I totally approve of a country that puts lime and chilli on almost all of its food, including popcorn. My main advice is to use fresh popcorn. Keep your kernels fresh in an airtight jar. If your popcorn is a little old, put the kernels in some water, then drain them again immediately. This will help to rehydrate your old corn. For a party, increase the amount to 500g (1lb 2oz) and the rest of the ingredients accordingly.

INGREDIENTS

Vegetarian
Serves 2

100g (3½oz)
fresh popcorn kernels
(fresher will pop better)

20g (¾oz) butter, melted

Juice of 1 lime

Sea salt

Splash of chipotle sauce
(bought or see recipe opposite)

1 Pop your corn in a large lidded saucepan, beginning on a high heat, then turning it down to medium as the pops get fewer, and removing the pan from the heat as soon as the popping stops –you don't want to burn the bottom. Shake the pan every so often but make sure the lid is on tightly.

2 Transfer the popcorn to a large bowl, add the melted butter and squeeze on the lime juice. Stir well and add salt to taste.

3 Finally, add some chipotle sauce to taste.

FLAVOUR VARIATIONS

Truffle oil and a little salt

Vanilla salt

Good-quality Hungarian paprika

Freshly grated Parmesan cheese
(use vegetarian Parmesan if necessary)

CRACK-COCAINE PADRÓN PEPPERS

I first had these at a Spanish restaurant called Dehesa in London. They are very mild chilli peppers, but once in a while you'll get a hot one, so it's a bit of a roulette. Don't worry, they are not as hot as normal chillies. You can order them from Spanish food importers or online. People describe them as being like crack cocaine, so addictive are they. There's a bit of a debate as to whether you grill or fry them. I tend to lightly fry them.

INGREDIENTS

Vegetarian
Serves 4

Olive oil, for frying
150g (5½oz) Padrón peppers
Good-quality sea salt
(such as Maldon)

1 Put a little olive oil in a frying pan over a high heat.

2 Throw in the Padrón peppers and cook until the skin is slightly blistered. Sprinkle on some sea salt and serve.

INGREDIENTS

Vegetarian
Makes 600ml (1 pint)

5–10 dried chipotle chillies, depending on how hot you want the sauce
450ml (16fl oz) boiling water
50ml (1¾fl oz) vegetable oil
1 brown or white onion, diced
2 cloves of garlic, crushed
500g (1lb 2oz) fresh tomatoes, placed briefly into boiling water and skinned
1 tbsp brown sugar
75ml (2½fl oz) cider vinegar
15g (½oz) salt
¼ tsp ground cinnamon

CHIPOTLE SAUCE

Although you can buy this, it's even better if you make it! Dried chipotles are available in most supermarkets. The best chipotle sauce I ever had was in Mexico. So good that I decanted it into a plastic water bottle and carried it home in my luggage. I eked it out for two years.

1 Soak the chipotles in the hot water for 30 minutes. Remove the seeds and stalks. Chop finely. Keep the water.

2 Fry the onion in the oil until soft, then add the chillies.

3 Add the rest of the ingredients, including the hot water. Simmer on a low heat for 30 minutes to 1 hour, depending on how concentrated you want your sauce.

4 Transfer to a food processor and purée.

5 Leave for a day and then recheck for seasoning.

BOMBAY MIX

INGREDIENTS

Vegetarian
Serves 10–20

Ghee or vegetable oil,
for cooking

3 tbsp each of red lentils,
Moong dahl, sunflower
seeds, almonds,
shelled pistachios,
cashews and peanuts

1 tbsp fennel seeds

2 small green chillies,
finely sliced

2 tbsp curry leaves,
dried or fresh

Handful of fresh
coriander leaves

2 tbsp desiccated coconut

100g (3½oz) green raisins
(often found in
Indian shops)

2 tbsp brown sugar
(palm or date sugar also
work well)

¼ tsp turmeric

Small pinch of citric acid,
to add sourness

Maldon sea salt, to taste

This is great with beer and as an appetiser for Indian food. Yes, I know you can buy it in the shops. But, like everything, it is so much better when you make it fresh. This is my version, which omits the doughy fried strands also known as seviya (little gram flour noodles, broken up). I tried to make them once, but it was too difficult without the correct Indian kitchen tool. (To get one, you can visit www.spicesofindia.co.uk/acatalog/Indian-Food-Sev-Maker-Sancha.html).

This recipe is a bit like the five-seed roast (see page 94) but with different spices and more fruit. It's got a lot of ingredients. If you can't find them all, adapt. The recipe requires patience with a frying pan but tastes so fresh that it's worth the effort. You'll need a fine mesh sieve – I use a fine chip basket.

1 Heat the ghee or vegetable oil in a frying pan on a medium–high heat.

2 Fry all of the ingredients on the list down to (and including) the coriander leaves, one type at a time, until golden. After each ingredient has been cooked, place on kitchen paper to absorb the oil and leave to cool.

3 Dry-roast the desiccated coconut in a frying pan without oil.

4 Once the fried ingredients have cooled, put everything in a bowl, add the rest of the ingredients and mix well.

5 The Bombay mix will keep for up to 1 week in a lidded container.

FIVE-SEED ROAST

I used to make this for my daughter because it was the only healthy snack she would consent to eat. Full of omega 3s and 6s, it is also good with drinks or sprinkled on salads and soups. Do feel free to change the proportions of seeds, so if you like pumpkin seeds best and hemp not at all, then add more pumpkins and skip the hemp (though you should still be aiming for 85g/3oz seeds in total).

INGREDIENTS

**Vegetarian
Serves 4**

25g (1oz) sunflower seeds

25g (1oz) pumpkin seeds

15g (½oz) sesame seeds

10g (⅓oz) linseeds

10g (⅓oz) hemp seeds

Couple of splashes Tamari or soy sauce

Couple of sheets of sushi seaweed (optional)

1 Put all the seeds, largest first, in a cast-iron or non-stick frying pan and dry-roast them with no oil over a medium heat. When all the seeds are lightly roasted and their natural oils begin to emerge, add the Tamari or soy sauce and mix well to coat the seeds before removing the pan from the heat. The sauce might seem to stick at first, but as it cools down it'll dry out again.

2 Transfer the seeds to a bowl and return the frying pan to the heat. Quickly roast the seaweed sheets in the dry frying pan – they're very thin and take just a few seconds to shrivel down – then crumble them into the bowl of seeds and mix in. Allow to cool before serving.

MARINATED OLIVES

This recipe uses bought olives, but if you are really swotty you can pick and cure your own. I have done this from my parents' olive tree in the south of France. It's not that difficult; just keep the olives in salted water and rinse every day, for 10 days, replacing the salt water. This removes the bitterness. Then pack into oil in a preserving jar as described in this recipe. For a variation, add herbs just before serving the olives.

Vegetarian
Serves 10–20

1 x 300g jar of Kalamata olives

1 x 300g jar of good-quality green olives in brine

Bottle of olive oil

1 lemon, cut into small sections

1 clove of garlic, peeled and finely chopped

1 Drain both jars of olives and transfer into a large, clean, wide-mouthed jar with a lid. Fill the jar with olive oil until the olives are covered. Add the lemon and garlic, screw on the lid and leave to marinate for up to 1 week.

2 Just before your guests arrive, spoon the marinated olives into little dishes. Have another dish on the side if the olives have stones (otherwise some people might put the stones from their mouths back into the olive dish, yuk!).

DUKKAH

This is a dry, nutty dip for sharing. It's usually served with a small bowl of olive oil and warmed pitta breads (to make your own, see page 99). You dip your bread into the oil, then into the Dukkah. Your bread then has an oily but cooling crust of nuts and herbs. Dukkah hasn't really caught on in Britain yet, but once it does, you'll be addicted. It originates from Arabian countries, where every family and shop makes their own version. Traditionally it is made with hazelnuts, but you can replace them with walnuts, almonds, cashews, pistachios or a mix, if you prefer.

INGREDIENTS

Vegetarian
Serves 4–6

100g (3½oz) hazelnuts

1 tsp coriander seeds

¼ tsp cumin seeds

2 tbsp Za'atar (a mix of thyme, marjoram, oregano and sesame seeds, available from Middle-Eastern stores)

2 tbsp dried mint

Sea salt, to taste

Pitta breads (see page 99) and olive oil, to serve

1 Dry-roast the hazelnuts, coriander and cumin seeds in separate batches in a frying pan over a medium–high heat.

2 Allow each batch to cool and then put them all together in a food processor or mortar and pestle.

3 Add the Za'atar and mint, then grind until it forms a crumbly mixture.

4 Salt to taste. Serve with a bowl of olive oil and some pitta bread.

BABA GANOUSH

Aubergines are probably my favourite vegetable. They are so adaptable: they can be puréed, fried, battered, roasted. Baba Ganoush is Arabic for 'food to spoil father with, like a child'. I love Arabic titles for food, they tell little stories in themselves. This dish is also known as the poor man's caviar. My version doesn't contain too much tahini, which I think can overwhelm the taste of the aubergine. Ideally you would roast the aubergines on a wood fire to get that smoky taste. You can also roast them inside an ordinary oven on a very high heat, over one of the gas rings of your hob on a low flame, or on a barbecue.

INGREDIENTS

Vegetarian
Serves 4

2 large or 8 small purple aubergines

50ml (1¾fl oz) olive oil

1 tbsp tahini

½ tsp ground cumin

1 garlic clove, peeled and crushed

Juice of 2 lemons, to taste

Handful of flat-leaf parsley

Sea salt, to taste

1 Roast the aubergines whole over a gas ring or in a very hot oven until the skin is black and loose and the interior is soft and scoopable. Peel off and discard the skin; put the flesh into a food processor. Pulse until puréed.

2 Add the rest of the ingredients and pulse again to mix. Transfer to a bowl, taste and adjust the seasoning to your liking. Serve with one or more of the optional toppings, if you like.

OPTIONAL TOPPINGS

Handful of pomegranate seeds

Drizzle of pomegranate molasses

Pinch of smoked paprika

Swirl of yoghurt

PITTA BREAD

Why make pitta bread when you can buy it so cheaply? Because the home-made stuff is sooo good. In fact, you and your family will eat it so quickly that you'll have a hard time saving it for the meal. My teen scoffed it straight out of the oven. You can make the pitta in advance and keep in an air-tight container or bag but, like all things baked, it's better warm and fresh. I serve it with dips or Dukkah (see page 97) and a dish of olive oil.

INGREDIENTS

Vegetarian
Makes 10

2 x 7g sachets fast-action
dried yeast

1 tsp white sugar

300ml (10½fl oz)
lukewarm water

450g (1lb) strong white flour
(though plain flour will do)

1 tbsp finely ground sea salt

1 tbsp olive oil

1 Mix together the yeast, sugar and lukewarm water in a jug or a bowl and allow to froth up. Put the flour, salt and oil in a large bowl and pour the frothy yeast mixture over the top. Mix everything together, and then knead the dough in the bowl for 10 minutes. Cover the bowl with a clean, damp tea towel or a plastic bag, and leave it to rise for 2 hours in a warm place.

2 After the 2 hours, uncover the dough. It will have risen up, so punch it back down and knead in the bowl for another minute. Then divide the dough into small round balls, each about the size of a satsuma. Cover the balls and leave to rest for 10 minutes in a warm place.

3 Preheat the oven to 260ºC (500ºF), Gas Mark 10, or its highest setting. If using an Aga, prepare the roasting oven.

4 With a rolling pin, roll the balls into flat circles or ovals. To do this, begin from the middle of the ball and roll away from you, then give the dough a quarter-turn and repeat. Keep doing this until you have a circular shape about 5mm (¼in) thick. This rolling technique works for all types of dough and pastry.

5 If you are making lots of pittas, then you will need to cook them in batches. While they're waiting to be cooked, the dough circles can be placed between squares of greaseproof paper and stacked.

6 Put the pitta dough circles on a lightly floured baking sheet, spaced 2–3cm (1in) apart, and cook for about 7–8 minutes. The circles will magically puff up, creating a pocket that you can slit open. Don't worry if a few of them don't puff up, they will still taste great.

FOCACCIA BREAD SHOTS

The French baker Richard Bertinet makes 'bread shots'. I've adapted his recipe to make it with focaccia dough instead. These are incredibly addictive. I make them quite small, with a little salty umami treat in the centre of each one. You can easily end up slinging quite a few of these in your mouth while drinking, I find.

Richard's kneading technique is quite different from the British approach. He makes a fairly wet dough and doesn't punch it down. In this way, you can achieve the airy quality of French bread. So don't worry if the dough looks too wobbly and wet, this will only make the final result very light.

Vegetarian

Makes about 15 bread shots

1 x 7g sachet fast-action dried yeast

1 tsp sugar (any type)

160ml (5½fl oz) lukewarm water

250g (9oz) strong white flour (with 12g of protein listed on packet)

10g (⅓oz) course semolina

5g (¼oz) sea salt

25ml (1fl oz) good-quality olive oil, plus 2 tbsp for greasing

Rosemary or coarse sea salt, for sprinkling

1 Mix together the yeast, sugar and water in a cup or jug and leave to froth up for 10 minutes in a warm place (like on the black enamel of an Aga or next to your preheated oven). I like to do this to make sure the yeast is live and kicking, rather than just mixing the yeast straight into the dough. Do make sure the water isn't too hot initially, though, or you will kill the yeast.

2 Mix together the flour, semolina, salt and olive oil in a bowl or in your food processor, then pour in the yeast mixture. Knead the dough in the bowl until it looks and feels elastic. (For more advice on kneading bread, see page 99.) Cover the bowl with cling film or a clean wet tea towel and leave to rise for 1 hour in a warm place.

3 One thing Richard emphasises is to treat your dough with care, gently. Tip your risen dough carefully onto a lightly floured work surface, trying not to tear it. Place a digital scale next to you and work quickly, cutting off pieces of dough of about 20g (¾oz), checking by placing them directly on the scale. A few grams more or less doesn't matter – you will eventually get your eye in and know how much to cut.

4 Take each piece of cut dough and tuck the sides/ends underneath to make a ball with a seam at the bottom. The seam is the weak part of the dough. Press your choice of topping into the top of the ball, in the centre.

5 Grease a roasting tin or deep baking tray (use one with deep sides to allow for rising) with olive oil, and place the dough balls onto it, making sure there is a gap of 2.5cm (1in) between each ball, as they will spread whilst cooking. Once your tray of balls is ready, cover with a clean wet tea towel or cling film and leave to rise for 30 minutes in a warm place.

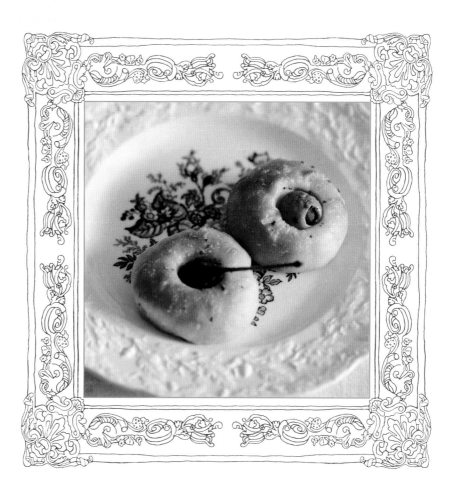

6 Preheat the oven to 220°C (425°F), Gas Mark 7. If using an Aga, prepare the roasting oven.

7 When the dough balls have risen, uncover them and press the toppings back down into the dough a little. Sprinkle with rosemary or coarse salt. Bake in the oven for 10 minutes or so, until golden. The focaccia shots are best served while still warm, though they will last for 1 day. I'm getting hungry just writing this!

OPTIONAL TOPPINGS

Sun-blush tomatoes, Stuffed green olives,
Black olives, Large caperberries,
Pickled garlic cloves

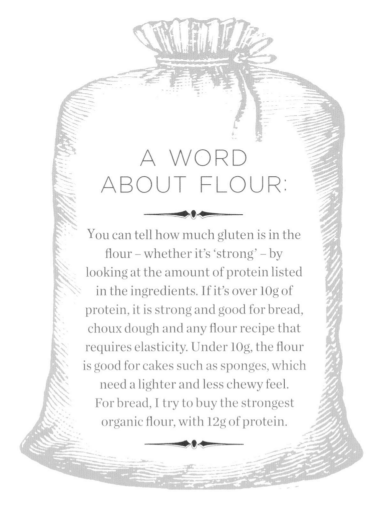

A WORD ABOUT FLOUR:

You can tell how much gluten is in the flour – whether it's 'strong' – by looking at the amount of protein listed in the ingredients. If it's over 10g of protein, it is strong and good for bread, choux dough and any flour recipe that requires elasticity. Under 10g, the flour is good for cakes such as sponges, which need a lighter and less chewy feel. For bread, I try to buy the strongest organic flour, with 12g of protein.

KNEADING BREAD FOR BEGINNERS

For a long time, I was a terrible baker. And the main reason was because I was too inexperienced/lazy to knead properly. So how do you know when you've kneaded enough? Here are two tricks:

1 The window test. If the kneaded dough can be stretched into a thin, translucent window 'pane' about 3cm (1¼in) square, then congratulations, you've passed the test.

2 Stick a thermometer into the dough. If it's sufficiently kneaded, the temperature should be about 32–35ºC (90–95ºF), and you're done.

3 After a while, you just sort of know when it's done. It's almost impossible to over-knead by hand, so give it more rather than less. It'll make your bread bouncier, airier. In an electric mixer, 10 minutes should be enough on the number 1 or 2 setting.

MARMITE ON TOAST WITH CRISPY SEAWEED

My parents once booked a 'dusk dinner cruise' on an Australian river. On arriving at the dock, they climbed into a rowing boat, thinking that this was the shuttle to the main boat. No, it was the dinner-cruise boat. There were only four guests; you couldn't have fitted anybody else in. For the aperitif, the skipper and his girlfriend served Vegemite sandwiches. My parents love Marmite (well, they did bring me up) and thought this was a wonderful canapé. They had a brilliant time, eating a simple menu while being rowed around the river, one of the highlights of their Australian trip.

When I did my Marmite-themed menu, I figured I just had to include Marmite on toast, something I eat every day. My mum told me she had recently eaten it with Chinese crispy seaweed on top, a surprisingly successful combination. Good for a party. It'll make people laugh too.

INGREDIENTS

**Vegetarian
Serves 4**

*4 slices of good-quality
sliced bread
(such as Vogel's linseed
and soya bread)*

*Good-quality butter
(I use Normandy
sea salt butter)*

Jar of Marmite or Vegemite

1 x 70g box of crispy seaweed

Freshly ground black pepper

1 Toast the bread and cut the slices on the diagonal into triangles. Butter the triangles and then spread sparingly with Marmite.

2 Sprinkle some crispy seaweed on top, grind on some black pepper and serve quickly, while still hot.

BLOODY MARMITEY

I made this cocktail for my themed Marmite menu, where every course contained some Marmite, including the welcome drink, the salad and the dessert! With a name like MsMarmiteLover, it was pretty inevitable. This adaptation of a Bloody Mary worked really well. Even Marmite-haters liked it. I have also on occasion added freshly grated horseradish root to a basic Bloody Mary. If you prefer not to use Marmite, add plenty of good sea salt instead.

Serves 1

25ml (1fl oz) vodka
1 generous tbsp Marmite
300ml (10½fl oz)
tomato juice
Squeeze of fresh lemon juice
Freshly ground black pepper
1 celery stick, to garnish
Ice cubes

1 Fill a tall glass with ice and pour in the vodka. Add all the other ingredients and mix well.

2 Decorate with a pretty stick of celery, which doubles up as a cocktail stirrer.

EDAMAME

These are Japanese pods that contain tasty beans; they are available at Japanese food stores and most health food stores. They are that rare combination of both tasty and healthy, and I serve them sprinkled with sea salt and crushed pink peppercorns. You can also serve them with a dipping sauce of Tamari/soy or Ponzu (a citrus soy sauce).

Vegetarian
Serves 4

150–200g (5½–7oz)
edamame pods

Maldon sea salt

1 tbsp pink peppercorns,
crushed

Tamari, soy sauce or Ponzu
(optional)

Simply place the pods in a bowl, sprinkle with the salt and crushed peppercorns and serve with a small dish of dipping sauce, if you like.

Nice Touches

Whether holding a dinner party or starting your own supper club, the small details make all the difference. Here are some of the tricks I use:

Pretty salt and pepper

Why stick to white salt and black pepper? There are so many kinds of salt, in different colours, including smoked salt, black Hawaiian salt, pink salt from the Himalayas, red salt, and sulphuric salt from India (a bit hardcore this one, but surprisingly good sprinkled on tropical fruit with a squeeze of lime).

As for pepper, I've used pink peppercorns, which have a unique taste, white Sichuan pepper, as well as the standard black pepper. Green pickled peppercorns are also a favourite garnish, fantastic in cheesy dishes. I'm a big fan of condiments in general, so I always put a few little dishes out on the table so that people can pick and choose.

Decorative butter

I will often put out flower or herb butter if I'm providing bread or a cake that needs butter. How much you make is up to you, depending on how many of you there are. It can also be stored in the fridge for a few weeks to use at a later date. You can mash it together with a fork or, even easier, mix in a food processor. I serve the butter in little mounds, but you can also roll it into a sausage, wrap in cling film, refrigerate and serve sliced. All of the flavoured butters that follow are also good on breads, to liven up a sandwich for instance.

Flower butter

Use any edible flower and mix with salted butter. Here's a list: violas, nasturtiums, rose petals, lavender, marigold petals, sweet rocket, borage and squash blossoms, as well as the flowers of herbs like chives, thyme, coriander, wild garlic and sage. These have a taste that is a milder version of the herb. With roses, don't use the bitter white heel of the petal.

Herb butter

Mix salted butter with the following:
- Dill, for salmon dishes
- Flat-leaf parsley and lemon, to make the classic Maître d'hôtel butter, great with steak, fish and scallops
- Wild garlic leaves, to use in pasta

OTHER FLAVOURS

Mix salted butter with:

Lemon zest, to serve with fish

Pink peppercorns, for a great addition to steak

Starters
&
Sides

I've called this chapter Starters and Sides because many of the dishes can be used as either. Influenced by meze and tapas, many restaurants are now serving 'small plates' to share rather than a big main course per person. I rather like eating that way, even though many restaurants use it as an excuse to give you a tiny amount of food for two-thirds of the price of a main course. With a supper club or at home, that's not a problem.

The chapter begins with baked dishes, which are good for supper clubs and dinner parties because you can assemble and even part-cook them in advance. I particularly love gratins. The name comes from the French *grater*, to scratch. You can pretty much cook anything gratin-style, baked in the oven with breadcrumbs or cheese sprinkled over the top. Gratins are a particularly good option for vegetarians: they won't feel deprived faced with a creamy bubbling dish. When I lived in Paris, nobody had any idea what to cook for me – the French are very dependent on meat. I'd suggest 'Why not a gratin?' and hear them sigh with relief. If you want your gratin really rich and sinful, cover your vegetable layer with double cream, but otherwise use vegetable stock. You can even use soya milk for vegans. I use seasonal vegetables, all of which are enhanced by slow cooking and the addition of cream. My salsify gratin (see page 115) uses a vegetable that is very popular in France, though you could replace the salsify with other fragrant vegetables such as Jerusalem artichokes or artichoke hearts.

There is also a selection of fried dishes in this chapter. For a supper club, fried food for any more than 5 or 6 people means there will be a delay. But I find people are willing to wait for food cooked in a vat of oil. Best to restrict yourself to one fried dish per supper, though.

BAKED JALAPEÑO POPPERS

I absolutely adore jalapeños, but it's so hard to get hold of them in this country.
You can use any mild large chilli instead for this recipe, as jalapeños are not very
hot. A 'popper' is a delicious stuffed pepper, eaten as a snack. Being baked, these
poppers are slightly healthier than those fried ones you get in the supermarket.
As an alternative to the sauce, you could serve the jalapeño poppers with
Tomatillo Salsa (see page 168), a lovely sour salsa of chopped soft tomatillos,
lime and salt, which cuts through the creaminess of the cheese.

INGREDIENTS

Vegetarian
Serves 4

400g (14oz) cream cheese
250g (9oz) Cheddar or
mozzarella cheese, grated
1 tsp garlic powder
¼ tsp ground cumin
½ tsp sea salt
½ tsp freshly ground pepper
12 jalapeño peppers
Butter or oil, for greasing

Sauce
200ml (7fl oz) soured cream
Splash of chipotle sauce
(see page 91) or
1 chipotle, chopped

1 Preheat the oven to 180°C (350°F), Gas Mark 4. If you use an Aga,
prepare the roasting oven.

2 Mix the cream cheese, grated cheese, garlic powder, cumin, salt and
pepper in a bowl. This mixture will act as the stuffing for the poppers.

3 Cut each jalapeño in half lengthways and remove the seeds. Fill each
half jalapeño with the stuffing mixture and place, stuffed-side upwards,
in a single layer in a lightly greased baking dish. Bake uncovered for 20–
30 minutes (or for 15–20 minutes in an Aga), until the cheese has melted.

4 To make the sauce, mix together the soured cream and the chipotle
sauce or chopped chipotle. Serve with the poppers.

THAI CORN FRITTERS
WITH SWEET AND SOUR CUCUMBER DIPPING SAUCE

INGREDIENTS

Vegetarian
if fish sauce is omitted
Makes 10–12 fritters
each about the size of
a flattened satsuma

*1 x 300g tin of sweetcorn,
drained, or
300g (10½oz) cooked fresh
sweetcorn kernels*

3 tbsp cornflour

3 tbsp plain flour

1 egg, lightly beaten

4 spring onions, finely sliced

*Handful of coriander leaves,
roughly chopped*

*1–2 kaffir lime leaves, snipped
up and stem discarded*

1 tsp sea salt

½ tsp freshly ground pepper

*20ml (¾fl oz) water,
if necessary, to bind*

*About 200ml (7fl oz)
groundnut or vegetable oil,
for frying*

Cucumber Dipping Sauce
*100ml (3½fl oz) white wine
or rice vinegar*

100g (3½oz) caster sugar

1½ tbsp water

*2 tsp Nam Pla fish sauce
(vegetarians can omit this,
but check the salt level)*

*⅓ cucumber,
peeled and very finely diced*

*1 carrot,
peeled and very finely diced*

*1–2 red bird's-eye chillies,
thinly sliced*

Who doesn't love these? I first came across them in Thailand, sold in packets of ten on the street. To serve as a starter for a supper club, you need to be organised. Have your mixture ready, then start frying at least 20 minutes before your guests are due to start eating. You could make them in advance and keep them warm or reheat them (in a frying pan or the microwave), but obviously freshly fried tastes best. The dipping sauce can be prepped and cooked in advance. It is so easy but very authentic tasting.

1 To make the dipping sauce, gently heat the vinegar, sugar and water in a small saucepan until the sugar has dissolved. Stir in the fish sauce, cucumber, carrot and chillies and simmer for 10 minutes. Allow to cool and pour into small saucers or ramekins. Set aside until needed.

2 In a bowl, mix the sweetcorn with the cornflour and plain flour. Add the beaten egg and season with salt and pepper. Add the spring onions, coriander and lime leaves and stir to bring the mixture together – if it's too dry, add a little water to help bind it.

3 Heat the oil in a frying pan over a medium heat. When the oil is hot, drop tablespoons of the mixture into the pan to make circular fritters. They don't have to be perfect circles, so don't stress! You will probably have to do this in a couple of batches.

4 Fry for a few minutes on each side, flattening slightly with a fish slice, until golden. Remove from the pan and drain on kitchen paper. Repeat with the rest of the mixture. These are best served immediately, or can be reheated when needed.

Serve with the cucumber dipping sauce.

VADAI WITH YOGHURT AND FLAKED JAGGERY

Vadai are Southern-Indian savoury fried dumplings, considered to be fast food. In North London, near Wembley, you can get plates of these very cheaply.

When I lived in Paris, I craved Indian food. The French are brilliant at French food, but when it comes to ethnic food, they often pretend it's a French meal, with a starter, main and dessert rather than an all-dig-in-at-the-same-time, shared-dishes approach. So on those days that I was homesick for a curry, I'd go to the Gare du Nord where, along the north-eastern side of the station, you find Rue du Faubourg St Denis, a haven of cheap and authentic Sri Lankan food, a cuisine very similar to that of Southern India.

This recipe is adapted from a beautiful cookery book called *Serendip*. For a supper club you can part-fry the vadai in advance and then put them back in the frying pan at the last minute to finish them off. I shave the jaggery with a sharp knife to make it into fine slithers, which juxtapose beautifully with the tangy yoghurt.

1 First make the sauce. Combine the yoghurt and flaked jaggery or palm sugar in a bowl and chill until required.

2 Drain the urad dahl and place in a bowl with all of the remaining ingredients except for the oil, coconut milk and onion. Mix until you have a thick paste. Add the diced onion. Then add, little by little, the coconut milk or water, until the point when it will be too difficult to make them into patties. Shape into ten balls, each about 5cm (2in) in diameter, flattening them into patties 1cm (½in) thick, and pressing your thumb through the centre to make a doughnut-like hole. Why the hole? It helps the vadai to cook more evenly throughout.

3 Heat the oil in a frying pan over a high heat. Fry the vadai until golden. Remove with a slotted spoon, let the oil drain, and serve hot with the chilled yoghurt and jaggery sauce.

BUTTERNUT SQUASH & FETA FILO TRIANGLES
EDGED WITH POPPY SEEDS

These tiny, flaky triangles can be served with drinks or as a starter. They are delicate and a little fiddly to make, but disappear very quickly once made.

Vegetarian
Serves 8–10

1 butternut squash, peeled, seeded and cut into 2.5cm (1in) cubes

50ml (1¾fl oz) olive oil

1 tsp sumac

2 star anise

Sea salt and freshly ground pepper

200g (7oz) feta cheese (or goat's cheese) cut into small pieces

Handful of chopped coriander leaves

1 x 270g packet of filo pastry

125g (4½oz) butter, plus extra for greasing

100g (3½oz) poppy seeds

Mint Dip
300g (10½oz) Greek yoghurt

2 tbsp dried mint

Juice of 1 lemon

Sea salt, to taste

1 Preheat the oven to 220°C (425°F), Gas Mark 7. If using an Aga, prepare the roasting oven.

2 Put the squash in a roasting tin, toss with the olive oil and scatter over the sumac, star anise, salt and pepper. Roast for 30 minutes in the oven until soft enough to push a fork through easily. (You will need the oven again later, but the next process takes some time, so you might like to turn it off for now.) Leave the squash until cool and then scatter with the feta and the chopped coriander.

3 Meanwhile, prepare a clean, damp tea towel and remove the filo pastry from its packet. You should work with just a small section at a time, leaving the rest under the damp towel to prevent it drying out and becoming flaky and impossible to work with. Cut the stack of filo pastry lengthways into thirds, so that each third is a long strip of about 5cm (2in) in width and made up of multiple layers. Take just a few of the layers from the top of one strip (keeping the layers together), and cover the rest of the pastry with the damp tea towel.

4 Melt the butter in a saucepan or the microwave. Use a pastry brush to brush butter all over the top of the filo strip. Put a teaspoon of the squash mixture onto one end of the strip, leaving the edges free. Fold the rest of the strip over on the diagonal, so that the mixture is encased in a triangle. Continue to fold the pastry round the triangle, working your way down the strip until you've given the triangle 2–3 folds of pastry on each side. Cut off the rest of the strip and press the edge down to seal the triangle. Repeat with another teaspoon of mixture on the remaining part of the strip. You will probably get two triangles out of each strip. Repeat with all the remaining pastry.

5 Preheat the oven to 200°C (400°F), Gas Mark 6. If using an Aga, prepare the roasting oven.

6 Put the poppy seeds on a plate. Brush the filo triangles all over with more melted butter and dip all the edges into the seeds so that they are speckled with the little black seeds.

7 Lay the triangles on a well-greased baking sheet, then bake in the oven for 20 minutes (or for 10 minutes in the Aga) until the pastry crisps up.

8 Meanwhile, mix together all the ingredients for the mint dip. When the triangles are ready, serve them hot with the mint dip.

GRATIN OF SALSIFY

Salsify is not a well-known ingredient in this country. It has a subtle, nutty taste and, when peeled, looks a little like asparagus.

**Vegetarian
Serves 4–6**

*Butter, for greasing
Juice of ½ lemon
1kg (2lb 3oz) salsify roots
600ml (1 pint) single cream
½ glass of white wine
Sea salt and freshly ground
white pepper
100g (3½oz) breadcrumbs
250g (9oz)
hard cheese, grated*

1 Preheat the oven to 180°C (350°F), Gas Mark 4. If using an Aga, prepare the roasting oven and position the bottom shelf.

2 Grease a shallow baking dish large enough to fit the salsify comfortably. Prepare a bowl of boiling water and squeeze in the lemon juice.

3 Peel the salsify roots and place into the bowl with the lemon water. This stops them from discolouring while you are preparing the rest of them. When all the roots are prepared, drain the lemon water and transfer the salsify into the baking dish, spreading them out neatly.

4 Pour in the cream and white wine and season with salt and pepper. Sprinkle the breadcrumbs and cheese all over the top.

5 Bake for 30 minutes in the oven until the top of the gratin is brown and bubbling.

DOLMAS

My mum's best friend Joy is a passionate cook. Although you could hardly meet anybody more English, she was married for a while to a Greek Cypriot – very unusual in the '60s – and lived as a housewife in Southgate, until the difference in their cultures became too difficult. One of the dishes she'd make, which seemed so exotic at that time, was dolmas, or dolmades (Greek for 'stuffed thing').

This is my version of Joy's recipe. If you have a vine, you can use fresh leaves, blanched briefly in boiling water. Otherwise, buy them in jars or tins, but remember to rinse the salt off them! If you don't have all the spices listed, don't worry. But don't try and use basmati rice. Says she who, having run out of the correct rice, once thought basmati would do. It didn't. The dolmas wouldn't stick together...!

These are perfect party food: easy to handle with your fingers but also nice served as part of a meze for mains or starters (though you might wish to halve the quantities if serving as a starter). This is also a dish you can prep in advance.

INGREDIENTS

Vegetarian
Serves 4 (Makes 24 dolmas)

Olive oil, for cooking
and drizzling

1 large onion or 3–4 shallots,
peeled and diced

2 cloves of garlic,
peeled and crushed

100g (3½oz) long-grain rice
(Not basmati! See intro)

150g (5½oz)
fresh mushrooms,
cleaned and chopped

1½ tsp ground cinnamon

1 tbsp dried dill

1 tbsp ground mace

½ tsp sumac

Sea salt

250ml (9fl oz) hot vegetable
stock, if needed

Juice of 1 lemon

2 tbsp raisins

2 tbsp pine nuts

2 tbsp pomegranate molasses

2 preserved lemons, diced

1 tbsp dried mint

Handful of chopped
flat-leaf parsley

1 x 680g jar (400g when
drained) of vine leaves, rinsed
(or up to 50 fresh vine leaves
if available)

Handful of chopped fresh
mint leaves (optional)

1 Heat the olive oil in a lidded saucepan over a low heat. Cook the onions until soft and translucent, then add the garlic and cook for a few minutes until also softened. Next add the rice and cook for 5 minutes. Add the mushrooms and cook for another 5 minutes, before finally adding all the spices and a tablespoon of salt. Remove from the heat, add the hot stock and stir once. Then cook gently, with the lid on the pan, for 15–20 minutes, stirring occasionally. The rice mixture is ready when small 'dimples' appear on the surface and most of the water has evaporated – the rice should still be slightly al dente.

2 Remove from the heat, add half of the lemon juice and adjust the seasoning. Mix well and leave the mixture to cool until you can handle it with bare hands. Then mix in the raisins, pine nuts, pomegranate molasses, preserved lemons, dried mint and parsley.

3 In the meantime, carefully extract your vine leaves from the jar (or take your fresh leaves) and put in a large bowl. Scald with boiling water and leave to soften for just 2 minutes (they will go hard if left for any longer), before refreshing in cold water. Drain in a colander.

4 Lay a vine leaf flat with the stem nearest you. Snip off the stem with scissors and put a teaspoon of the rice mixture at the base of the leaf, in the middle. Fold both sides in over the mixture and roll up the leaf from the bottom to the top to make a sausage-shaped roll. It should be moist enough to seal itself. Place the rolled leaves with the 'seal' facing down so that they don't unravel. Repeat with the remaining leaves and mixture. When you reach the small, fragile leaves at the bottom of the jar, use two overlapping, like a patchwork. At this point, the rolled vine leaves can be frozen for up to 2 months if you wish. Otherwise put in the fridge to chill until ready to serve.

5 Serve the dolmas cool, drizzled with olive oil and the juice from the other half of the lemon. Garnish with fresh chopped mint if you like.

TEMPURA

Vegetarian
if prawns are omitted
Serves 4
Enough batter for
about 16 items

_____

16 items to tempura
(your choice of vegetables
or prawns, see intro)

1 egg, beaten

140ml (5fl oz) fizzy
or soda water, iced

70g (2½oz) cornflour

70g (2½oz) rice flour
(or use plain flour if needs be)

¼ tsp sea salt

Pinch of ajinomoto
(optional; this adds
an umami flavour)

Ponzu, or soy sauce mixed
with wasabi, to serve

Equipment
Deep-fat fryer, or a deep
heavy-based saucepan
with a chip pan

I love tempura, a Japanese method of frying vegetables and seafood in a very light batter. It is wonderfully crisp and savoury. The traditional things to 'tempura' are prawns (cut the tendons underneath to make them straight, not bendy), finely sliced peppers, aubergines, carrots and sweet potatoes. I also make tempura avocado slices. Yes I know that sounds a bit '70s, like 'baked avocado', but it tastes great, the soft butteriness of the avocado flesh contrasted with the crispy batter. I also batter mild chilli peppers, and herbs such as basil, sage and shiso (a bitter Japanese leaf). With any leaves, you batter just one side and leave the other side green.

Tempura batter must be light. Ideally you should be able to see the vegetable or prawn through the batter. Don't worry about lumps. Lumps are good. Lumps are tasty! It also doesn't matter if the items stick together in the fryer – untangling the lacy tempura with your chopsticks is part of the fun. And I think the traditional dipping sauce that you get at Japanese restaurants is boring and a bit tasteless. A bit too subtly Zen for my liking. I prefer Ponzu juice (a citrusy soy sauce), or try adding some wasabi to your soy sauce to make it nicer.

1 Prepare your choice of vegetables and/or prawns.

2 Mix the beaten egg with the cold water, then sift in both types of flour, salt and ajinomoto (if using) and stir gently to make a batter. Be careful not to over-stir the batter, or the gluten won't activate. The icy water prevents the batter from absorbing too much oil when it is fried.

3 Heat the oil in a deep-fat fryer or a deep, heavy-based saucepan to 190ºC (375ºF). (For more advice on deep-frying, see page 83.) You can test for the correct temperature by dropping a little of the batter into the oil; if the oil is hot enough it should drop halfway to the bottom and then float back up.

4 Lightly dip each vegetable or prawn in the batter, then deep-fry until crisp and lightly golden. Drain on kitchen paper. Serve straight away with the dipping sauce.

KUSHI KATSU:

JAPANESE MOTORWAY CAFÉ SARNIE

I served Kushi Katsu (which is Japanese for 'deep-fried food on sticks') at a Japanese-themed evening, with Japanese mayonnaise and Tonkatsu sauce, the latter being the equivalent of English HP sauce. I told everybody I was giving them Japanese motorway cuisine! Emma Reynolds, who owns the Japanese restaurant Tsuru in London, helped me out with this recipe. It's perfect hangover food, just like a bacon sarnie with brown sauce. It's good to know that the Japanese can do junk food too! I've done a vegetarian version here, but you could replace the vegetables with chunks of chicken, beef or fish.

Vegetarian
Serves 4

*1 large shiny aubergine,
cut into large cubes*

*2 red onions,
peeled and quartered*

*100g (3½oz) mushrooms,
cleaned and quartered*

*2 sweet potatoes, peeled and
cut into bite-sized chunks*

100g (3½oz) plain flour

*100g (3½oz) Japanese panko
breadcrumbs*

1 egg, beaten

*750ml (1 pint 6fl oz)
vegetable or groundnut oil,
for deep-frying*

To Serve

8 slices of soft white bread

*Japanese mayonnaise or
normal mayonnaise*

Tonkatsu sauce or HP sauce

Equipment

4 wooden skewers

Deep-fat fryer, or
a large deep frying pan

1 Thread the pieces of aubergine, onion, mushroom and sweet potato alternately onto wooden skewers. Spread out the flour on a flat plate and the breadcrumbs on another. Put the beaten egg in a wide, shallow dish (a large baking dish is ideal). Roll the skewered ingredients first in the flour, then the beaten egg, and lastly in the breadcrumbs.

2 Heat your oil in a large, deep frying pan or a deep-fat fryer to 190ºC (375ºF). (For more advice on deep-frying, see page 83.) Fry the skewers until golden.

3 To serve, place each skewer between two slices of bread with a squirt of mayo and some Tonkatsu sauce. Once it's sandwiched, carefully pull out the skewer, leaving the chunks behind. Or you could instead serve the skewer on a layer of shredded green cabbage.

STEAMED ARTICHOKES
WITH DIJON MUSTARD DRESSING

I love theatrical food that involves labour on the part of the diner as well as the cook. Cooking globe artichokes – a member of the thistle family – involves trimming the points from the prickly leaves and steaming or boiling the artichoke in lemony water (the lemon helps to retain the green colour). The diners then pull off each leaf and dip it into a dressing, until they get to the bristly 'choke'. This they discard, leaving just the tender heart.

Artichokes are both an aphrodisiac and a digestion aid; they contain a compound called Cynarin, which enhances the sweetness of other foods. It's a kind-of miracle fruit. If you eat artichoke and then drink plain water, the water will taste sweeter. Artichokes also contain anti-oxidants, which are anti-ageing; when I eat them, I feel like I'm getting younger by the minute!

I serve the tender, perfumed artichokes with a Dijon mustard, olive oil and lemon dressing, which is how I had them as a child travelling through France.

**Vegetarian
Serves 4**

*4 globe artichokes
Juice of 1 lemon
200ml (7fl oz) extra-virgin
olive oil
3 tbsp Dijon mustard
1 clove of garlic,
peeled and crushed
(optional)
Sea salt*

1 Wash the artichokes and snip off the points of the spiky outside leaves. If you are a dab hand, then pull aside the middle leaves and scoop out the hairy choke with a sharp spoon. I don't bother; you can do it when you are eating.

2 Bring a large pan of water to the boil, add salt and squeeze in half the lemon juice. Boil the artichokes until a leaf will come off easily – normally about 20 minutes, depending on how fresh the artichokes are.

3 Meanwhile, pour the olive oil into a bowl and mix the Dijon mustard into it. Once well mixed, squeeze in the remaining lemon juice and whisk. Keep whisking until it forms a thick mustardy sauce. Add salt to taste. You can also add crushed garlic if you wish. I've given quite modest proportions for this dressing, but you could probably make more, as people can often get through a considerable amount.

4 Once the artichokes are cooked, drain them upside down for 10 minutes. Serve them whole, accompanied by a bowl of the dressing. Have another large plate on the table for the leaves that will be discarded.

INGREDIENTS

**Vegetarian
Serves 4**

8 poblano chillies

Seeds from ½ pomegranate

Handful of chopped
flat-leaf parsley

Handful of chopped
coriander

Stuffing

Olive oil, for cooking

1 medium onion,
peeled and diced

3 cloves of garlic,
peeled and crushed

8 peppercorns

2 cloves

1 cinnamon stick or ½ tsp
ground cinnamon

2 tbsp whole blanched
almonds

2 tbsp raisins

8 tomatoes, finely diced

1 pear, cored and finely diced

1 peach, destoned and
finely diced

Walnut Sauce

20 walnuts, fresh if possible

Milk, for soaking

100g (3½oz) breadcrumbs

150g (5½oz) fresh goat's
cheese

225ml (8fl oz) soured cream
or crème fraîche

1 tsp ground cinnamon

Equipment

Food processor
(or pestle and mortar)

CHILLIES EN NOGADA

This is a dish from the movie *Like Water For Chocolate* that I cooked at my 'Film and Food' themed night, where I quoted dishes from famous foodie movies. Normally this dish is served with meat, but mine is a vegetarian version. Poblano chillies, which aren't too hot, are hard to get hold of in Britain, so I ordered them from www.southdevonchillifarm.co.uk. If you can't find them, use green or red peppers, jalapeños or grilled slices of aubergine instead.

1 Prepare the walnuts the night before, if possible. Put them in milk and leave to soak overnight. The following day, their skins should come off easily. Otherwise just grind up your walnuts, ideally without skins, though I've found it doesn't really matter that much. Put the walnuts into a pestle and mortar or a food processor, add the remaining sauce ingredients and mince finely. Transfer the sauce to a bowl and set aside until needed.

2 Put your chillies in a dry frying pan and cook over a high heat until the skins blister. Turn them until all sides are black and blistered, but make sure they don't burn through the shiny skin. Then put the chillies into a plastic bag, seal and leave for 15 minutes. This makes the skin easy to peel off.

3 Meanwhile, make the stuffing. Heat some olive oil in a saucepan over a low heat and gently cook the onion and garlic until soft and translucent. Grind together the peppercorns, cloves, cinnamon and almonds with the pestle and mortar, or in the food processor. Add to the onion and garlic mixture and heat through. Add the raisins, tomatoes and other fruit until you have a firm mixture. Allow to cool.

4 Preheat the oven to 180°C (350°F), Gas Mark 4. Remove the chillies from the plastic bag and peel away the skin. Slit each chilli neatly and carefully remove the seeds, leaving the top with the stem intact. Fill them with the cool stuffing mixture. Bake in the oven for 20 minutes.

5 Place the stuffed chillies on plates, cover with walnut sauce and garnish with pomegranate seeds and parsley or coriander.

BEEF AND SPRING ONION CHINESE DUMPLINGS
(FROM MAMA LAN'S SUPPER CLUB)

Mama Lan's Supper Club is a mother and daughter team based in North-West London. Mama Lan comes from a long line of chefs in China. Her children are now grown-up. The supper club, at her daughter Ning Ma's house, has given her renewed purpose, for once again she has people to cook for. During meals, Mama Lan and Ning will often give live cooking demonstrations and offer guests the chance to have a go! On the evening that I went, she showed me how to make Chinese dumplings. She makes them with meat, but for a vegetarian option stuff them with unusual fillings such as roasted butternut squash and water chestnuts. Fusion it up!

INGREDIENTS

Serves 4
Makes about 20

*200g (7oz) plain flour,
plus extra for sprinkling*

*100ml (3½fl oz)
lukewarm water*

Vegetable oil, for frying

*Chinese rice vinegar,
to serve*

1 Put the flour in a large, deep bowl and add the lukewarm water a small cupful at a time, mixing between additions. Once the flour and water are mixed, bring the dough together, remove from the bowl and knead on a lightly floured surface until it becomes smooth. This takes about 10 minutes by hand. The dough should be really soft but not wet to the touch – a bit like freshly made pasta. Cover and leave to rest while you make the stuffing.

2 To make the stuffing, put all the ingredients apart from the spring onions and ginger in a large bowl. Use a spoon to mix until the meat takes on a patty consistency – when it holds together well and the texture resembles sausage meat. Add the spring onions and ginger to the meat and mix well.

Stuffing
100g (3½oz) beef mince
1 egg, lightly beaten
1 tbsp sea salt
1 tbsp dark soy sauce
1 tbsp water
½ tbsp sesame oil
½ tbsp vegetable oil
6–8 fine spring onions,
thinly sliced
Piece of root ginger
the size of a pound coin,
peeled and finely chopped

3 Uncover the dough and place on a flat floured work surface. Sprinkle flour on the dough and cut into 4 equal-sized pieces. Take one piece and roll into a sausage about 2cm (¾in) wide. Put the other three pieces back into the bowl and cover so that their surface doesn't go hard.

4 Cut off a thumb-sized piece of dough from the 'sausage'. Sprinkle with flour, so that it doesn't stick, then flatten it out on the table with the palm of your hand and use a rolling pin to roll into a small disc about the thickness of a pound coin. Hold the disc in the palm of your hand and put a spoonful of the meat filling in the centre of the disc. With your finger and thumb, nip the sides together, making a crescent-shaped dumpling. Repeat with the rest of the dough and meat mixture.

5 To cook the dumplings, you can either boil or pan-fry them for different results. To boil, place in a pan of boiling water and cook for 15 minutes, rather like cooking little ravioli. After 5 minutes, add 100ml (3½fl oz) cold water into the boiling pan, then the same again after 10 minutes. Then drain and serve.

6 To pan-fry them, heat up a little vegetable oil in a frying pan, add the dumplings to the pan and fry for just a minute or so. Then fill the pan with cold water – be careful because the pan may spit. Boil for 15 minutes, then carefully pour away as much water as you can, holding the dumplings in place with a spatula or spoon. Place the pan back on the heat, add a little more oil, and fry until any remaining water disappears and the dumplings have a golden base. This takes a little longer than the simple boiling method, but the resulting texture is soft and light on top, supported by a delicious crunchy base.

Enjoy the hot dumplings with a little Chinese rice vinegar!

SAVOURY YOGHURT GRANITA

WITH CARAMELISED PINE NUTS, PRESERVED LEMONS AND TORN BASIL

This is an unusual way of using yoghurt, as a starter. It's a light and tangy, sweet and sour appetiser that leaves one feeling refreshed and eager for the main course, like a savoury slush puppy. You can change the herbs if you like – use coriander, mint or flat-leaf parsley – and also the nuts. You should try to get a contrast of flavours and textures, salty with sour and sweet, cold brittle flakes with syrup and crunch.

INGREDIENTS

**Vegetarian
Serves 4**

*600g (1lb 5oz) yoghurt
(Goat's if you have
access to it)*

100g (3½oz) pine nuts

40g (1½oz) brown sugar

1 preserved lemon, diced

Handful of basil leaves, torn

Drizzle of balsamic syrup

*Sprinkle of sea salt
(or vanilla salt if you have it)*

1 Pour the yoghurt into a shallow dish and put into the freezer. Take it out every 20 minutes and fork the yoghurt into flakes, replacing it in the freezer when done. This process will take 1–1½ hours overall to get the right consistency, which is icy but not smooth.

2 Meanwhile, put the pine nuts in a pan with the sugar and caramelise them on your hob over a medium–high heat. Carefully pour the caramelised pine nuts onto greaseproof paper and allow them to cool down. They will have stuck together so, once cool, break them up.

3 Put a portion of the yoghurt granita into the middle of each plate and decorate with the caramelised pine nuts, preserved lemon pieces and some torn basil leaves. Squeeze a vein of balsamic syrup around the edge of the plate.

GAMMODOKI
(FROM HORTON JUPITER)

Horton's supper club The Secret Ingredient is in an East-End council flat. He serves vegetarian Japanese food with a twist. Here's his recipe for Gammodoki. He says: 'I first found it in a cookbook at the age of 25. I couldn't cook a thing – as Armando Ianucci says, "a tin of tomatoes and any vegetable – SHAZAM! An acceptable pasta sauce." One afternoon I found myself standing in a public library stealing a book on Japanese cooking because I thought it was about time I could do something else to impress the ladies other than being 'a god in the sack' [that's a genuine quote] and Japanese fud is SUPER-sexy.'

INGREDIENTS

Vegetarian
Serves 4
(Makes 16–24)

1 x 340–400g packet of tofu

5 large carrots,
peeled and grated

5 dried shiitake mushrooms,
soaked in cold water overnight
(keep the water for an
alternative sauce
– see variations –
or use for stock)

3 tsp sesame seeds,
lightly toasted or dry roasted
in a non-stick pan

2–3 tsp sea salt

Any extras your imagination
suggests, such as ¼ onion,
peeled and finely chopped,
or green beans (optional)

2 eggs

500ml (18fl oz) vegetable oil,
for frying

1 Wrap the tofu block in a clean tea towel and place under a heavy weight for 30 minutes or so, then do this again using a fresh tea towel – this is important, else the Gammodoki will be wet through and, upon frying, you'll find an abstract mess in the pan!

2 Meanwhile, place the grated carrot in layers between sheets of kitchen paper and also place under a weight to press out excess water.

3 To prepare the Ponzu dipping sauce, squeeze the lemons and lime into a bowl, then add 1 tablespoon of rice vinegar at a time, tasting the mixture, until the vinegar starts to take the edge off the citrus. Then do the same for the soy sauce, slowly adding and tasting, and stopping just before the soy becomes too dominant, so that you get a nice mixture of the flavours. Add some finely chopped red chilli if you fancy. Set aside until needed. You can actually make this sauce well in advance and leave it for a few months; it just gets better! It will last in the fridge for a year or so, but is best served at room temperature.

4 Extort the water from the shiitake mushrooms by pressing them in a sieve, then chop them finely.

5 Making sure that the water has left the tofu, remove the tofu from the tea towel, place it in a large bowl and mash it like so much of your brain, then knead it back into a dough before adding and mixing in the grated carrots, sesame seeds, salt and anything else your imagination suggests (for instance, finely chopped onions will add more of a western Kentucky-fried loveliness to the finished item, or green beans will make the Gammodoki crunchier). Whisk the eggs and mix them thoroughly into the blend.

Another nice sauce for the Gammodoki is a sweet and sour sauce made from the reserved mushroom soaking water. Heat the water gently in a saucepan over a low heat and add some caster sugar, mirin (a kind of sweetened cooking sake – if you can't find this, you might substitute actual sake and sugar, or a small amount of sweet sherry), rice vinegar, light soy sauce, and 1–2 tablespoons of cornflour to thicken the sauce. Briefly reheat the Gammodoki in the sauce before serving.

Or you can make a simple ginger sauce from 500ml (18fl oz) water, 4 tablespoons of light soy sauce, 4 tablespoons of mirin or sugar, a pinch of salt and 1 tablespoon chopped root ginger. Bring this to the boil in a saucepan, add the Gammodoki and simmer gently for a few minutes to absorb the flavours.

Ponzu Dipping Sauce
Juice of 4–5 lemons and 1 lime
Rice vinegar, to taste
Dark soy sauce, to taste
1 red chilli, seeded and finely chopped (optional)

6 To form the Gammodoki, roll a small ball of the mixture in your hands and hold it in the 'O' formed by an 'ok' hand gesture with one hand, then use thumb and two forefingers of the other hand to press the sides flat, so that you're left with a small round flat patty. Repeat with the rest of the mixture.

7 Heat the vegetable oil for a few minutes in a saucepan over a medium heat. Lower the patties into the hot oil and deep-fry gently. (For more advice on deep-frying, see page 83.) You can fry them until they're a light golden colour and then serve (more authentic), or you can remove them from the oil, turn up the heat, and then re-fry at a much hotter temperature to make them nice and crispy on the outside (especially good if you've added onions).

Serve the Gammodoki hot with the Ponzu dipping sauce.

YUZU CEVICHE

This is my twist on a dish that is traditional both in Japan and Latin America, though each version has slightly different flavours. Here I've mixed the two. Ceviche cooks fish not by heat but with citrus. Every time I've served this dish at The Underground Restaurant, people want more. It's a perfect starter: *refreshing*, *zingy* and *unusual*.

Yuzu is a floral Japanese citrus fruit that is rarely available fresh in this country. You can buy small jars of it in Oriental shops, or the juice is sometimes available. You can replace with a combination of lime, lemon and orange juice if stuck. Ponzu is another Japanese ingredient that is so addictive once you have discovered it. It's a kind of soy sauce with citrus. Nice just poured over avocado or rice. Put these ingredients together about 30 minutes before your guests arrive. The fish will take approximately that long to 'cook' in the citrus juice.

INGREDIENTS

Serves 4–6

600g (1lb 5oz) very fresh fillets of white fish, such as sea bass

75g (2½oz) white miso

3–4 umeboshi plums, quartered

Juice of 2 limes or kaffir limes

½ tbsp Yuzu flesh or juice

25ml (1fl oz) Ponzu

50g (1¾oz) pickled ginger (pink or red)

Handful of coriander leaves

1 Slice the fish into thin slices and place in a bowl.

2 In another bowl, mix together all the remaining ingredients apart from the pickled ginger and coriander leaves. Pour the mixture over the fish, making sure you coat every bit. Leave in the fridge for 30 minutes to marinate.

3 To serve, add a little pickled ginger to the top and decorate with coriander leaves.

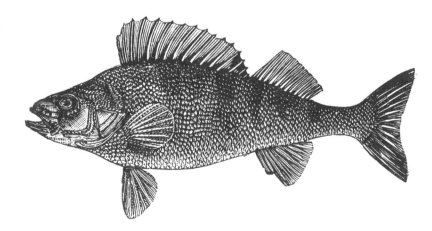

Soups

One of the first things you need to make great soup is stock. You can use powdered stock or stock cubes, but believe me, real stock tastes so much better. To make the base, you need to make what classic French cooks call a *mirepoix*: a mixture of onions, carrots and celery. After that, use anything you've got hanging about – for instance, vegetables going limp in your vegetable box.

Tip: refresh limp vegetables such as carrots by cutting off one end and leaving that end in cold water. The carrots will stiffen up.

The only rule: don't add starchy vegetables like potatoes. When making soup, I season a little at the start while cooking the initial onion, garlic and spice mixture. Then I keep tasting throughout the rest of the cooking and adjusting the salt and pepper levels. I often cook huge vats of soup, and seasoning for that amount is a skill in itself. It's essential to keep tasting, beginning, middle and end.

Marmite French Onion Soup

Where I was brought up in Highgate, there used to be a French man who cycled around wearing a blue and white striped T-shirt. He sold onions and strings of garlic. The onions were from Brittany and were so good fried that I had a hard time not eating all of them out of the pot before they could even be used in a dish. So if you can, get decent organic onions for this perfect winter soup.

Vegetarian
Serves 4

Olive oil, for frying

1.2kg (2lb 10oz)/4 very large onions, peeled and finely sliced into rounds

3 cloves of garlic, peeled and finely chopped

1 bottle of white wine

500ml (18fl oz) vegetable stock (see page 137)

2 bay leaves, fresh if possible

1 tbsp Marmite

200g (7oz) Cheddar cheese (or Tomme), grated

½ baguette, sliced

Freshly ground black pepper

Handful of flat-leaf parsley sprigs

1 Heat the olive oil in a large saucepan over a low–medium heat, add the onions and cook until soft and translucent. Add the garlic and cook for a couple of minutes until also translucent. Pour in the white wine and the stock, bring to the boil, then reduce the heat, add the bay leaves and Marmite and leave to simmer for 1 hour.

2 Preheat the grill on high. Sprinkle the Cheddar cheese over the baguette slices and place on a baking tray under the grill until the cheese is melted and bubbling.

3 Ladle the soup into bowls and place a couple of the cheesy croutons in each bowl. Grind in some black pepper and decorate with a few parsley sprigs.

Vegetable Stock

This stock is the basis for most of the soups on the following pages. When straining the stock, just leave it to strain without pressing the vegetables, and you will end up with a clearer stock that can be served as a simple bouillon, or clear soup. Bouillon is the original *restaurant*: the word means 'to restore'. After the French revolution, when people no longer had private cooks, they often went to places where they could have their *restaurant*, a healthy clear soup.

INGREDIENTS

**Vegetarian
Makes about 1.5 litres
(2½ pints)**

2–3 tbsp olive oil

1–2 large onions (some people leave the skins on to darken the stock), chopped

450g (1lb) celery, chopped

450g (1lb) carrots, washed but left unpeeled, then chopped

3 cloves of garlic, peeled and sliced

1 bay leaf

10 black peppercorns

2 tsp sea salt

4.5 litres (8 pints) water

60ml (2fl oz) Tamari, Maggi or soy sauce

1 Heat the olive oil in a large saucepan over a medium heat. Cook the onion, celery and carrots until soft. Then gradually add the garlic and the optional vegetables, if using, along with the bay leaf, peppercorns and salt. Pour in the water, bring to the boil, then reduce the heat to a simmer. After 1 hour, add the soy sauce. Simmer for another hour.

2 Strain the stock through a sieve into a large container. Leave it to filter through the sieve, and when it's cool enough, press down the vegetables to extract the last juices. If you wish to make bouillon (see introduction above), just leave it to strain without pressing. Once made, you can freeze this stock for up to 3 months.

OPTIONAL INGREDIENTS

Mushrooms, leeks, fennel, celeriac, any greens (even limp salad), herbs, broccoli

Roasted Cherry Tomato and Garlic Soup

I love Heinz tomato soup though it's completely different – sweeter, thicker, creamier – to home-made tomato soup. I use cherry tomatoes for this, but use whatever fresh tomatoes you can get hold of.

**Vegetarian
Serves 4**

Olive oil, for oiling
*500g (1lb 2oz)
cherry tomatoes*
1 head of garlic
1 fresh bay leaf
1 tbsp oregano
Good-quality sea salt
*500ml (18fl oz) vegetable
stock (see page 137)*
*Handful of basil leaves,
to garnish*
*Focaccia (see pages 100-1),
to serve*

Equipment
Freestanding or
hand-held blender

1 Preheat the oven to 220ºC (425ºF), Gas Mark 7.

2 Oil a baking tin with olive oil and place the cherry tomatoes in it. Put in the head of garlic and the bay leaf. Sprinkle oregano and salt over the tomatoes. Bake in the oven for 45 minutes until the skins are browned and crispy. Remove from the oven and allow to cool until you are able to handle the tomatoes.

3 Now, this bit is fiddly: peel the crispy skins off the tomatoes. Discard the skins and catch the flesh and juice in a large saucepan. You can strain out the seeds if you like, but I don't bother. Squeeze the cloves from the roasted garlic head into the pan. Use a hand-held blender to whiz the tomatoes and garlic in the pan.

4 Pour in the stock. Cook over a medium heat for 10–15 minutes, tasting and adjusting the salt levels as the soup warms. Serve in bowls with a basil leaf in the centre of each and some focaccia on the side.

Sorrel Soup

Sorrel has such a subtle taste. I was given some by my friend Scarlett, who has an allotment. I try to use local allotmenteers as much as I can. The trick with sorrel soup is to keep the beautiful green hue...I manage this by reserving some of the sorrel and adding it at the end to get a two-colour effect.

INGREDIENTS

**Vegetarian
Serves 4**

90g (3oz) butter

1 large onion,
peeled and finely diced

2 tbsp plain flour

150ml (5½fl oz)
double cream

500g (1lb 2oz) sorrel,
washed and chopped

500ml (18fl oz) vegetable
stock (see page 137)

Sea salt and freshly ground
black pepper

Extra cream or yoghurt,
to garnish

Equipment
Freestanding or
hand-held blender

1 Melt the butter in a saucepan over a low heat and cook the onion slowly until soft and translucent. Add the flour, cream, two-thirds of the sorrel and a bit of stock and cook, stirring, for about 10 minutes. Add the rest of the stock, turn up the heat and bring to the boil, then turn the heat back down and simmer for 30 minutes.

2 Remove from the heat. Transfer the soup to a blender or whiz it in the pan with a hand-held blender. Return the soup to the saucepan and return to the heat. Simmer for 5 minutes, stirring, then taste and season with salt and pepper.

3 Transfer one-third of your soup into a separate large bowl. Add the remaining sorrel to this and blend. This portion will be a darker green than the rest of the soup.

4 Divide the larger, lighter-coloured portion of sorrel soup among bowls, then add a ladle of the darker soup to each bowl. This will give you two colours. You can also add a swirl of cream or yoghurt if you like.

Thai Green Spinach Soup

INGREDIENTS

Vegetarian/vegan
if fish sauce is omitted
Serves 4–6

Thai Green Paste

4 tbsp groundnut oil

2 small shallots, peeled

3 cloves of garlic, peeled

*4 pound-coin-sized slices of
galangal or root ginger
(or both), peeled*

*3 stalks of lemongrass,
outer layers discarded*

*3 red bird's-eye chillies,
stemmed and seeded*

*½ tsp ground turmeric or
2–3cm (1in) piece of peeled
fresh turmeric root
if you can get it*

*1 tsp brown sugar
or palm sugar*

1 tsp paprika

3 tbsp tamarind paste

300g (10½oz) baby spinach

*Large bunch of coriander,
well washed (use the stems
as well as the leaves)*

Broth

*Groundnut or vegetable oil,
for cooking*

1 x 400ml tin of coconut milk

*500ml (18fl oz) fish or
vegetable stock (see page 137)*

*4 tbsp Nam pla fish sauce
(omit for vegetarians)*

*Fresh mint leaves and lime
wedges, to garnish*

Equipment

Food processor

Always a favourite, this one. The great thing about soup for a supper club or dinner party is that you can make a big vat of it beforehand, then just heat it up. This is a creamy but spicy soup that is also good for vegans, as it uses only coconut milk (though make sure you omit the fish sauce!).

1 Put all the ingredients for the Thai green paste in a food processor and whiz throroughly until well chopped and combined.

2 Heat a little groundnut or vegetable oil in a large saucepan over a low heat and add the paste. Warm gently, then pour in the coconut milk, stock and fish sauce, mix until combined and allow to warm through.

3 Add your choice of vegetables to the broth and simmer for 10 minutes. If including rice noodles, add these at the very end to avoid the soup going sludgy. Ladle the soup into bowls and garnish with mint leaves and lime wedges.

OPTIONAL INGREDIENTS

Small pea-sized aubergines
(available in Asian shops),
thinly sliced carrot batons,
mangetout, beansprouts, rice noodles

Cockaleekie
without the Cock!

I made this typically Scottish soup for a Burn's Night dinner. It was delicious and healthy. The prunes, bizarre though they may sound, add contrast and interest to this simple dish.

INGREDIENTS

**Vegetarian
Serves 4**

Olive oil, for cooking

300g (10½oz) leeks, finely chopped

2 onions, peeled and finely chopped

2 cloves of garlic, peeled and crushed

Handful of fresh herbs (such as parsley, tarragon and thyme)

700ml (1 pint 4fl oz) vegetable stock (see page 137)

Sea salt and freshly ground black pepper

Handful of prunes, cooked in stock, stones removed

2 tbsp chopped curly parsley

1 Put some olive oil in a pan over a low–medium heat, add the leeks and onions and cook gently until soft, taking care not to let them burn. Add the garlic, herbs and the stock. Turn up the heat, bring to the boil, then turn the heat back down and simmer for 30 minutes.

2 Scoop out a little of the soup and put in a small bowl. Add the prunes to this bowl, leaving them to become warm.

3 Meanwhile, taste and season the soup, then ladle into bowls. Put 2–3 warmed prunes in each bowl and garnish with curly parsley.

Magic Wizard Pumpkin Soup

INGREDIENTS

**Vegetarian
Serves 4**

*1 large pumpkin
(about 1kg/2lb 3oz),
peeled and cubed*

6 tbsp olive oil

*1 medium onion,
peeled and thinly sliced
across the grain*

1½ tsp ground cinnamon

*1½ tsp chilli flakes
(I use Japanese chilli spice mix)*

2 star anise

*2 cloves of garlic,
peeled and finely sliced*

*700ml (1 pint 4fl oz)
vegetable stock (see page 137)*

*Sea salt and freshly
ground pepper*

Garnish

100g (3½oz) Greek yoghurt

*2 tbsp pumpkin seeds,
dry-roasted and tossed
in soy sauce*

*Drizzle of cold-pressed nut oil
(such as hemp, pumpkin seed,
hazelnut or walnut)*

*Handful of roughly chopped
flat-leaf or curly parsley*

I served this soup for my Harry Notter/Halloween-themed night. The beautiful rich shades of pumpkins, seasonal in the autumn, are reminiscent of the orange-hued leaves on the trees. There are lots of different types of pumpkins: kabocha, turban, Jack-o'-lantern, or squashes such as butternut squash. For a magical touch, like something from a fairy tale, serve the soup in small hollowed-out pumpkins. Cut off the top and set aside, then rub the pumpkins with salt and oil and bake in the oven at 200°C (400°F), Gas Mark 6 (or the Aga roasting oven) for 15–20 minutes. Once baked, pour in the soup and replace the top as a hat.

1 Preheat the oven to 200°C (400°F), Gas Mark 4. If using an Aga, prepare the roasting oven. Drizzle the pumpkin cubes with 3 tablespoons of the olive oil and roast in the oven for 20–30 minutes until soft.

2 Meanwhile, heat the remaining olive oil in a saucepan over a medium heat. Cook the onion until soft and translucent, then add the cinnamon, chilli flakes, star anise and garlic and cook for 10 minutes, stirring continuously so that the mixture doesn't burn. Season to taste.

3 When the pumpkin cubes are ready, remove from the oven and add to the saucepan. Stir them around so that they absorb the spices. Pour in the vegetable stock. Cook for at least 30 minutes (can be longer: the flavours will only deepen with time). Taste and adjust the seasoning.

4 Serve the soup hot, in bowls or hollowed-out pumpkins, with a generous tablespoon of Greek yoghurt, a large pinch of roasted pumpkin seeds, a drizzle of cold-pressed nut oil and a scattering of chopped parsley.

Salads

*I*n France they often serve salad as a starter. You can also serve salad with a main course. Salad is supposed to help your digestion, activating the digestive enzymes.

I often crumble a little Maldon sea salt over the salad just before serving. This adds crunch as well as flavour. As for salad dressings, a great tip is to make them in a jam jar – that way, you can put the lid on and shake and blend the dressing easily. Afterwards, just keep the leftover dressing in the fridge.

French Beans with Tofu & Walnut sauce

This is a Japanese-influenced salad that makes French beans a little more interesting than just boiling them to death, à l'Anglaise.

INGREDIENTS

**Vegetarian
Serves 4**

*400g (14oz) fine French
beans, topped and tailed*
Handful of walnuts
1 x 400g packet of silken tofu
2 tbsp white miso
Few drops of sesame oil
Japanese soy sauce or Ponzu

Equipment
Food processor

1 Steam the beans in a saucepan of salted water for a few minutes until tender.

2 Put the walnuts in a food processor and whiz until finely chopped. Then add the tofu and white miso and whiz again to combine.

3 Lay the beans out in a row on each plate and sprinkle the tofu and walnut mixture across them down the centre. Shake on a few drops of sesame oil and soy sauce and serve.

Palm Heart Salad

I discovered palm hearts when trekking through the Amazon jungle in South America. The guides would strip the 'cabbage' palm trees and expose the hearts – still beating – tender white tubes reminiscent of artichoke or asparagus. They are basically baby tree trunks! In Florida, palm hearts used to be a poor people's food but now, like oysters, they have become an expensive luxury.

In this country we can buy palm hearts tinned. Be careful to buy only the harvested palm hearts, not the wild ones, as the stripping has destroyed trees in the forest to the point that they are now an endangered species.

Vegetarian
Serves 4

1 x 410g tin of palm hearts, drained and cut into 1cm (½in) slices

4 tbsp olive oil

Juice of 1 lemon or 1 lime

Sea salt and freshly ground pepper

Handful of black olives, pitted and sliced

Handful of walnuts, broken into quarters

Handful of roughly chopped coriander leaves

1 Combine the palm hearts, olive oil, lemon or lime juice, salt and pepper.

2 Leave in the fridge for 30 minutes or so, to let the palm hearts absorb the flavours. Then mix in the rest of the ingredients and serve.

Mint, Coriander, Onion & Pomegranate Cachumber

A cachumber is a bit like an Indian salsa, and goes very well with Indian food. In this one, the white, green and pink of the ingredients is very pretty and refreshing. I served this at my 'Night of the senses' meal with dahl, rice and aubergine, and Indian pumpkin curry. This course represented 'touch', so I asked my guests to eat with their hands as they do in India. There is an elegant technique: you use your fingers, rather than your palm, to ball the rice/curry/cachumber. Eating with your hands makes it a much more sensual experience; you experience the feel as well as the taste of your food. Try it!

Vegetarian
Serves 4

Mix all of the ingredients together in a bowl. Season with salt to taste, then chill until ready to serve.

2 onions, peeled and diced

Bunch of coriander, leaves only, roughly chopped

Bunch of mint, leaves only, roughly chopped

Seeds of 1 pomegranate

Juice of 1 lemon

1 tsp ground cumin

Sea salt, to taste

Really Great Caesar Salad

I served this at my 'I love New York' meal, which I held on the anniversary of that fateful date: 9/11. My cousin Jimmy, who lives in New York and was restaurant manager of The Tavern on the Green, left his job after the disaster to help coordinate the food effort at the site:

'During that time I was tabbed by the Office of Emergency Management in NYC to be one of the coordinators of the food effort, as we had to serve about 40 thousand meals a day on the site, as it was considered a rescue effort upon initiation. Only after about 5 days did we figure out that everyone was dead. I knew a lot of the chefs and had run the catering at a football stadium, so they knew I had the ability to organise food for large groups, thus they called me. I ended up working on the project about 3 months.

The restaurant at the top of the building was called Windows on the World and former employees from Tavern on the Green worked there. Unfortunately many of the people who perished were friends of ours. Surviving members of the staff have organised a restaurant called Colors.'

I happened to be having a supper on September 11th and, although it was controversial, for me it seemed strange to let the date go by without acknowledging it. A classic Caesar salad includes chicken, so this is a vegetarian version. Cos or romaine lettuce is essential to get the right sweet, crispy combination with the glossy, salty dressing.

Serves 4

1 large (or 2 small) cos or romaine lettuce(s), leaves washed and chopped into 7.5cm (3in) pieces

Croutons
½ loaf of stale bread or baguette, cut into 2.5cm (1in) cubes
Glug of olive oil
1 clove of garlic, peeled and crushed
Sea salt

Caesar Dressing
2 small garlic cloves, peeled
1 egg
1 tbsp Dijon mustard
1 tbsp anchovy essence or 1 anchovy fillet from a tin, finely chopped
100–125ml (3½–4½fl oz) groundnut oil
Juice of ½ lemon
60g (2oz) Parmesan cheese, freshly grated
Freshly ground black pepper

1 First make your croutons. Preheat the oven to 180ºC (350ºF), Gas Mark 4. If using an Aga, prepare the roasting oven. Lay the cubes of bread in a baking tray and toss with olive oil, garlic and salt. Roast for 5–10 minutes until golden.

2 Rub a large salad bowl with a clove of garlic. Once this is done, you can crush the remaining garlic ready to use.

3 To make the dressing, boil ('coddle') the egg in a saucepan of water for 1 minute, before cracking it into a bowl – you will use both the uncooked white and the yolk. Add the mustard and garlic and whisk until smooth. Add the anchovy essence, then slowly whisk in the groundnut oil. Add the lemon and half the Parmesan. Season with pepper (not salt, as the anchovy should provide enough saltiness.)

4 Place your lettuce leaves in the garlic-rubbed bowl and toss in the dressing. Top with the croutons and scatter with the rest of the Parmesan cheese.

Broad Bean, Feta & Mint salad

There used to be a cheap, homely Greek restaurant near to my dad's office, which served this spring-like salad. My dad's office was on Exmouth Market in Clerkenwell. It was a working-class fruit and veg market until Clerkenwell became fashionable in the '90s, housing designer boutiques and restaurants like Moro, which brought authentic Spanish and Northern African food to London. The Greek restaurant picked up on the 'bourgeoisification' of the area, put up their prices and became a chic destination. Use good-quality feta for this salad if you can.

INGREDIENTS

**Vegetarian
Serves 4**

400g (14oz) broad beans
(fresh or frozen)

4 tbsp good-quality
extra-virgin olive oil

1 x 200g packet of feta
cheese, cut into cubes

Handful of fresh mint
leaves, torn

Sea salt and freshly
ground pepper

1 Simmer the broad beans in a saucepan of salted water until tender. When cooked, shell the broad beans and put them in a bowl.

2 Add the olive oil and the feta. The warmth of the beans will meld lightly with the cheese and the dressing. Season the salad and sprinkle some mint leaves over the top.

Pear, Walnut & Gorgonzola Salad

I served this as a starter for an Italian meal. Pears with blue cheese is a classic combination that can't fail. If you don't like blue cheese, replace with Pecorino, another classic combination.

Vegetarian
if vegetarian
Gorgonzola is used
Serves 4

---

*2 ripe pears, peeled,
cored and halved*

*100g (3½oz) Gorgonzola
cheese, cut into cubes*

*Handful of walnuts,
broken into large pieces*

Dressing
1 tbsp white wine vinegar

4 tbsp walnut oil

*1 tsp pink peppercorns,
roughly crushed*

Maldon sea salt

1 Take each pear half and use a sharp knife to make a number of lengthways cuts, leaving a couple of centimetres uncut at the narrower end. Fan out the pears.

2 Put a fanned-out pear on each plate, add the cheese cubes and walnut pieces. Whisk together all the ingredients for the dressing and drizzle over the top.

Mâche with Egg
& Dijon Mustard Dressing

Vegetarian
Serves 4

3 tbsp mild Dijon mustard

1 clove of garlic,
peeled and crushed

Juice of ½ lemon

Sea salt

75ml (2½fl oz)
good-quality olive oil

400g (14oz) mâche
(also known as corn salad
or lamb's lettuce),
washed and dried

2 eggs

I learnt this salad from my daughter's French grandmother. She came from a poor family; her husband had died and she had to bring up ten kids on her own in an HLM, or council flat. She was a tough woman who once had a job wringing chicken's necks, which she did with casual aplomb, but she could cook like a dream…earthy peasant dishes infused with the innate food knowledge that all French people seem to possess, rich or poor. One day at lunchtime, I watched her whip together a salad dressing à la Lyonnais in the bottom of a large bowl. This dressing requires a large amount of Dijon mustard and not too much vinegar or lemon. Prior to this, I had always believed vinaigrettes were loosely amalgamated. This was the first time I'd seen a dressing that was an emulsion, a revelation. Here is the recipe for this simple but warming salad. Although this recipe serves four people, the finished salads are quite small – perfect as an accompaniment, but if you want them more substantial you may need to double the ingredients.

1 Make the dressing in a large bowl by stirring together the mustard and garlic. Add a squeeze of the lemon juice and the sea salt. Slowly whisk in the oil and it should pull together in a mayonnaise-type mixture. If it splits, add a few drops of hot water. Add the mâche to the bowl.

2 Lightly boil the eggs in a saucepan of water until soft-boiled. This takes about 4 minutes – the whites should be hard, the yolks soft. Peel the eggs and chop them into the bowl. Mix everything to combine and serve immediately. The warm runny yolk, the softness of the leaves and the slippery dressing make a wonderful combination.

Grilled Halloumi
& Roasted Pepper Salad

I'm very interested in urban food and how some great food is being made and foraged in cities. My friend Andy Mahoney (@handyface) makes cheese, including halloumi, in his Peckham flat. You don't have to go to Cyprus to taste it home-made! It's very easy to make and not as rubbery as the supermarket version. I've asked him to give demonstrations at The Underground Farmers & Craft Market at my house. Check out his blog if you want to have a go: http://handyface.wordpress.com/2010/09/05/halloumi-3/. In the summer barbie season, it's always good to have a packet of halloumi in your fridge. This salad is a great barbecue alternative for vegetarians, as the cheese doesn't melt when hot.

INGREDIENTS

Serves 4

2 red peppers, seeded, cored and cut into strips

1 x 250g packet halloumi, drained and sliced

6 tbsp olive oil

Juice of 1 lemon

Handful of chopped flat-leaf parsley

Sea salt and freshly ground pepper

1 Preheat the grill or prepare the barbecue. Grill the peppers until their skins are bubbly and roasted, and blackened along the edges. Lightly season the grilled peppers.

2 Grill the slices of halloumi until lightly golden on each side.

3 Combine the grilled peppers and halloumi in a bowl, dress with the olive oil and lemon juice and garnish with parsley.

Vegetarian Main Courses

Here you will find a collection of vegetarian main courses. It's not a second best option: good vegetarian food is not worthy brown slop; it's as tasty, colourful, rich and exciting as meat and fish recipes. I can assure you, after trying some of these, you won't feel deprived. I've included baked dishes, rice and pasta dishes and curries. For a vegetarian, a curry is a salvation – most of India is vegetarian. For an Englishwoman, I think my curries are pretty good. My Asian guests have enjoyed them anyway! Serve the curries with rice, cachumber (see page 148) and cucumber raita. It's definitely worth making your own curry powder, a mix of whole and ground spices (see page 166). It will automatically make your curry taste fresher and more authentic.

BAKED VACHERIN (FONDUE FOR CHEATS)

Love cheese fondue and can't be arsed to cook it? Vacherin is your friend. It's a seasonal cheese produced in France and Switzerland between November and February. The type you want is Vacherin Mont d'Or, which comes in a wooden box in two sizes – small or large. You can also eat it uncooked with a spoon from a cheeseboard but it's perhaps more impressive as a baked hot dish. I find a small box is good for 2–3 people, a large for 7–8. This dish takes about 10 minutes to make. Great for a dinner party after you get in from work and are too tired to cook. It's also perfect for a supper club, partly because the communal nature of the dish means that it encourages chatter and sharing between guests.

**Vegetarian
Serves 2–3**

*400g (14oz) small waxy
potatoes, such as
Exquisa or Charlotte*

Sea salt, for rolling

Olive oil, for greasing

*1 small Vacherin Mont d'Or
cheese (in a wooden box)*

½ glass of dry white wine

*1 clove of garlic, peeled
and cut into slivers*

*Selection of silverskin
onions, mini gherkins,
caperberries and pickled
green peppercorns,
to serve*

1 Preheat the oven to 220°C (425°F), Gas Mark 7. If using an Aga, prepare the roasting oven.

2 Wash the potatoes and roll them in salt, pressing quite firmly so that it sticks to them.

3 Put your salty potatoes into a baking tin greased with olive oil. Bake in the oven for 40 minutes.

4 Meanwhile, take the cheese in its wooden box, remove the lid and fit it underneath so that the box is sat in it. Then wrap the bottom of the box in foil, leaving the top open.

5 Pour the wine into a saucepan over a low heat, add the slivers of garlic and heat gently for 5 minutes. This will soften the garlic. Remove the softened garlic slivers from the wine with a slotted spoon and press them into the top of the cheese. Cut a couple of slits in the top, then pour the wine onto the cheese.

6 About 10–15 minutes before the potatoes are finished, reduce the oven temperature to 180°C (350°F), Gas Mark 4. Add the box of cheese to the oven and cook for 10–15 minutes until the top is bubbling.

7 To serve, put the Vacherin (still in its box) in the middle of the table with a spoon in it. Serve with a dish of the hot potatoes and small dishes of the pickles, which your guests can pick and choose as they wish. The cheese can be scooped onto the potatoes on people's plates.

EGGPLANT PARMESAN (MELANZANE ALLA PARMIGIANA)

This dish is a pain in the butt to make but well worth it. When I made it for 30, it took me 6 hours to fry the aubergine slices. I must admit, to get through the ordeal, I resorted to the Keith Floyd school of cookery: I swigged constantly on a bottle of red wine, while standing over my Aga, spattered with oil. The dish involves my favourite vegetable, lots of frying, lots of layers. It's a heavy, satisfying dish that is even nicer the following day.

Vegetarian
if vegetarian
Parmesan is used
Serves 4

*1 portion of tomato sauce
(see page 180)*

*700g (1½lb) shiny purple
aubergines (about 3 large
ones), sliced thinly and salted*

Bottle of olive oil, for cooking

*Sea salt and freshly
ground pepper*

*1 tsp oregano and/or thyme
(optional)*

*Plain flour, for coating
aubergines*

*1 bottle of good-quality
red wine*

*200g (7oz) good-quality
mozzarella cheese,
thinly sliced*

*200g (7oz) Parmesan cheese,
freshly grated*

1 Cook your tomato sauce following the method on page 180 or defrost it if you have some in the freezer.

2 Salt the aubergine slices lightly, then leave to sweat and drain in a colander for 30 minutes. You can weigh them down by putting a dish and tins of beans on top, which aids squeezing the bitter water from them. (If there is still a lot of water when you come to fry them, they will smoke up the kitchen, so drain well or dab dry with kitchen paper.)

3 Put a bowl of olive oil next to the hob. Aubergines soak up loads of oil and you will need it to hand. Heat up a frying pan with a generous amount of the olive oil. I also season the olive oil with some salt and pepper (and oregano or thyme, if you like). This is easier than trying to season the whole dish. Obviously take into account that the aubergines have already got some salt on them.

4 Coat your aubergine slices in flour, then gradually fry all the slices on both sides. This is hot work. Drink the red wine.

5 Preheat the oven to 190°C (375°F), Gas Mark 5. If using an Aga, you will cook the dish at the bottom of the roasting oven.

6 Put a thin layer of the tomato sauce in the bottom of a baking dish. Layer up the aubergine slices and pour the rest of the tomato sauce over them. Put some slices of mozzarella on the top and sprinkle with Parmesan. Bake in the oven for 1 hour until brown and bubbling.

7 Serve hot, cut into squares, with a green salad and more red wine.

QUENELLES

The cheat's fondue recipe was easy, so if you fancy stretching yourself, this is a much more difficult dish, from Lyon. The term *quenelle*, denoting a rugby-ball shape, is often used for desserts, but the Lyonnais quenelle is larger, longer. It's basically a dumpling. I don't do the traditional *brochet* version (*brochet* means 'pike', a river fish) but *quenelles nature*, with cheese.

Most Lyonnais don't make their own quenelles. 'We don't make them, we buy them, they are hard work,' one told me. But the older generation still know how to do it.

This kind of dish is the heavy style of French cuisine that is no longer fashionable, usurped in the '80s by nouvelle cuisine. Personally I still love it. I love eating so much rich heavy food that you break out in a rash of hives and need a trou normand between courses in order to survive the meal. A trou normand is a little glass of eau de vie, such as Calvados, which, the theory goes, makes a 'hole' in the food in your stomach so that you can fit more food in. It's for reasons like these that I love the French!

I make these quenelles with a tomato sauce, but they can also be done with the traditional Sauce Nantua.

INGREDIENTS

Vegetarian
if vegetarian
Parmesan is used
Serves 4

Quenelles
200ml (7fl oz) milk
*50g (1¾oz) butter, softened,
plus extra for greasing*
75g (2½oz) plain flour
*3 large eggs,
plus 2 very cold egg whites*
*150g (5½oz) Parmesan or
Emmental cheese*
1 tsp freshly grated nutmeg
1 sprig of thyme
2 cloves of garlic, peeled
*Sea salt and freshly ground
pepper, plus 1½ tbsp coarse
sea salt*

Tomato Sauce
2 tbsp olive oil
2 x 500g boxes of passata
*3 cloves of garlic, peeled and
crushed*
1 fresh bay leaf
*Sea salt and freshly ground
pepper*

Equipment
Food processor

1 If possible, prepare the tomato sauce in advance, as tomato-based sauces are always better the day after they're made. Put all the sauce ingredients together in a saucepan over a low heat and simmer for 1 hour. The sauce will keep for 4–5 days or longer in the fridge.

2 To make the panade (paste) for the quenelles, put the milk and half the butter in a saucepan with a little salt and pepper, set over a medium–high heat and bring to the boil. Then turn down the heat to low and vigorously stir in the flour with a wooden spoon until the mixture pulls away from the side of the pan. It will look similar to choux pastry. This is hard, as the mixture is so dense. Your arm will hurt. But don't give up!

3 Whisk in one egg and finish stirring it in with a spatula. Remove the pan from the heat and allow to cool to room temperature.

4 Transfer the quenelle mixture to a food processor, add the Parmesan or Emmental and whiz to blend. Then add the remaining butter, the nutmeg and some salt and pepper. With the motor running, add the two remaining whole eggs and the two cold egg whites. Scrape the mixture into a bowl and put in the fridge for 2 hours. Also put two large spoons in the fridge to chill – you will use these to make the quenelles.

5 Forming and cooking the quenelles is a skill in itself, but doesn't actually take too long to learn. Remove the quenelle mixture from the fridge and use one of the chilled spoons to scrape some mixture up the side of the bowl. Then, with a scooping gesture, turn the spoon onto the other spoon, passing the mixture back and forth between the two spoons to make the classic rugby-ball shape. Repeat with the rest of the mixture. Don't worry, you will get the hang of it. There are some videos on YouTube that demonstrate the technique. If it is too much of a faff, then simply roll the mixture into sausage shapes.

6 Preheat the oven to 200°C (400°F), Gas Mark 6. If using an Aga, prepare the roasting oven.

7 Bring 3 litres (5 pints 6fl oz) of water to the boil in a large saucepan. Lower the heat so that the water comes back to a gentle simmer, then add the thyme, garlic and coarse salt. When all the quenelles are shaped, gently lower them into the simmering water and poach for 10 minutes until you see them begin to puff up and float. Remove with a skimmer or slotted spoon. Drain the quenelles well and dry with kitchen paper.

8 Grease a porcelain baking dish with butter and lay the quenelles in it, in a single layer, leaving space between them. Cover with the tomato sauce and bake for 20 minutes on the bottom shelf of the oven until browned and bubbling.

BASIC CURRY SPICE MIX

Vegetarian
Makes enough powder
for a curry for 4

Spice Mix
1 cinnamon stick

1 star anise

1 tsp coriander seeds

1 tsp cumin seeds

1 clove

½ tsp fennel seeds

¼ tsp chilli powder or
2 whole red chillies

10 curry leaves

½ tsp paprika

½ tsp turmeric or 2.5cm
(1in) piece of fresh turmeric,
peeled and finely chopped

5 cardamom pods, crushed
and shells discarded

Brown Curry Sauce
Ghee or vegetable oil,
for cooking

1 tsp mustard seeds

Small piece of root ginger,
peeled and finely chopped

2–3 cloves of garlic,
peeled and crushed

2 onions, peeled and
processed to a pulp

Equipment
Food processor
(or pestle and mortar)

This spice mix is a basic powder that can be used in many curries. By adding root ginger, garlic and onions, it will give you the brown sauce that can be used as a base for most curries. Add tomatoes to that and you get another basic curry sauce. Add coconut milk, yoghurt or double cream (with or without the tomatoes) and you have a mild creamy sauce. (When the spice mix is used in the recipes on the subsequent pages, you need just the powder, not the extra ingredients for the brown curry sauce.) All curries are best garnished with coriander leaves.

1 Put all the ingredients for the spice mix in a frying pan without oil, and dry-roast over a medium–high heat for a minute or so to bring out the flavours. Then grind them up in a food processor or mortar and pestle. This spice powder can then be kept for up to 3 months. You can follow the next step to turn it into a brown curry sauce or you can use the powder in the curry recipes that follow.

2 To turn the powder into a basic brown curry sauce, add some ghee or vegetable oil to a frying pan and fry the spice powder with the mustard seeds (which will spit and pop a little), root ginger, garlic and onions. Cook for about 10 minutes, until the onions have absorbed the spices and caramelised a little, then add your choice of meat or vegetables and simmer in the sauce until cooked.

CHILLI SIN CARNE WITH ALL THE WORKS

*Vegetable or groundnut oil,
for cooking*

*1 large onion,
peeled and diced*

*2 cloves of garlic,
peeled and crushed*

*1 red pepper,
seeded and thinly sliced*

1 tsp ground cumin

1 tsp ground coriander

1 stick of cinnamon, ground

*1 tsp oregano (Mexican
oregano if you can get it)*

*2 x 400g tins of
chopped tomatoes*

*100g (3½oz) dried pinto
or black beans, soaked and
cooked until soft, or 1 x 400g
tin of pinto beans*

*2 dried ancho or chipotle
chillies, more if you
like it spicy*

*50g (1¾oz) dark chocolate
(I use Green and Black's Mayan
Gold), broken into pieces*

Sea salt, to taste

*Handful of fresh
coriander leaves*

*2–3 fresh jalapeño peppers
or large mild green chilli
peppers, seeded and grilled,
to garnish (optional)*

*Soured cream and grated
Cheddar cheese, to serve*

Here is a recipe for chilli without meat. Inspired by my travels in Mexico, I held a Mexican night at The Underground Restaurant. I bought all the right ingredients, the proper 'masa harina', which is the special cornflour that they use in Mexico, and a tortilla press. The whole building smelt like Mexico. To end the meal with a bang, Petra Chocstar, who runs a chocolate emporium from a converted ice-cream van, parked in my driveway. People went outside to get pudding through the hatch!

Now I must explain something: I may not eat meat but I never, never eat things like TVP (textured vegetable protein). I think it's disgusting, horribly processed and tastes similar to meat. Some people put it in their chilli sin carne but I never would. My chilli is pure bean! I like it with all the works, but if you don't have time, you can just serve it with rice or on its own. You can also buy ready-made wheat or corn tortillas. Corn and beans are typically native American foods, and together make complete protein.

1 Heat the oil in a saucepan over a low heat and cook the onion and garlic gently until soft and translucent. Add the red pepper and fry until soft. Add the spices, tomatoes and the beans and leave to simmer for 1 hour or more.

2 Meanwhile, soak your dried ancho chillies or chipotles in a cup of hot (not boiling) water. Once soft, remove from the cup (reserving the water) and remove the stems, seeds and membranes. Chop or tear into pieces and purée in a blender. Add to the bean mixture along with the reserved water. Also add the chocolate.

3 Once the beans are cooked, taste the mixture and adjust the salt level to your liking.

4 This dish gets even better if kept overnight. To serve, snip some coriander leaves over it and garnish with the grilled jalapeños, if using.

5 Serve the bowls of chilli with a scoop of soured cream and scoops of salsa and guacamole (see recipes overleaf). You can also sprinkle a handful of Cheddar cheese on top, which will melt on the hot chillies. Serve with the tortillas (see recipe on page 169), or you could instead serve with rice.

**Vegetarian
Serves 4**

*1 large mild green chilli
(preferably jalapeño)*

4 ripe tomatoes

1 small onion

Sea salt

*Juice of 2 limes
(or lemons if you
don't have limes)*

*Handful of chopped
fresh coriander*

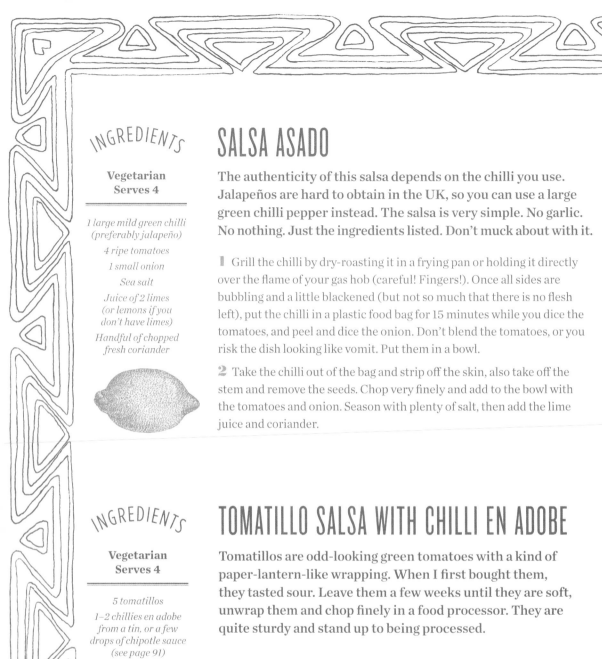

SALSA ASADO

The authenticity of this salsa depends on the chilli you use. Jalapeños are hard to obtain in the UK, so you can use a large green chilli pepper instead. The salsa is very simple. No garlic. No nothing. Just the ingredients listed. Don't muck about with it.

1 Grill the chilli by dry-roasting it in a frying pan or holding it directly over the flame of your gas hob (careful! Fingers!). Once all sides are bubbling and a little blackened (but not so much that there is no flesh left), put the chilli in a plastic food bag for 15 minutes while you dice the tomatoes, and peel and dice the onion. Don't blend the tomatoes, or you risk the dish looking like vomit. Put them in a bowl.

2 Take the chilli out of the bag and strip off the skin, also take off the stem and remove the seeds. Chop very finely and add to the bowl with the tomatoes and onion. Season with plenty of salt, then add the lime juice and coriander.

**Vegetarian
Serves 4**

5 tomatillos

*1–2 chillies en adobe
from a tin, or a few
drops of chipotle sauce
(see page 91)*

Juice of 2 limes

Handful of coriander leaves

Sea salt

Equipment

Food processor

TOMATILLO SALSA WITH CHILLI EN ADOBE

Tomatillos are odd-looking green tomatoes with a kind of paper-lantern-like wrapping. When I first bought them, they tasted sour. Leave them a few weeks until they are soft, unwrap them and chop finely in a food processor. They are quite sturdy and stand up to being processed.

Put all the ingredients in a food processor and blend together for instant authentic Mexico!

**Vegetarian
Serves 4**

---

2 ripe avocados

*1 small red onion,
peeled and diced*

*1 jalapeño or red chilli, grilled
(see method for Salsa Asado
opposite) and finely chopped*

Juice of 2 limes

*Handful of chopped fresh
coriander*

1 tsp sea salt

GUACAMOLE

**I'm a purist about guacamole. I think it should be chunky not
smooth, and without garlic.**

Remove the skin and stones from the avocados, scoop out the flesh and
chop finely. Put in a bowl, mix with the rest of the ingredients and taste
to check the seasoning.

**Vegetarian
Makes 12–14**

---

*300g (10½oz) cornflour
(masa harina, not cornmeal)*

About 150ml (5½fl oz) water

CORN TORTILLAS

1 Put the cornflour in a bowl and gradually add the water, mixing them
together. The dough shouldn't be too crumbly or too wet. Divide it into
little balls, each the size of a satsuma. The dough dries out quickly, so
keep it in a plastic food bag as you make the tortillas.

2 If you're using a tortilla press, cut two sheets of baking parchment
the size of the press and put a ball of dough between them. Then slot
this into the press. The paper prevents the ball of dough from sticking to
the press. Pull down the lever and the ball will flatten into a round shape.
If you don't have a press, then flatten with a heavy flat-bottomed pan.

3 Take a cast-iron frying pan or crêpière and dry-roast the flattened
tortilla over a low heat. If you are doing several tortillas, moisten a
clean tea towel and keep the tortillas wrapped once warmed, while
you finish the rest.

TWITTER CURRY

(FROM SPICY HARDEEP SINGH KHOLI)

One week I felt a bit lost for menu ideas. So I asked an open question on Twitter: '*What should I cook this week?*'

Hardeep Singh Kholi, the comic writer and broadcaster, a finalist in *Celebrity Masterchef* answered me '*Smoked aubergine and pea curry.*'

'*Wanna cook it?*' I asked. '*Guest chef?*'

'*Love to,*' came the response. I could hardly believe it.

Hardeep came over the day before the dinner, '*Curry is always better if cooked the day before.*' He wore a shocking-pink turban and smelt great, an exotic blend of aromas. He was quickly very flirty, breathing with a meaningful look, '*This situation is making me HOT,*' to the point that he took off his top and, bare-chested, continued to stir a vat of curry while taking calls from his agent on his Blackberry. Multi-tasking, he did everything at top speed, spinning out advice: '*Always include whole as well as ground spices for an authentic curry.*'

Hardeep confessed that he was recently divorced. I had a near brush with his special brand of hirsute and turbaned romance, which quite shocked me, food geek that I am, more interested in his spice technique than a quickie. Nevertheless, the man is a wonderful cook! I'm still not sure to this day whether it was all a joke.

On the evening of the meal, my guests did a double take when Hardeep helped out with the front-of-house '*Isn't that…?*' they said, open-mouthed. You gotta hand it to him, he's a game guy!

Here is Hardeep's recipe, followed by recipes for the sides: a salad and a chutney.

4 large aubergines

200g (7oz) butter or ghee

½ tsp turmeric powder

½ tsp chilli powder

4–5 cardamom pods

2 cinnamon sticks

½ tsp freshly ground black pepper

½ tsp whole cumin

½ tsp ground cumin

2 large onions, peeled and diced

6 plum tomatoes, diced

3–4 green chillies, finely chopped

2 x 250g bag of frozen petit pois

Sea salt

Handful of roughly chopped coriander leaves

1 First of all, roast your aubergines. We simply put both whole aubergines on the hotplate of the Aga and turned them over until the skin on each side had gone blackened and bubbly. You could replicate this by using a cast-iron pan over a gas hob, or you could blacken the aubergines on a wood barbecue. This gives the aubergine a wonderful smoky taste. Once done, remove from the heat and allow to cool, then strip off the skin, cut off the stem, and scoop out the soft flesh into a bowl. Set aside.

2 Heat the butter or ghee in a saucepan over a low heat and gently fry all the spices. Shortly afterwards, add the onion, tomatoes and chillies, turn the heat up to medium and cook for 15 minutes. Then add the peas and aubergine flesh. Simmer for 30 minutes, adding salt to taste. Finally stir in the coriander. Serve with the Sikh salad and kissing chutney on the following page.

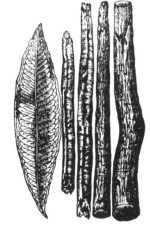

**Vegetarian
Serves 4**

50ml (1¾fl oz) white wine
or cider vinegar

3 Granny Smith apples,
peeled and cored

1 green chilli, seeded

Handful of fresh
chopped coriander

Sea salt and freshly
ground pepper

Equipment

Food processor

KISSING CHUTNEY

I served this chutney in a rose ice bowl (see page 290), which
caused guests to gasp with pleasure and surprise.

Put all the ingredients in a food processor, pulse until combined but still
chunky, then season to taste. Serve with the Twitter curry.

**Vegetarian
Serves 4**

2 medium red onions,
peeled and sliced

3–4 ripe tomatoes, sliced

1–2 green chillies,
seeded and finely sliced

125ml (4½fl oz) white wine
or cider vinegar

Handful of chopped
coriander leaves

Salt and freshly ground
black pepper

SIKH SALAD

I served this collection of recipes as part of my 'Indian Summer'
flower menu, so I added rose geranium leaves and marigold petals
to the salad, which made it look even prettier.

Simply mix together all the prepared ingredients
in a large bowl. Serve with the Twitter curry.

COCONUT DAHL

**Vegetarian
Serves 4**

---

2 tbsp ghee or vegetable oil

1 tbsp curry spice mix
(see page 166 or store-bought)

2.5cm (1in) piece
of root ginger,
peeled and finely chopped

2 cloves of garlic,
peeled and crushed

¼ tsp coriander seeds

250g (9oz) red lentils
(make sure there are no stones)

350ml (12fl oz) water

1 x 400ml tin of coconut milk

Sea salt, to taste

Handful of chopped
coriander leaves

I cooked in some unusual places before starting The Underground Restaurant: at squat cafés, at cooperative community cafés, at protest camps such as the anti-G8 camp in Stirling, Scotland in 2005. There is a certain type of food, which I'll call 'squat slop', and which often consists of one-pot dishes like stews and curries. It's filling, it's cheap and it can expand to feed the 5000. Some squats use 'skipped' food – that is, from dumpsters. Supermarkets throw out perfectly good food, still in the packets. Activists who can't abide waste, and squatters – who tend to be poor – go round the back of the supermarket and reclaim the unused food. Don't be shocked! An ex-boyfriend of mine once found four bottles of champagne! Unfortunately, some supermarkets cottoned onto this practice and deliberately ruined the food by squirting detergents. Such a waste! At least give it to homeless shelters...

However, just because you are cooking for a little community café or a camp or squat doesn't mean you should let your standards drop. Dahl is a standard lentil dish, which every vegetarian Indian or Nepalese lives on...it's healthy and cheap. This Coconut Dahl is a more luxurious version, and it's also pretty quick because red lentils don't need soaking.

1 Heat up the ghee in a saucepan and gently fry the curry spice mix over a low–medium heat, then add the ginger, garlic and coriander seeds. Add the red lentils, along with the water and the coconut milk. Simmer for 30 minutes, tasting occasionally and adjusting the salt.

2 Adjust the liquid levels, depending on whether you like a thick dahl or a liquid one. Stir regularly and serve garnished with fresh coriander.

TINDA MASALA

I first tasted tinda, baby pumpkin, in a curry at a very cheap restaurant called Tayyabs, in London's East End. Tayyabs was one of the first London restaurants to build an authentic tandoor oven to make naan breads. It's best known as a restaurant that specialises in meat, but the tinda masala could make a vegetarian cry, it's so good. You'll need to go to Asian shops to get hold of these tiny satsuma-sized pumpkins with their slightly sharp, citrussy taste. You could also use tinned tinda or, failing that, this recipe might work with young marrows or round courgettes (normal courgettes are too watery).

INGREDIENTS

**Vegetarian
Serves 4**

*100g (3½oz) ghee or butter,
or 100ml (3½fl oz) vegetable
oil, plus extra to serve*

½ tsp mustard seeds

*2 tbsp curry spice mix
(see page 166 or store-bought)*

*1 tsp amchur (dry mango
powder, a souring agent)*

1 red chilli, finely sliced

*4 cloves of garlic,
peeled and crushed*

*2.5cm (1in) piece of
root ginger,
peeled and finely chopped*

*16 small smooth tindas,
peeled and cut into quarters
(if using tinned, wash and
quarter)*

Sea salt, to taste

*10 small fresh tomatoes,
quartered*

*300ml pot of yoghurt
or tin of coconut milk*

*Handful of fresh chopped
coriander*

1 Heat the ghee, butter or oil in a saucepan over a low heat and drop in the mustard seeds. When they begin to pop, add the curry spice mix, the amchur and the red chilli. Stir briefly, then add the garlic and ginger and continue to stir so that the mixture doesn't stick at the bottom. Add the tindas and cook over a low heat until they are tender, stirring gently now and again to stop the curry sticking. Add half of the fresh tomatoes. Taste and adjust the salt.

2 When the tindas are almost ready – that is, tender – add the rest of the tomatoes, the yoghurt or coconut milk and the coriander to the pan. Continue to cook for 5–10 minutes. The curry should look slick and oily, so feel free to add more oil or ghee. Check the seasoning, garnish with fresh coriander and serve.

JEWELLED BASMATI

The brightly coloured rice that you get in Indian restaurants is something I long wanted to imitate. I tend to use a rice steamer to cook rice. That way, there are no mistakes and the rice is always fluffy and the grains stay separate. Just put the rice in the steamer and measure out the same amount in water. Do pay for the best-quality rice; it's a false economy otherwise. I like to serve rice and curries with an extra jug of ghee to pour over. No calorie-counting here!

Vegetarian
Serves 4

400g (14oz) best-quality
basmati rice

400ml (14fl oz) water

Sea salt

Pinch of orange powdered
food colouring

50g (1¾oz) cashew nuts,
roughly chopped

Butter or ghee, for cooking
cashews (optional)

Handful of fresh
coriander leaves

Handful of sour cherries
(optional)

Equipment
Rice steamer (optional)

1 Put the rice and the water in a rice steamer and add a little salt. Steam for 10–15 minutes until cooked. You can also cook the rice in a saucepan according to the packet instructions.

2 When the rice is cooked, add a pinch of the orange powder and stir it in gently with a fork. Some grains will stay white, some will go yellow, some orange and some dark orange.

3 You can sauté your cashew nuts in a little butter or ghee if you like. Scatter them on top of the rice and garnish with coriander and sour cherries, if using.

BUTTERNUT SQUASH
& BLUE CHEESE RISOTTO

At first I encouraged guest chefs at The Underground Restaurant. This sometimes worked and sometimes didn't. An Italian friend cooked a butternut and blue cheese risotto for my guests one Saturday. She gave me a sample of the dish and very nice it was too. But cooking for large numbers of people on an unfamiliar oven (an Aga) is a whole different ball game. On the night in question, I didn't realise at first, but the risotto she made burnt on the bottom. My first clue was guests saying, 'Hmm, this is very er...smoky tasting.' When I tasted it myself I was horrified and embarrassed. A risotto is tough to make for large numbers of people. Still a great recipe, though. Just watch it like a hawk and keep stirring until it's glossy.

INGREDIENTS

Vegetarian
Serves 4

Olive oil, for cooking

1 onion, peeled and diced

2–3 cloves of garlic, peeled and crushed

1 fresh bay leaf

1 large butternut squash, peeled and diced into 3cm (1¼in) cubes

400g (14oz) risotto rice, such as carnaroli or nano vialone

2 glasses of white wine

400ml (14fl oz) hot vegetable stock (see page 137)

100g (3½oz) butter, cut into cubes

200g (7oz) blue cheese (such as Colston Bassett stilton), cut into 2cm (¾in) cubes

Handful of flat-leaf parsley

Sea salt and freshly ground black pepper

1 Heat the olive oil in a saucepan and cook your onion and garlic, with the bay leaf, until they are soft and translucent. Add the butternut squash, turning the cubes so that they pick up the lovely garlic flavours. Add the rice and sauté a little until it goes translucent.

2 Pour in the white wine and keep stirring for about 5 minutes until it's absorbed. Then gradually add the stock, a cup at a time, until fully absorbed by the rice. Once the rice has swollen and tastes cooked (with perhaps a small, nutty centre still – you don't want it to feel soggy in the mouth and it does continue to cook in its own heat as you serve it), beat in the butter and season the risotto with salt and pepper. Stir half the blue cheese cubes into the risotto.

3 Serve in bowls with the rest of the blue cheese scattered on top. Garnish with flat-leaf parsley and add another turn of black pepper, if you want.

HOME-MADE
FRESH PASTA

I could eat pasta for every single meal, that's how much I love it. I'd like to propose that you make your own. It's not that hard. Granted, it is time-consuming and not something you will be doing every week. But it's worth it for special occasions. Get the kids involved too. I make my pasta in a food processor. You can obviously also make it by hand.

Vegetarian
Serves 6–8

300g (10½oz) pasta flour ('00' preferably) or strong white flour

1 tsp sea salt

3 large eggs, beaten

Equipment
Food processor (optional)
Pasta machine

1 If using a food processor, put the flour and salt in the machine and pulse. With the motor running, gradually add the beaten eggs to the mixture, a gloopy drop at a time. The mixture should look like couscous. If it looks lumpy, add more flour.

2 Once it does look like couscous, turn off the food processor and gather up the dough into a ball, then knead for 10 minutes. If the dough looks dry while you are kneading it, cover with a clean damp tea towel and leave it for 30 minutes to hydrate. Look, feel, get to know your dough. It will tell you what it needs.

3 If making the pasta by hand, put the flour in a mound on a clean work surface. Make a well in the centre and add the salt and the beaten eggs. Using a fork, mix the sides with the eggy centre, eventually bringing the mixture together into a ball. Then knead for 10 minutes.

4 Wrap your ball of pasta in cling film and rest for 30 minutes at room temperature.

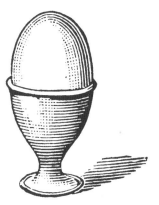

5 Screw your pasta machine to a work surface with the handle closest to you. Unwrap the ball of pasta and flatten it slightly. Run it though the machine on the widest setting, then fold the pasta 'tongue' in half and thread it through the widest setting again, with the unfolded end of the tongue going through first. Repeat this about ten times – you will feel the pasta becoming more elastic. You may hear a little pop sound at the folded end just as you finish threading it through for the last time. This pop means it's definitely done. If you don't hear it, just make sure you've rolled it though at least ten times. If the rollers stick, sprinkle some flour over them.

6 Now run the pasta through the machine slowly on each setting, not folding it this time. Keep going until the last setting, by which time your pasta will be three times as long as it was. You need long arms for this or get somebody to help! If it becomes unmanageably long, you can cut it in half once.

7 The pasta is now ready to use. To make cannelloni, lasagne sheets, ravioli or tortelloni, keep it whole. You can make fettuccini by running it through one of the other rollers on the machine. Cover the pasta immediately, to prevent it drying out before you need to use it again.

8 If you are making stuffed pasta (see page 270), I'd use it straight away, as it dries out very quickly and becomes hard to bend. You can then freeze the made-up tortelloni or ravioli for up to 3 months, sprinkled with flour. For spaghetti/fettuccini, cut it up, make a nest and let it dry or freeze sprinkled with flour.

SPINACH & RICOTTA CANNELLONI

Vegetarian
if vegetarian
Parmesan is used
Serves 4
Makes about 16 tubes

---

*1 portion of fresh pasta
(see pages 178–9), rolled into
strips and cut into rectangles
of about 10 x 7cm (4 x 3in)*

*Handful of freshly grated
Parmesan cheese (optional)*

Stuffing

*700g (1½lb) fresh spinach,
washed (or use frozen)*

*Large pinch of freshly grated
nutmeg*

400g (14oz) ricotta cheese

*Sea salt and freshly ground
pepper*

Tomato Sauce

(Makes 500ml/18fl oz)

Olive oil, for cooking

1 onion, peeled and diced

*3 cloves of garlic,
peeled and crushed*

*2 x 400g tins
chopped tomatoes*

2 fresh bay leaves

Sea salt

A nice use of the home-made pasta on the previous pages is to make it into little rolls called cannelloni. It's a question of cutting it into squares, putting a strip of filling down the centre and sealing the ends together with water to make a tube. However, I would only roll it in the pasta machine to setting number 5 or 6, not number 7 for the really fine pasta. You can also use dried cannelloni for this recipe – the 'no boil' type is good. Who can be bothered to boil the slippery little buggers before trying to stuff them?

The tomato sauce here is my basic tomato sauce for pasta. You will also use it for the Melanzane alla Parmigiana recipe (see page 162). I probably cook it about three times a week. It's my Death Row sauce. By which I mean, if I was about to die, I'd want spaghetti with a garlicky tomato sauce as my last meal. The proportions here make 500ml (18fl oz), enough for this cannelloni dish, but I tend to make larger amounts and freeze portions in those stand-up freezer bags designed for liquids. Tomato sauce is always better a day after it's made (that's why I love spaghetti for breakfast!), so it's good to have extra to hand.

1 First make the tomato sauce. (Make it a day in advance if possible.) Heat the olive oil in a saucepan and cook the onion and garlic until soft and translucent. Add the tomatoes and the bay leaves, and season well with salt. Simmer for 1 hour. Set aside until needed, or allow to cool and store in the fridge for 4–5 days, or freeze for up to 3 months.

2 For the cheese sauce, melt the butter in a saucepan over a low heat, then add the flour and stir to make a roux. Gradually, still on a low heat, whisk in the milk until you have a smooth sauce. Season with nutmeg, salt and pepper, then add the cheese. Keep stirring until it has all melted. Take the pan off the heat and set aside until ready to assemble the dish.

3 To make the stuffing, put the spinach into a large pan on a low heat. Allow it to reduce and sprinkle some nutmeg over it. Take it off the heat and allow to cool. Once cool, mix in the ricotta. Season with salt and pepper.

4 Preheat the oven to 180°C (350°F), Gas Mark 4. If using an Aga, prepare the roasting oven with the middle shelf positioned.

Cheese Sauce (Optional)

30g (1oz) butter

30g (1oz) plain flour

500ml (18fl oz) whole milk

Pinch of freshly grated nutmeg

Sea salt and freshly ground pepper

100g (3½oz) Cheddar cheese, grated

5 Oil an ovenproof dish or baking tin and spread a layer of the tomato sauce across the bottom. Begin to construct the cannelloni by putting a tablespoon of the spinach and ricotta mixture into the middle of a pasta square and spreading it evenly in a line down the centre. Turn the pasta square so that you can seal two edges over the mixture to make a tube. Repeat with the rest of the pasta and mixture until you have about 16 of these cannelloni tubes, then place them side by side in the baking dish on top of the tomato sauce. Once they are lined up, pour the rest of the tomato sauce over the top of the cannelloni, followed by the cheese sauce. If you prefer to omit the cheese sauce, you can sprinkle with some grated Parmesan cheese instead.

6 Cover the dish with foil and bake in the oven for 30 minutes, then remove the foil and increase the oven to 200°C (400°F), Gas Mark 6 (or if using an Aga, move the dish to the top shelf). Cook for a further 10 minutes until brown on top.

IL TIMPANO

Il timpano is Italian for 'drum'. When the fresh pasta is laid tightly across the top of this pie, it can look and sound like the skin of a drum. I made this pasta pie for a 'Film and Food' night, at which I 'quoted' dishes from foodie films. This dish comes from a film called *Big Night* about two Italian brothers who try to set up an authentic Italian restaurant in America in the '50s. They make a special meal to impress a famous visiting musician and the pièce de résistance is this dish, *Il timpano* – 'A secret recipe from their home village' in Italy. The actor, director and writer of the film, Stanley Tucci, owns an Italian restaurant in real life, where in fact this dish is made. There is a wonderful unedited sequence at the end of the film in which Stanley makes a frittata for the kitchen staff. The whole film is a delight.

If you want, you can order the special 6-litre (imperial) 'timpano' bowl from here: http://www.amazon.com/Enamelware-Timpano-Basin-Blue-Marble/dp/B001R5AQT2.

I used a big metal dish that I happened to have, but make sure you use one that fits in your oven! You don't want to spend hours preparing this and then find the dish won't fit. (Not that that happened to me, of course).

This dish takes a while to make, but again, if you want something spectacular and theatrical to serve, then this is your baby.

INGREDIENTS

Vegetarian
Serves 10–12

2 portions of fresh pasta dough (see pages 178–9)

Plain flour, for dusting

Olive oil, for greasing the bowl and tossing the rigatoni

1kg (2lb 3oz) dried rigatoni

Sea salt and freshly ground pepper

1kg (2lb 3oz) tomato sauce (see page 180)

300g (10½oz) provolone cheese, cubed

8 hard-boiled eggs, peeled and cut into quarters

100g (3½oz) Pecorino cheese, grated

4 eggs, beaten and seasoned with salt and pepper

1 For this recipe you will need a large circle of pasta to line your timpano bowl. So do not run your fresh pasta dough through the machine. Instead, follow the recipe on pages 178–9 up to the stage where the dough has been left to rest for 30 minutes. Then, on a floured work surface, roll the dough outwards from the centre, rotating it a quarter-turn after each roll, to get a large enough circle to line the entire bowl, plus enough to overlap the top of your bowl.

2 Oil your timpano bowl and line it with the pasta dough, pressing it gently, so that it doesn't break, into the edges. Leave the excess hanging down outside the bowl.

3 Part-cook the rigatoni, for two-thirds of the time stated on the packet instructions, then drain, return to the saucepan and toss with olive oil, salt and pepper. Mix half of the tomato sauce with the part-cooked rigatoni.

4 Preheat the oven to 180°C (350°F), Gas Mark 4. If using an Aga, prepare the baking oven.

5 Pour a thick layer of the tomatoey rigatoni into the pasta-lined timpano bowl. Then add a layer of provolone cubes, followed by a layer of egg quarters and a sprinkling of Pecorino cheese. Repeat with the rigatoni, then more provolone, more egg and more cheese. Continue in this way, ending with a layer of rigatoni. Leave a 2–3cm (1in) gap at the top of the bowl.

6 Pour the remaining tomato sauce over the pasta. Pour over the beaten eggs. Bring up the overhanging pasta and fold over the top of the pie, pinching it together in the middle to make a seal. Trim away any excess.

7 Cook in the oven for 1 hour. Then cover the top with foil and bake for another 30 minutes. It's useful to check the internal temperature with a probe thermometer at this point. It should be at least 50°C (120°F) inside. If not, continue cooking until it is.

8 Remove the pie from oven and allow to rest for 30 minutes. Then, oooh, the tricky bit: turn it over onto a plate. You might need someone to help you do this. To serve, cut a circle in the middle; this will help the pie to stay together. Cut into wedges and serve with salad.

REALLY GOOD MAC & CHEESE

'Mac and Cheese' is what the Americans call macaroni cheese. It was the only school dinner I ever looked forward to! Pretty much everything can be changed in this recipe – the ingredients I've suggested are just an indication. You don't have to use Cheddar cheese; use whatever type you have in the fridge. You can make it slimming by using half-fat milk instead of the whole milk and cream. But really, this is a lovely comforting winter's dish, perfect for eating in front of the telly, while watching something a bit crap like *I'm A Celebrity*. It's great duvet food and it's great supper-club food.

Vegetarian
Serves 4

500g (1lb 2oz)
large macaroni
Sea salt
30g (1oz) unsalted butter
3 tbsp plain flour
250ml (9fl oz) whole milk
600ml (1 pint) single cream
450g (1lb) strong
Cheddar cheese, such as
Montgomery or Greens
of Glastonbury, grated
1 heaped tbsp
wholegrain mustard
(or any type you have)
Pinch of freshly
grated nutmeg (optional)
1–2 tbsp green
pickled peppercorns
Sea salt and ground
white pepper

1 Preheat the oven to 200°C (400°F), Gas Mark 6. If using an Aga, prepare the roasting oven.

2 Boil the macaroni in a saucepan of salted water. Cook it for a little less time than suggested on the packet instructions, about 5 minutes, as the macaroni will continue to cook in the oven.

3 Meanwhile, put the unsalted butter and the flour in another saucepan. Heat gently and stir it around, making sure it doesn't burn. Once it has formed a paste, gradually whisk in the milk until the sauce becomes a thick liquid. Then add the single cream and 300g (10½oz) of the cheese. Add the mustard and a pinch of nutmeg shavings, if you wish, and season to taste. When the cheese has melted, add the pickled green peppercorns, then remove the pan from the heat.

4 Drain the macaroni and spread out in a buttered baking tin or other ovenproof dish.

5 Pour the sauce over the macaroni and sprinkle the rest of the cheese on top. Bake in the oven for 15–20 minutes until the cheese on top is brown and bubbling.

6 Serve with salad, such as rocket or lamb's lettuce, drizzled with walnut oil and lemon juice, and a glass of chilled white wine, Gewürztraminer perhaps.

CRÊPES

Crêpes, rather than pancakes, are the nearest thing the French have to snack food, which is possibly why 'French women don't get fat'. As a street food, crêpes are folded into moist triangles, so hot that they burn your hands. These crêpes are Breton-style, also known as *galettes* or *crêpes au Sarrasin* (comparing the dark colour of the flour with the dark skin of the Saracens), cooked with cider rather than milk, with lacy edges and a wonderful sour alcoholic taste to the batter. I did an Anti-Valentine's singles night at The Underground Restaurant, which coincided with Shrove Tuesday/Pancake Day. It was called 'F**k Valentines, let's eat pancakes!' I had space for 15 girls and 15 men. Only three men came, one of whom already had a girlfriend!

INGREDIENTS

Vegetarian
Serves 4

110g (4oz) buckwheat flour

1 egg, plus 1 yolk

275ml (10fl oz) cider, preferably French sparkling cidre brut

15g (½oz) butter, melted

Pinch of sea salt

Xanthan gum (optional)

Choice of Fillings

300g (10½oz) good-quality Cheddar cheese, grated

Handful of field mushrooms, fried in butter and garlic

Finely sliced onions, fried

1 Mix the flour, egg and yolk together with half of the cider. Whisk until the batter is lump-free, then add the rest of the cider, the melted butter and the salt.

2 If you were using normal flour, it would be important not to overbeat, as it activates the gluten and makes the pancakes tough. But buckwheat flour has no gluten, so it's not a problem here. However, if you want, you can add a little xanthan gum to help make the pancakes stronger and stretchier.

3 Prepare your chosen filling(s).

4 When cooking the crêpes, the usual pancake rules apply: the first crepe is always crap.

5 Find the largest, flattest frying pan you possess, or a crêpière. Dip a little kitchen roll in melted butter or use an empty butter paper to rub grease all over your pan (these WW2 habits that I learnt from my grandmother die hard). Put a ladle of the batter in the pan, tipping the pan so that the batter spreads finely over the whole surface. You want a thin crêpe not an American-style pancake. Let it cook on one side.

6 At this point, you can either add your fillings right away or you can make a stack of crepes ready to reheat later (adding the fillings at the last minute). If serving immediately, add your filling on top. Fold the crêpe in half or into quarters and cook for a couple more minutes to let the filling heat through.

7 Serve the crêpes hot, garnished with flat-leaf parsley and freshly ground pepper.

Fish
Main Courses

*f*ish is very good for your health. In fact, according to evolutionary scientists, eating a seafood diet led to the rapid growth of the human brain two million years ago.

But of course we have to be careful about fish, as many species such as the Bluefin tuna are in danger of extinction due to trawler nets. Even line-caught doesn't necessarily mean some folksy guy with a fishing rod; it can mean rows of industrial lines. The film *The End of the Line* exposes industrial overfishing, which is so serious that it is estimated that the world will run out of fish by 2048. Do we really want our children to grow up without fish? I'm careful to eat certain types of fish such as sardines, pilchards, coley, mackerel, tilapia, brown trout and seabream and I check with the fishmonger that my fish comes from sustainable sources.

Many confident cooks are frightened of working with fish, but no need, these recipes are easy and accessible and at the same time, impressive!

GRATIN DAUPHINOISE WITH SMOKED SALMON

Serves 4

1 clove of garlic, peeled

Butter, for greasing

4 large potatoes (such as Charlotte, Maris Piper, Desirée or King Edwards), peeled and thinly sliced

250g (9oz) smoked salmon (optional)

2 fresh bay leaves

600ml (1 pint 2fl oz) double cream

Sea salt and freshly ground pepper

If I have a signature dish, this is probably it. I've spent a lot of time in the Lyon area of France, not too far from the Alps, and not too far from the Dauphine region from whence this dish comes. Despite the delicate treatment of the potatoes, it is hearty mountain food, designed to get you through a cold night under a thick duvet. I have a bay tree, and the intensity of flavour is remarkable when you use fresh bay leaves. Accompanied with a green salad, scattered walnuts, a walnut oil dressing and a crisp white wine, gratin dauphinoise embraces both comfort and elegance. The version below is interleaved with smoked salmon. You can, of course, make it without the smoked salmon if you want a vegetarian dish.

1 Preheat the oven to 180°C (350°F), Gas Mark 4. If using an Aga, use the bottom shelf of the roasting oven.

2 This dish is more elegant if you slice the potatoes very thinly with a mandoline, or you can use the slicing attachment on a food processor.

3 Rub a baking dish or tin with the garlic clove, and then discard the clove. Grease with butter. Arrange a layer of potato slices prettily in the bottom, like fish scales.

4 Salt the layer lightly. Then add a layer of smoked salmon. Repeat with the rest of the potatoes and salmon, salting lightly as you go. You shouldn't have more than three layers altogether, as you need room at the top for the cream, so don't overfill the dish. Just three layers also keeps it from being too stodgy.

5 Place the bay leaves on the top layer and season. Pour over the double cream; this should cover the potatoes and the bay leaves generously. Cover the dish with foil and bake in the oven for 30 minutes. Then remove the foil and bake for another 15 minutes, which will brown the top. If you stick a skewer in the potatoes, they should be soft and yielding.

CURING YOUR OWN SALMON

This is very easy. Surprisingly so. The food writer Tim Hayward has a smoking shed in his back garden and offered me the use of it. But I had to cure the salmon first. I served it for my Burn's Night supper at The Underground Restaurant and the rest at a brunch. It was the best smoked salmon I have ever tasted. You can also cure other fish in the same way; in Greece they cure very fresh sardines and eat them with Ouzo.

INGREDIENTS

**Makes 2kg
(4lb 6oz)**

1kg (2lb 3oz) good-quality
sea salt (I use sel grise)

1kg (2lb 3oz) sugar
(I used sugar left over from
candying citrus fruits)

Large handful of herbs
(such as tarragon, flat-leaf
parsley, basil and dill)

2kg (4lb 6oz) very fresh
whole side of salmon, head,
tail and skin removed

Selection of spices (such as
juniper and peppercorns)

Drizzle of gin or Pernod
(optional)

1 Mix the salt, sugar, herbs and spices together. Spread a thick layer of this mixture all over a large dish, such as a shallow-sided baking tin, one that is long enough to fit the side of salmon. Lay the salmon on top of this mixture, then put the rest of the mix directly onto the fish. Drizzle the fish with alcohol if you wish.

2 Place another, similar-sized, dish on top of the salmon and weigh it down with tins or weights. Put the sandwiched salmon in a cool place or the fridge for 12–24 hours.

3 After this time, bring it out, take off the weights and remove the top dish. Scrape the salt/sugar/herb/spice mix off the salmon into a bowl and drain the water from the bottom dish.

4 You will notice that your fish is now quite stiff. Turn the salmon over and repack it with the salt/sugar/herb/spice mix from the bowl. Replace the top dish and the weights and put it back in the fridge for another 12–24 hours.

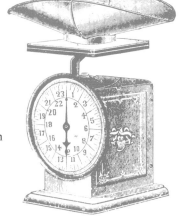

5 Bring out the fish, take off the weights and dish and scrape off the mixture. Rinse the fish and pat dry. Wrap in cling film. You can now eat the salmon as it is or take it to be smoked.

GRILLED SARDINES WITH MINT

I never really liked sardines until I visited Portugal, where for the first time I ate them fresh (not tinned) grilled with blistering, crispy, oily skins, contrasted with mint leaves and a crisp, green Vinho Verde, a young Portuguese wine. It's the perfect dish for a hot summer's day, good on the barbecue, but also easy to do in the oven. Serve the sardines with roast potatoes and a tomato salad, or they are also very good on buttered toast!

Serves 4

4 large whole sardines or 8 small ones, gutted

50ml (1¾fl oz) olive oil

Large handful of fresh mint leaves, torn

2 lemons, one sliced and the other cut into wedges

Sea salt and freshly ground pepper

1 Preheat the oven to 220ºC (425ºF), Gas Mark 7. If using an Aga, position the top shelf of the roasting oven. Alternatively, light your barbecue.

2 Sprinkle the sardines with olive oil and torn mint leaves, tucking some mint and lemon slices into their cavities. Season with salt and pepper.

3 If cooking in the oven, lay the sardines in an ovenproof baking dish and roast for 10–15 minutes until bubbling. Alternatively, you can grill the sardines on a barbecue for 5 minutes on each side.

Serve with wedges of lemon to squeeze over the fish.

SALT-BAKED FISH

I love salt. To me, the message should not be 'reduce salt', but use good salt that has all the minerals in it. (Though 'drink more water' is a better message!)

In the salt flats of Ile de Ré, in the west of France, they have salt that they call fleur de sel, flower of salt, reminiscent of violets. For cooking I most commonly use sel grise, a large-grained salt, still damp from the Guérande coast where it is harvested. I have all flavours and textures of salt, which I use for different dishes: black lava salt from Hawaii; pink Himalayan rock salt, sulphuric Indian salt (to put on fruit), smoked salt, the delicate flakes of Maldon sea salt, green-tea salt, herb, spice and citrus salts. I also love different peppers: the classic freshly ground black peppercorns, white zingy Sichuan pepper, fragrant pink peppercorns, white pepper for pale sauces.

In South America I visited the salt cathedral in Tunja, Colombia, located in a cavernous underground salt mine, where you can lick the walls! I also toured the Salar de Uyuni in Bolivia, blindingly white, snowy kilometres of salt from a dried inland sea.

Salt can be used to bake meat, fish and vegetables – I've cooked potatoes on a bed of salt, which leaves the skins crispy. This recipe encases fish in mounds of salt, creating a mini oven that leaves the flesh tender and tasty. Sea bass works well, or red snapper looks really pretty with the white of the salt, also sea bream and tilapia. Do choose a fish that isn't too bony, as it's difficult to extract the bones once cooked. You can leave the scales on because the skin will be removed to eat it. Use cheap, coarse sea salt to encase the fish. Save the good stuff for seasoning.

INGREDIENTS

Serves 4

4 x small 250g (9oz) or 1 x large 1kg (2lb 3oz) sea bass, red snapper or other firm fish, washed and gutted

3 lemons, zested and sliced

Handful of thyme leaves

1–2 tbsp fennel seeds, ground

2 tbsp olive oil

2–3kg (4½– 6½lb) coarse sea salt

4–5 egg whites

Selection of herbs (such as bay leaves, thyme sprigs, rosemary sprigs, lavender sprigs and fennel)

Lavender, to garnish

1 Preheat the oven to 220°C (425°F), Gas Mark 7. If using an Aga, prepare the roasting oven.

2 Wash the fish and pat dry with kitchen paper. Put most of the lemon zest in a bowl with the thyme and fennel seeds. Use this to stuff the cavities of the fish. Also put some olive oil and lemon slices into the cavities.

3 Mix the salt with the egg whites; the texture should be like fine sand or wet snow. You can add a little water if needs be, but not so much that the salt dissolves. Put a layer of this in the bottom of an oven dish, pressing it down firmly with your hands, then place the stuffed fish on top. Sprinkle your chosen herbs and the remaining lemon zest over the skin of the fish.

4 Then spread the rest of the salt compactly, like a thick blanket, over the bodies of the fish, as if they are in a salty clay adobe oven. Make sure there are no holes; you want to seal the fish in, though you can leave their heads and tails exposed.

5 Bake in the oven for 40 minutes. To check the fish is cooked, plunge a metal skewer into the middle. If it comes out warm, the fish is ready.

6 Leave the dish to rest for 5 minutes. Then you can crack open the salt casing and peel back the skin of the fish, lifting out the meat. Or impress your guests by serving the fish still in their salt shells and letting everyone else do the work. Garnish with lavender.

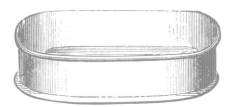

MARMITE CHEESE
ON SMOKED HADDOCK

I made this dish for my Marmite menu, in which everything – every course, every dish – used Marmite as an ingredient. Mostly I used Marmite as a seasoning, like soy sauce, but smoked haddock is strong enough to take a thick slathering of Marmite. It all depends on how hardcore you are with Marmite. This recipe is a bit like Welsh rarebit, but with fish instead. I've also tried to reflect the classic Marmite jar colours of yellow, brown, red and green in the presentation of this dish.

Serves 4

*800g (1lb 12oz)
smoked haddock fillet,
cut into 4 even portions*

Jar of Marmite

*4 tbsp mustard
(wholegrain if possible)*

*200g (7oz) strong
Cheddar cheese, grated*

3–4 tomatoes, sliced

Freshly ground black pepper

*Handful of chopped flat-leaf
parsley, to garnish*

1 Preheat the oven to 180°C (350°F), Gas Mark 4. If using an Aga, prepare the roasting oven.

2 Rinse your smoked haddock fillets and pat dry with kitchen paper. Place in an ovenproof baking dish. Spread Marmite onto the fish, as thickly or thinly as you like. Then spread the mustard on top. Cover with the grated cheese and finally add slices of the tomato. Grind black pepper over the top. Bake in the oven for 25 minutes.

3 Serve garnished with flat-leaf parsley.

SPAGHETTI AL CARTOCCIO

Serves 4

200g (7oz) clams (palourdes
are best, preferably fresh
but use tinned if stuck)

Olive oil, for cooking

2–3 shallots,
peeled and finely chopped

4 cloves of garlic, peeled
and crushed (plus extra if
you're a garlic-lover)

Handful of flat-leaf parsley

2 glasses of white wine

500g (1lb 2oz)
good-quality spaghetti or
linguine (good-quality pasta
with an 11-minute cooking
time is essential, or it may
end up overcooked)

Sea salt and freshly
ground black pepper

Equipment

Lots of greaseproof paper

This is a dish I used to have with my parents on a Sunday
afternoon. As a special treat we would go to an Italian restaurant
in Chelsea for 'spaghetti in a bag'. It was always a magical moment
when the bag was opened at the table and all the hot steam
poured out...

1 Soak your vongole (clams) in salted water for at least 1 hour, preferably
longer, until you need them. This opens up the shells and helps to rinse
them of sand and grit. Change the water several times.

2 Heat a little olive oil in a saucepan over a low–medium heat and
cook the shallots until soft and translucent. Add plenty of crushed garlic
(I mean plenty) and cook for a little longer. Roughly chop your flat-leaf
parsley – not too fine, you want to see the shape of the leaf – and add
to the pan. Pour in the white wine and simmer for 5 minutes.

3 Fill another pot with water, add salt and bring to the boil. Add your
pasta (about 100–150g/3½–5½oz per person) and cook it for 7–8 minutes.
Be really careful not to go over this amount of time. Immediately remove
from the heat and pour it into a colander. Splash some olive oil over your
pasta and stir through so that the strands don't stick together. Set aside.

4 Preheat the oven to 200°C (400°F), Gas Mark 6. If using an Aga, prepare
the roasting oven.

5 Rinse the clams under fresh running water. Any that don't shut, discard.
Any that are very broken, chuck. You really don't want to take risks with
shellfish. Add the clams to the shallot/garlic/parsley mixture and heat gently.
The shells should start to open very quickly. If any remain shut, remove them
and discard. Stir so that the shells get some of the lovely oily garlicky mixture
inside them.

6 Cut out four half-metre squares of greaseproof paper. Lay a handful
of your partly cooked pasta in the middle of each square of greaseproof
paper. Dump a scoop of the vongole sauce on top, then bring up the sides
of the paper and twist together. Put your bundles of spaghetti on a baking
tray and bake in the oven for 5 minutes.

7 Serve a parcel of vongole on each plate...spectacular and delicious!

THAI-STYLE FISH IN BANANA LEAVES WITH COCONUT RICE

This is an 'en papillote' style recipe, meaning the fish is wrapped up and cooked. You can use any firm fish fillet – I've used monkfish, sea bass, salmon and sea trout. It's an impressive-looking dish and I think people just like to unwrap things; it's reminiscent of birthday presents and pass-the-parcel!

Serves 4

2 large banana leaves (available in Asian stores, or use foil or baking parchment instead)

4 x 150–200g (5½–7oz) fish fillets (not too large, or it's hard to wrap them)

1 x 400ml tin of coconut milk or coconut cream

8 small red bird's-eye chillies

1–2 stalks of lemongrass, outer layers discarded and hearts finely sliced

4 spring onions, finely sliced into strips

Handful of fresh coriander leaves

Coconut Rice

400g (14oz) best-quality Thai jasmine rice

1 x 400ml tin of coconut milk

Sea salt

Equipment
Cocktail sticks

Rice steamer

1 Preheat the oven to 200°C (400°F), Gas Mark 6. If using an Aga, prepare the roasting oven.

2 Cut both banana leaves in half. Blanch the leaves to make them more flexible, by putting the pieces into boiling water for a few minutes, then draining.

3 Lay out the leaf pieces (or foil/baking parchment, if using) and place a fish fillet onto each one. Spoon some of the coconut milk on top, add a couple of whole chillies, some slices of lemongrass, a few strands of spring onion and some coriander leaves. Carefully fold the banana leaves into parcels, pinning them closed with the cocktail sticks.

4 Place the fish parcels in a baking dish and cook in the oven for 40 minutes. If the leaves split a little, it's a shame but not a major crisis. Just try to make sure that the liquid stays in the packets. If some escapes, spoon it out to drizzle over the rice.

5 Meanwhile, prepare the coconut rice. If you use a steamer, don't put the coconut milk in first! I made this mistake and the steamer wouldn't work. Instead, cook the rice as normal, then add the coconut milk to the cooked rice at the very end. Or use 200g (7oz) coconut powder instead and add it to the rice at the start. If you cook your rice in a saucepan on the hob, the coconut milk doesn't cause a problem, so boil the rice according to the packet instructions but add the coconut milk and reduce the water to compensate for the extra liquid.

6 To serve, spoon a mound of coconut rice onto each plate, then place a fish parcel alongside for your guests to unwrap for themselves.

STARGAZY PIE

I made this dish for an evening when I recreated the shipboard meals in Patrick O'Brian's *Master and Commander* books, which were set in the eighteenth century, during the time of Nelson. I served this pie along with other authentic dishes with evocative names, such as hard tack, portable soup (an early stock cube), mushroom ketchup, dogsbody (peas pudding) and boiled baby (a steamed suet pudding). Many of the guests came dressed up as pirates. I gave them a ration of rum but, as landlubbers, I felt they were probably safe from scurvy!

When combining a few of these recipes together (some with pastry on the bottom, others without), I can see why they are not on menus all the time; they're very time-consuming to make. However, it was well worth the effort. I added pastry stars and a moon to the top of this pie and moulded the edges into wavelike shapes.

Deep breath. Are you ready? Set aside some time for this.

Serves 6–8

Shortcrust Pastry

285g (10oz) plain flour, plus extra for dusting

1 tsp salt

180g (6½oz) butter, cut into cubes, plus extra for greasing

90ml–120ml (3–4fl oz) water, iced

Filling

4–8 pilchards, sardines or small herrings, depending on size when 'canoed' (which means they've been gutted and boned but retained their heads and tails)

Sea salt and freshly ground pepper

½ onion, peeled and chopped

1 First, decide whether you want pastry at the top and bottom of your pie. It's nicest to have both, but bear in mind that the pastry at the bottom will not be crispy like the top, so it can make the whole pie a little stodgier. If you choose not to have any at the bottom, halve the quantities for the pastry ingredients.

2 To make the pastry, sift together the flour and salt and put into a food processor. Add the butter and pulse to combine, then gradually add iced water and pulse until the mixture comes together. Remove the pastry from the machine, form into a ball and wrap in cling film. Chill in the fridge for 20 minutes or more, while you prepare the pie filling.

3 Make the sauce by melting the butter in a saucepan over a low–medium heat and adding the flour to make a paste (a roux). Cook this for a moment, then whisk in the white wine and stock. Bring the sauce to the boil, continuously stirring or whisking to get rid of lumps. Remove from the heat to add the cream, then boil again before turning down the heat and simmering the sauce until thickened. Add the parsley and allow the sauce to cool.

4 Season inside the cavities of the fish and stuff with onion, parsley and slices of lemon. Preheat the oven to 180°C (350°F), Gas Mark 4. If using an Aga, prepare the roasting oven.

5 If putting pastry at the bottom, take it from the fridge and divide into three

Handful of flat-leaf parsley

1 lemon, sliced

3 hen's eggs or 6 quail's eggs, hard-boiled, peeled and chopped into halves or quarters, plus 1 beaten egg, for glazing

Sauce

30g (1oz) butter

1–2 tbsp plain flour

75ml (2½fl oz) dry white wine

250ml (9fl oz) fish or vegetable stock (see page 137)

300ml (10½fl oz) double cream

Handful of chopped flat-leaf parsley

Sea salt and freshly ground pepper

Equipment

Food processor

Large pie dish or circular oven dish

equal parts. Set one piece aside, then combine the other two pieces and roll out into a large disc that will fit your pie dish with plenty hanging down over the sides. Grease the dish with butter, then line with the pastry. Next, place the stuffed fish in the pie dish with the heads sticking out on one side and, if long enough, the tails sticking out on the other side. The bodies of the fish will be encased in the pie. The fish can face in all directions and can sit across each other. (If you've chosen not to put pastry at the bottom, simply arrange the fish directly onto the dish.) Fill in the gaps around the fish with the egg chunks, then pour in the sauce.

6 Roll out the remaining pastry to make the lid for the pie. Place it over the fish, cutting slits for the heads and tails to stick through. Where the lid meets the base, press the edges of the pastry together into slightly overlapping wave shapes. Shape any scraps of pastry into crescent-moons or stars and use beaten egg to stick them onto the top of the pie. Brush the whole pie with beaten egg.

7 Bake in the oven for 30–40 minutes (if your fish are bigger, probably 40 minutes) until the pastry is golden. Plunge a thermometer or skewer inside the pie; try and push it into the flesh of one of the fish. If it measures 70ºC (160ºF), or the skewer is piping hot when you pull it out, the pie is cooked. If not, return to the oven for a little longer before testing the temperature again. Serve the stargazy pie hot, with new potatoes and a watercress salad.

Meat
Main Courses

*Y*es, I know, I don't eat meat. Although I don't like to shove it down people's throats, to proselytise and stand on my soapbox about animal rights, it is better for the planet if we eat less and better quality meat.

My main reason for not eating meat is that it doesn't feel right to me, to eat animals. I'm not one of those vegetarians who likes meat but doesn't eat it purely for moral reasons. Eating meat is all a bit too real, which might be seen as hypocritical when I advocate 'reality' – that is, cooking from scratch, going back to basics, making your own – in all other areas of food. The fashion now is for nose-to-tail eating, using every part of the animal that has been killed to feed us. That's obviously the most moral option if you do eat meat. However, the idea of eating brains, tripe and organs drives fussy arses like me even further into the vegetarian corner. And there is no doubt that factory farming, the way that many animals are treated, to provide cheap meat, is appalling. I believe the current way we treat industrially farmed animals will, in the future, be considered as barbaric as putting children up chimneys.

So...I've asked other supper clubs to provide guest recipes. They hail from all over the globe, from Argentina and New Zealand to London. They span the breadth in terms of training too: the recipes are from talented home cooks as well as professionals like Nuno Mendez (who trained at El Bulli) and Ben Greeno (Noma). I couldn't tell you if they are any good, I haven't tasted them! But the testers told me they were delicious.

SPICED SLOW-ROASTED LEG OF LAMB
WITH MUJADARA (FROM THE SHED)

This East-London supper club is run by a very young couple who seat guests in their garden shed. Nicola works for a gourmet-food company and Andrew is a lawyer. In the winter months they bring their guests indoors.

Serves 4–6

1 large leg of lamb (2kg/4lb 6oz on the bone)

1 head of garlic, sliced in half horizontally

1 onion, peeled and sliced into thick discs

Sea salt and freshly ground pepper

Marinade

2 tbsp olive oil, plus extra for rubbing

1/2 tsp sea salt

1/2 tsp freshly ground black pepper

1 1/2 tbsp red wine vinegar

1/2 tbsp ground cumin, plus extra for sauce

1/2 tbsp smoked paprika

1/2 tsp soft light brown sugar, plus extra for sauce

3–4 fat cloves of garlic, peeled and roughly chopped

1 Make a few small incisions in the fattiest parts of the lamb, being careful not to go too deep. Combine all of the marinade ingredients and rub all over the lamb, ensuring a little goes into the incisions. Leave to marinate in the fridge for 12–18 hours or overnight.

2 Remove the lamb from the fridge 1 hour before cooking, and preheat the oven to as hot as it will go. Place the sliced head of garlic and onion in the base of a large roasting tin.

3 Brush the chopped garlic from the marinade off the surface of the lamb so that it doesn't burn in the oven. Rub a little more olive oil and salt onto the meat, then place the lamb on top of the vegetables in the tin and put in the oven, uncovered. Immediately turn down the oven temperature to 150ºC (300ºF), Gas Mark 2. After 40 minutes, pour 500ml (18fl oz) hot water over the meat and return to the oven for 3–4 hours, basting the whole joint with the cooking liquid every 40 minutes or so.

4 When the lamb is in danger of falling off the bone at the slightest touch, remove from the oven and leave in a warmish place to rest for 15 minutes while you make your sauce. Strain the cooking liquid from the tin into a saucepan and skim the surface to remove excess fat. Boil rapidly over a high heat until the sauce has reduced to your desired consistency, adding a little more sugar, cumin and seasoning if you think it needs it.

5 To serve, slice big chunks of lamb – it should almost fall off the bone of its own accord – and serve with the Mujadara (see recipe overleaf), and a big gutsy tomato chutney, if you like.

MUJADARA

INGREDIENTS

Vegetarian
Serves 4–6

50g (1¾oz) butter

*1 large white onion,
peeled and diced*

*125g (4½oz) Puy lentils,
rinsed*

2 tsp sea salt

*250g (9oz) good-quality
basmati rice, rinsed*

1 tbsp olive oil

Garnish

1 tbsp butter

*1 large white onion,
peeled and thinly sliced*

4 tbsp plain Greek yoghurt

*Handful of fresh herbs,
such as coriander
and flat-leaf parsley*

A Lebanese rice and lentil dish perfect for veggies and carnivores alike.

1 Melt the butter in a saucepan over a low–medium heat and cook the diced onions until soft and beginning to caramelise a little. Remove from the heat and set aside.

2 Meanwhile, bring 1 litre (1¾ pints) of water up to the boil in a separate lidded saucepan, add the lentils and salt and simmer for 20 minutes. Add the rice and caramelised onions, then check the water level – it needs to be around 2cm (¾in) above the level of the food, so if necessary, add a little more. Cook, covered, over a low heat until the rice and lentils are cooked through and the water has evaporated. Remove from the heat, add the oil and stir to incorporate. Put the lid back on to keep it warm if not serving immediately.

3 While your lentils and rice finish cooking, prepare the garnish. Melt the butter over a low heat in a large frying pan, and add the onions. When the onions begin to soften, turn up the temperature and allow to caramelise.

4 To serve, put the rice onto a large serving platter and scatter with the caramelised onions and blobs of Greek yoghurt. Add the herbs.

CASA SALTSHAKER LOCRO
(FROM CASA SALTSHAKER, BUENOS AIRES)

American Dan Perlman runs Casa Saltshaker in Buenos Aires, a city which, like London, is a thriving hub of supper clubs or *puertas cerradas* (closed door restaurants). Dan is one of the leading supper-club hosts there; he runs cooking classes and is an avid blogger and documenter of the supper-club scene. Locro is a traditional stew of northern Argentina, made with corn and squash and normally using the 'bits and pieces' from meat cuts and offal. This is a slightly more elegant version. The dried white corn might be difficult to get hold of in the UK, but look in ethnic stores or online, or see if you can find dried hominy instead. If you can't find it, replace with extra fresh sweetcorn kernels. Dan makes his own chilli oil for serving the dish by soaking a teaspoon of dried chilli flakes in a tablespoon of olive oil for 2–3 hours while everything else is cooking.

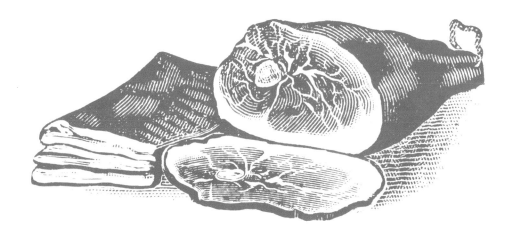

Serves 6

175g (6oz) dried white corn, cracked if available

2 medium white onions, peeled and coarsely chopped

2 cloves of garlic, peeled and thinly sliced

2 x 5mm (¼in) thick slices of smoked bacon, cubed

1 chorizo or other slightly spicy sausage, sliced

2 x 2.5cm (1in) thick osso bucos or similar cut (rump, shoulder roasts – something that will hold together when braised for a couple of hours)

2 cobs of fresh yellow sweetcorn, kernels cut off

1 tsp sweet paprika

1 tsp ground cumin

2 fresh bay leaves

½ tsp freshly ground black pepper

200g (7oz) butternut squash, peeled and finely diced

200g (7oz) batata (white yam) or sweet potato, peeled and finely diced

1 large baking potato, peeled and finely diced

2 plum tomatoes, cut into small wedges

Drizzle of chilli oil

Sea salt, to taste

1 Soak the white corn in 500ml (18fl oz) of water for at least 12 hours, or overnight.

2 Put the onions, garlic, bacon, sausage, and osso buco in a large cooking pot. Cook over a medium heat until the onions are soft and translucent. Add the fresh corn kernels, the paprika, cumin, bay leaves, a little salt and the pepper. Continue to cook, stirring regularly, for roughly 10 minutes. Add the soaked white corn kernels, water and all (may as well add this for extra corn flavour). Pour hot water into the pot so that it comes about 5cm (2in) above the level of the ingredients. Add the remaining vegetables and the tomatoes, stir, and bring to a boil. Reduce the heat and simmer, covered, stirring every 15–20 minutes, for at least 2 hours.

3 At this point, take off the lid and remove the bay leaves. Fish out the osso bucos, cut the meat into bite-sized pieces and discard the bones, then return the pieces of meat to the pot (unless they were boneless to begin with, in which case, dice them up at the start).

4 Continue to stir over a low heat, using the back of a wide spoon or spatula to press the ingredients against the sides of the pan. This will get the starchy vegetables and tomato to disintegrate into the soup. The corn and meat tend to resist being mashed, which is fine. As you continue to stir, mash and cook, the soup should gradually become thicker and thicker. Continue until it's a nice, rich stew consistency. Add salt to taste.

5 Serve in bowls and drizzle a little chilli oil over the top if you like things spicy.

QUINTESSENTIAL CHICKEN (FROM BEN GREENO)

Ben has travelled and trained in some of the world's top restaurants, finally working as a sous chef at Noma, this year named as the world's best restaurant. Noma uses only local ingredients from Scandinavia, eschewing garlic and Mediterranean ingredients. Ben did a short stint as a guest chef at Nuno Mendez's The Loft project and went on to open his own supper club in London. I asked him for a chicken recipe and this is what I got: it uses all aspects of a chicken, so I guess it's quintessentially chicken.

Serves 4

8 chicken wings

500ml (18fl oz) chicken stock

50g (1¾oz) butter

4 breast-sized pieces of chicken skin

8 chicken gizzards

8 chicken hearts

16 morel mushrooms

4 pickled walnuts

4 hen's eggs

Splash of vinegar

200g (7oz) chicken glaze (made by simmering roasted chicken wings in water for 5 hours, straining the liquid and then reducing to sauce consistency)

20g (¾oz) pickled elderberries

150g (5½oz) sourdough, toasted and cut into pieces

Sea salt and freshly ground pepper

1 Preheat the oven to 160°C (325°F), Gas Mark 3. Put the chicken wings in an oven dish with most of the stock and half the butter and braise in the oven for about 45 minutes until tender. Leave to cool until you can handle the wings, then pull the bones out carefully. Set aside.

2 Adjust the oven temperature to 180°C (350°F), Gas Mark 4. Bake the pieces of chicken skin for 25 minutes until crispy. Meanwhile, boil the gizzards in a saucepan of water for 15 minutes, so that they soften. Trim the bottoms off the hearts.

3 Wash the morels, ensure that all the dirt is out of them, then leave to dry. Slice each pickled walnut into three pieces.

4 Poach the eggs for 5 minutes in simmering water with a little vinegar. Reheat the chicken wings in a saucepan containing a little of the stock. Melt the butter in a frying pan over a low–medium heat. When it is foaming, add the hearts, gizzards and mushrooms and cook for about 2–3 minutes until golden. In a separate saucepan, melt the chicken glaze and add the elderberries.

5 Divide the walnuts, chicken wings, gizzards, hearts and mushrooms between four deep bowls. Add a poached egg on top of each, then pour over the chicken and elderberry glaze. Finally, throw on the chicken skin and pieces of sourdough.

SHIN OF BEEF RAGÙ (FROM SHEEN SUPPERS)

Lara Newman lives on the outskirts of London in Sheen and runs a superb suburban supper club with her partner. Her kitchen is an explosion of pink: a pink fridge, dishwasher, kettle, knives, coffee maker. Despite the Barbie colour scheme, Lara is a serious cook!

Serves 6

Olive oil, for cooking

*1 celery stick,
roughly chopped*

*3 large white onions,
peeled and roughly chopped*

*1kg (2lb 3oz) shin of beef,
trimmed and cut into 3cm
(1¼in) chunks*

80g (3oz) plain flour

*16 good-quality,
ripe tomatoes,
skinned and roughly chopped*

*1 bottle of full-bodied,
hearty Italian red wine*

*1 large, hand-sized,
home-made bouquet garni
(any herbs but include thyme
and flat-leaf parsley at least)*

Large glug of Marsala

*Handful of finely chopped
flat-leaf parsley*

*150g (5½oz) Pecorino
cheese, grated*

*Sea salt and freshly
ground pepper*

1 Preheat the oven to 170°C (325°F), Gas Mark 3. If using an Aga, prepare the baking oven.

2 In a big ovenproof pot, heat a little olive oil and gently cook the celery and onion for 8–10 minutes, or until soft. Brown the meat well in a separate pan and then add to the pot. Sprinkle in the plain flour and stir well to cover the meat and vegetables. Add half of the tomatoes, all of the red wine and the bouquet garni. Bring to a gentle boil, give the bottom of the pan a good scrape, put on the lid and transfer to the oven. Cook for as long as possible – at least 3 hours, ideally 4–5. Give it a good stir every now and again, scraping the bottom of the pot well. Halfway through, add the Marsala and stir well.

3 Once removed from the oven, use a spoon to break up the meat a little more – this should require no effort, as it will be completely tender by now. Add the remaining tomatoes and simmer for 20 minutes over a medium heat. You shouldn't need more liquid, but if you do, more tomatoes or a little water can be added.

4 You can serve immediately or you can allow the ragù to cool and then reheat and finish later, or even the following day (the flavours will have developed and it will taste even better).

5 When ready to serve, add a handful of parsley, the grated Pecorino and salt and pepper to taste. Serve with home-made pasta (see pages 178–9) or gnocchi.

PORK BELLY
WITH SAGE AND FENNEL STUFFING
(FROM PLUM KITCHEN, NEW ZEALAND)

Serves 4

1kg (2lb 3oz) pork belly
(weigh after the bone has
been removed); ask your
butcher to score the rind at
1cm (½in) intervals

2 meaty butcher's
pork sausages
(about 200g / 7oz in total)

1 tbsp chopped sage

2 tsp fennel seeds,
lightly crushed in
a mortar and pestle

20g (¾oz) dried apple
slices, chopped into
1cm (½in) chunks

1 clove of garlic,
peeled and crushed

1 small egg

25g (1oz) fresh breadcrumbs

Sea salt and freshly
ground black pepper

Splash of olive oil

Apple Sauce (Optional)

4 Granny Smith
or Bramley apples

50g (1¾oz) butter, softened

Pinch of sugar (any type)

Sea salt, to taste

In 2010, the first supper clubs started in New Zealand; within a short space of time they were bombarded with press and TV requests. I was getting e-mails from them asking, 'What shall we do?' My advice: relax and enjoy the attention!

1 Ensure your pork is at room temperature by taking it out of the fridge about 30 minutes before you want to start cooking. This will also allow the skin to dry out a little, which makes for better crackling.

2 Preheat the oven to 230°C (450°F), Gas Mark 8.

3 Skin your sausages and mix the meat with the sage, 1 teaspoon of the fennel seeds, the apple chunks, garlic, egg and breadcrumbs and a generous amount of seasoning. Place the pork skin-side down and sprinkle with salt and plenty of black pepper. With the long side of the pork towards you, spread the sausage mixture evenly down the middle, leaving a 3cm (1¼in) gap at each end to allow the filling to expand. Roll the pork up, rolling it away from you, and tie at regular intervals with string. The skin scoring should now be parallel to the two ends, so you can easily slice the pork when it is cooked. Not only does this look attractive, but it means your crackling will slice cleanly without shattering.

4 Rub a little olive oil onto the pork skin and sprinkle with the remaining fennel seeds and more salt. Place in a roasting tin with about 2cm (¾in) of water in the bottom of the tin. Top this water up as necessary throughout the cooking process. Roast in the oven for 20 minutes, then reduce the heat to 170°C (325°F), Gas Mark 3 and roast for a further 1½–2 hours.

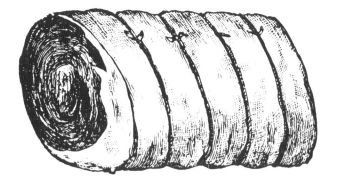

5 If you want to make the apple sauce, leave the skin on the apples and slice them across the middle with a small sharp knife. Rub all over with a little softened butter, and place skin-side down in a small roasting dish with a little water in the bottom. Roast in the oven for about 40 minutes, until the apples are collapsing, then take out of the oven and push through a sieve. Beat the apple pulp with a little more butter until smooth, adding a pinch of salt and sugar.

6 You can tell if the pork is cooked by piercing it with a skewer. If the skewer doesn't come out hot to the touch, then cook the meat for a little longer. Pork belly has quite a high fat content, which combined with the sausage meat ensures that it will stay moist even if it stays in the oven for longer. Once the skewer comes out hot, if the crackling is not as crispy as you like, simply place the pork under the grill for a couple of minutes and it will bubble up nicely.

7 Let your meat rest in a warm spot, with a loose covering of foil, for 15–20 minutes before slicing down between the scores in the crackling. Delicious served with the apple sauce.

RAMBLING SUNDAY ROAST OF
PORK BELLY
WITH BLACK PUDDING, THYME AND HONEY PARSNIPS AND CIDER GRAVY (FROM THE RAMBLING RESTAURANT)

This recipe is from the Rambling Restaurant which, although it does ramble to other locations, is based mostly in Camden, North London, at the house of the hostess, food blogger 'Food Rambler'. You have to find the address through literary clues…here's one: Llareggub – the favourite fictional place of a Welsh poet. There's a blue plaque on the outside wall of her house commemorating this famous poet.

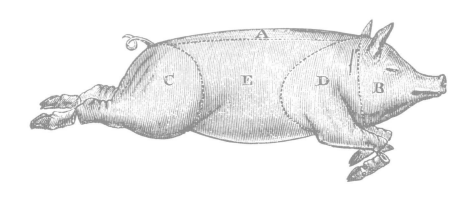

INGREDIENTS

Serves 4

1.5kg (3lb 4oz) pork belly joint, boneless but with fat

3 sprigs of fresh thyme, leaves only

8 juniper berries

2 cloves of garlic, peeled and crushed

Maldon sea salt and freshly ground black pepper

1 tsp fennel seeds

8 parsnips, peeled and cut in half widthways, then into quarters lengthways

Few splashes of olive oil

4 tbsp honey

1 English Cox apple

50g (1¾oz) salted butter

20g (¾oz) caster sugar

1 x 500ml bottle of medium dry organic cider (half for the gravy and half for the cook)

200ml (7fl oz) vegetable stock (see page 137)

1 savoy cabbage

250g (9oz) black pudding, sliced

Equipment

Hand-held blender

1 Preheat the oven to 220°C (425°F), Gas Mark 7.

2 Grind two-thirds of the thyme leaves with the juniper berries, garlic, salt, pepper and fennel seeds in a pestle and mortar. Score the pork belly rind, pour over a splash of boiling water and rub the mixture into the cracks and over the rest of the meat. Roast the pork in the oven for 20–30 minutes, skin-side up, until the crackling has really crackled. Then turn down the oven to 160°C (325°F), Gas Mark 3, and carry on cooking for 1½–2 hours, until the meat is really tender.

3 Boil the parsnips in a large saucepan of water for about 5 minutes, until tender. Take the pork out to rest and turn the oven up to 200°C (400°F), Gas Mark 6. Drain the parsnips, toss with olive oil, the remaining thyme and the honey. Roast in the oven for 20 minutes.

4 Meanwhile, peel, core and slice the apple. Fry in butter, sprinkled with sugar, until caramelised.

5 Transfer the pork to a plate or board and pour half the cider into the roasting tin. Deglaze the tin by heating gently over the hob and using a wooden spoon to scrape any bits from the bottom and edges, mixing them in with the juices and cider. Add the stock, a couple of roasted parsnip pieces and the buttery apple. Allow to boil until reduced, then strain into a jug and blend with a hand-held blender.

6 Boil up the savoy cabbage leaves, fry up the black pudding in the apple pan and serve with a couple of slices of pork, the parsnips and the gravy. Treat yourself to the rest of the cider.

DUCK BREAST
WITH RHUBARB COMPOTE
(FROM LEX EATS)

An Australian cook in London, Alexis Coleman, by day a lawyer, has started up a charming supper club in Holloway. Her duplex flat is beautifully decorated with vintage suitcases, girly high heels, an old record player. The same attention to detail goes into her table settings: for tablecloths she uses brown Kraft paper and writes little instructions and notes on it. There is generosity: you are given wonderful dessert wines gratis and her cooking is fantastic. There is a whole breed of innovative Antipodean chefs – Bill Granger, for instance – and it seems that this refreshing approach to food has also filtered down to home cooking, judging from what's coming off the stoves of Alexis and also my sometimes sous-chef Angie Ma.

The tartness of rhubarb is perfect to cut through the flavour of rich fatty meats like duck. This compote also works well with roast lamb and pork. You can make the compote the day before, then reheat and season just before serving. It will keep in the fridge for several days.

INGREDIENTS

Serves 4

25g (1oz) unsalted butter
Glug of olive oil
4 duck breasts
Sea salt and freshly ground pepper

Rhubarb Compote
20g (¾oz) unsalted butter
Glug of olive oil
5 shallots, peeled and thinly diced
(continued opposite)

1 To make the rhubarb compote, put the butter and a good glug of olive oil in a deep frying pan or saucepan over a medium heat. Add the shallots and a pinch of salt, then add the ginger. Sauté until the shallots are soft but not too brown. Add the rhubarb, sugar, lemon zest and juice and a few generous glugs of balsamic vinegar. Cook over a medium heat until the rhubarb is soft. Be careful not to overcook, or the rhubarb will lose its shape. Season just before serving.

2 Preheat the oven to 180–200°C (350–400°F), Gas Mark 4–6.

3 In a hot frying pan (if possible, use an ovenproof one), melt the butter and a glug of olive oil. Season the skin of the duck breasts with salt and pepper. Place the duck breasts in the pan, skin-side down and fry for 3 minutes on either side, until the skin is crispy. Then transfer the duck to the oven (either put the pan straight in the oven, or transfer the meat to a baking tin) to finish it off for about 7–10 minutes, depending on how well-done you like your duck.

1 generous tbsp grated root ginger (keep fresh ginger in the freezer – it will keep for longer and is easier to grate when frozen)

3–4 stalks of rhubarb, sliced into 1–2cm (½–¾in) pieces (if the stalks are very thick also halve them lengthways)

60g (2oz) caster sugar

Zest and juice of 1 lemon

1 generous tbsp balsamic vinegar

4 Let the duck breast rest for a few minutes, covered or wrapped in foil. To serve, slice the duck breasts and add a dollop of rhubarb compote to each portion. In my experience, a little bowl of extra compote on the table is always welcome! Enjoy with a medley of seasonal spring vegetables such as asparagus, spring greens, leeks and broad beans.

SLOW-COOKED SIRLOIN STEAK WITH WHOLEGRAIN NUT CRUST, ROASTED BABY BEETS AND BABY SPINACH CATALAN, SERVED WITH TRUFFLE POTATO PURÉE (FROM THE LOFT)

Nuno Mendez is from Portugal but rarely cooks Portuguese food, being more influenced by Japanese ingredients and the innovative cooking of El Bulli, where he worked for a while. His supper club, The Loft, was as masculine as mine is feminine. It was housed in a brick-walled modern warehouse, and in the bathroom his toiletries were expensive, his towels immaculate. There was no clutter, no knick-knacks, no dust-gatherers. Nuno started up The Loft as a test kitchen for his new restaurant in the East End of London, Viajante. He draws inspiration from the East End, which has always been a landing point for waves of new immigrants who introduce new cuisines and cultures. Since the '80s, it's also been a place where artists lived, rents were cheap, and whole streets were squatted. I know areas that are like a punk Coronation Street, people in and out of each other's houses all day. (One of these houses was where the National Portrait Gallery award-winning photograph 'Woman reading possession order' was taken by Tom Watson). I lived for a while in a squatted swimming pool in London Fields, in one of the changing rooms: this area was where many art projects were spawned. Charles Saatchi started his gallery on Brick Lane with Gilbert & George-influenced artists such as Toby Mott.

Hackney is a vibrant and wacky part of London, and it's no surprise that many London supper clubs are located there.

Serves 4

Steak

*2 x 380g (13oz) sirloin
steaks, cut in half*

2 tbsp olive oil

Handful of thyme leaves

2 tbsp red wine vinegar

2 tbsp red wine

*Sea salt and freshly
ground pepper*

Beets

6 baby beets

*Large handful of
thyme leaves*

4 tbsp olive oil

250ml (9fl oz) water

Wholegrain Nut Crust

225g (8oz) butter, melted

175g (6oz) chopped hazelnuts

*250g (9oz) wholegrain
mustard*

Potato Purée

*4 potatoes,
scrubbed but skin left on*

4 tbsp double cream

2 tbsp butter

*2 tbsp truffle butter
(optional)*

Spinach Catalan

Butter, for cooking

*150g (5½oz) onions,
peeled and chopped*

*150g (5½oz) golden raisins,
soaked in hot water*

125g (4½oz) pine nuts

*400g (14oz) baby spinach
leaves, stems removed*

1 Preheat the oven to 50°C (120°F) or its lowest setting. Season the steaks well and marinate with the olive oil, thyme, red wine vinegar, red wine and seasoning. Slow-roast in the oven for 1 hour.

2 Remove the steaks from the oven and turn up the temperature to 120°C (250°F), Gas Mark ½. Drizzle olive oil over the baby beets, cover with foil and slow-roast for 1 hour. Once cooked, peel and quarter them.

3 Meanwhile, mix together all the ingredients for the wholegrain crust and set aside.

4 Boil the potatoes in their skins in a saucepan of salted water until tender and cooked through. Then peel the potatoes and mash them with the cream, butter and truffle butter, if using. Adjust the seasoning to taste and keep warm.

5 To prepare the spinach Catalan, caramelise the onions in a little butter, add the golden raisins and pine nuts, season with salt and pepper and mix with the spinach.

6 Finally, sear the steaks on a hot griddle to reheat and caramelise them. Spread 2 tablespoons of the crust on top of each piece of steak and put under a hot grill for a couple of minutes.

7 To serve, arrange a line of spinach straight across four large plates, put a nice pile of beets in the centre and place the crusted steak on top. Serve with the hot potato purée on the side.

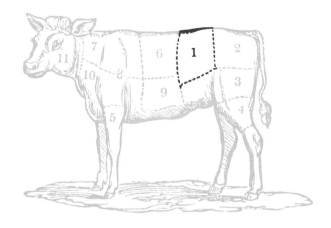

Desserts

*D*esserts are a bit like clothes: if you have a decent haircut and shoes, it doesn't matter so much what you wear. People don't remember middles so much. Some girls don't like to order their own desserts, preferring to eat their boyfriends', whereas others would kill their own mother for a decent pudding. Get the 'afters' right, make it spectacular, for that is the last memory of the meal that guests will take away with them. I also think, if you eat a proper pudding, you eat less sweets. The French eat pudding rather than nipping out to the newsagents several times a day for a packet of Smarties. (French sweets are awfully adult anyway.) So providing a decent dessert is practically a health option! Oh and have you tried Marmite chocolate? It's a total yes/no conflict, so wrong and yet so right. I love it.

Mousse au Chocolat Orange
with Cointreau and Choc-dipped Physalis

When I lived in Paris, I set myself the onerous task of a 'chocolate mousse survey' at all the local restaurants. This and crème caramel are almost always on a French dessert menu, along with fruit, yoghurt and cheese. Mousse is also a good supper-club dessert, as you can prep it the day before and get it out of the way. I always think of sweet-and-sour physalis as 'syphilis fruit', but I can eat them by the boxful. They are so pretty and delicate and make a posh garnish.

Serves 4

150g (5½oz)
orange-flavoured chocolate
(such as Green & Black's
Mayan Gold),
broken into squares

100g (3½oz) physalis fruit

5 eggs, yolks and whites
separated

2 tbsp Cointreau

Equipment

Silicone mat or baking
parchment

Electric whisk

4 ramkeins

1 Melt the chocolate in a glass bowl set over a saucepan of simmering water (don't let the bottom of the bowl touch the water, or the chocolate might go grainy). If you have an Aga, you can just leave the bowl on the black enamel and the chocolate will melt. Once melted, remove from the heat.

2 Take the physalis and pull back the paper leaves, twisting them behind the fruit. Dip the tip of one end of each fruit into the melted chocolate and leave to dry on a silicone mat or a sheet of baking parchment.

3 Add the egg yolks, one by one, to the remaining melted chocolate in the bowl and mix gently. Also mix in the Cointreau.

4 Beat the egg whites in a separate bowl until they form soft peaks. Fold them carefully into the melted chocolate and egg yolk mixture. Then pour the mixture into ramekins and leave to chill for at least 2 hours before serving with the choc-dipped physalis on the side.

Tarte Tatin
with Crème Fraîche Ice Cream

This is another classic French dessert with a slightly scary flippy-over bit at the end. When making these for The Underground Restaurant, I half-prep them in advance, then finish them off in the oven while the main course is out. I'm not an apple pie lover, but this is basically toffee-apple tart. It's really sweet and sticky and the lightly acidic crème fraîche ice cream is the perfect counterfoil. You need a large, deep, heavy-based, ovenproof frying pan for this dish, with a handle that can go in the oven.

INGREDIENTS

Serves 4–6

Juice of 2 lemons

1kg (2lb 3oz)/about 8–10 eating apples (such as Cox, Russet or Braeburn)

125–175g (4½–6oz) unsalted butter, slightly softened

125–175g (4½–6oz) caster sugar

4–6 star anise

200g (7oz) puff pastry, rolled to a disc the same dimensions as your frying pan

Crème fraîche ice cream, to serve (see pages 228–9)

1 Squeeze both lemons into a large bowl. Peel and core the apples, then halve them and put in the bowl of lemon juice to prevent them going brown.

2 Smear butter generously over the frying pan, up the sides too. Sprinkle sugar over the top in a nice thick layer (this will be the toffee bit, so if you like lots of toffee, put extra butter and sugar).

3 Remove your apple halves from the lemon juice and embed them in the butter/sugar mixture, with the holes (where the cores were) facing downwards. Pack the apples in tightly. Tuck a few star anise between the apples.

4 Preheat the oven to 220ºC (425ºF), Gas Mark 7. If using an Aga, prepare the roasting oven.

5 Put the frying pan over a medium flame on your hob. Keep an eye on it; this will caramelise. You have to be brave here and keep it going for about 15 minutes – you want a deep golden caramel colour and texture to develop. Once this has happened, leave the pan to cool, then plop your pastry disc on the top of the pan, tucking in the edges. Place the pan in the oven and bake the tart for 15 minutes or until the pastry has risen.

6 Here is the tricky bit: find a plate slightly larger than your frying pan and lay it over the top. Holding the handle firmly and keeping the plate pressed tightly to the pan, flip them both over. The plate will now be on the bottom and the frying pan on top. Lift the pan off to reveal a gorgeous, sticky, toffee-apple tart. If some of the apples have become displaced, don't worry, just take a fork and prod them back into place.

7 Cut into slices while hot and serve with a scoop or quenelle (see page 165 for this technique) of Crème Fraîche Ice Cream.

Crème Fraîche Ice Cream

Sweet but tart, this ice cream goes well with Tarte Tatin and also with meringue. I have an ice-cream attachment for my Kitchen Aid food processor. With a decent ice-cream maker, the texture of my ice cream has really improved.

Scooping ice cream is a skill. I worked for a week as an ice-cream seller at a festival. You have to master a technique in which you make a long, snail-like curl, to make the ice cream look bigger than a firmly packed scoop. This is harder to achieve than it looks.

It helps to be small to work in an ice-cream van. Your view of the outside world, and its view of you, is restricted to a tiny hatch. There is a little step up onto which kids haul themselves. All the parents are under the impression that their kids are cute. They give them the money and let them take their own ice cream. The child then climbs down from the step, holding the ice cream in their wobbly, pudgy mitt. The ice cream promptly drops off the cone. The parent returns, complaining defensively that 'The ice cream wasn't put on properly.' You replace it.

In general, kids want cones (shove the ice cream down firmly for little kids, due to aforesaid problem) and adults have cups. But ice-cream vans bring out the kid in everyone:

'Do you mind a cup?' I asked an adult.

'Yes, I mind. I want a cone,' whimpered this fully grown adult, reverting to five years old.

I ended up flirting for Britain through that little hatch, wearing brightly coloured clothes, calling out 'Cute dad alert,' and enticing the mummies to order themselves Chocolate Martini shots. But by Day Three I was having to ask each customer to repeat their order at least four times.

'It's a bloody festival,' I'd explain wearily, 'What do you expect? Efficiency?'
I started calling cones 'scones' and confusing mint choc-chip with caramel and
chocolate. The strawberry, being 'natural' was confusingly not pink, but beige.
Bring on the colourings and E-numbers, I say! Some of these parents, however,
were buying ice creams for their kids at 9 a.m. Then they'd wonder why the little
buggers were so hyper...

1 Warm the milk, sugar and salt in a medium-sized saucepan over a
medium heat. Be careful not to let the mixture boil.

2 In a separate bowl, whisk the egg yolks. Pour a little of the warm milk
mixture into the egg yolks, whisking. (This is called 'tempering' and stops
the eggs from scrambling when you eventually add them to the saucepan.)
Once you've tempered the eggs, pour them into the saucepan with the rest
of the milk mixture.

3 Stir the mixture constantly over a medium heat, using a wooden spoon
or spatula to scrape the bottom as you stir, until the mixture thickens and
coats the spoon – this should take about 10 minutes. Then pour the custard
through a fine sieve or strainer into a clean bowl to remove any eggy bits.
Sit the bowl in a larger dish of iced water and stir while the mixture begins to
cool. Once lukewarm, put in the fridge to chill thoroughly for 30–45 minutes.

4 Once chilled, take the bowl from the fridge and whisk in the crème
fraîche, then freeze the mixture in your ice-cream maker according to
the manufacturer's instructions. When complete, the ice cream will keep
for about 1 month, perhaps longer, in your freezer.

5 A good serving tip is to take your ice cream out of the freezer and put it
in the fridge 30 minutes before you want to serve it. This way it will soften
evenly, not just around the edges. Also buy a decent ice-cream scoop. Pay
at least £15. The cheap ones just don't do it.

6 Scoop the ice cream onto the Tarte Tatin, or whatever dessert you want
to serve it alongside.

Bergamot Posset
with Crystallised Thyme & Lavender Shortbread

Serves 4

Bergamot Posset
400ml (14fl oz) double cream
100g (3½oz) caster sugar
Zest and juice of
1–2 bergamots

Lavender Shortbread
50g (1¾oz) icing sugar, plus extra for dusting biscuits
185g (6½oz) plain flour, plus extra for dusting work surface
60g (2oz) cornflour
30g (1oz) ground almonds
250g (9oz) butter, diced
40g (1½oz) lavender sugar
Purple food colouring or violet liqueur (optional)

Crystallised Thyme
8 thyme sprigs
1 egg white
Caster sugar, for dipping

Equipment
4 ramekins or glasses
Food processor (optional)
Biscuit cutters of your choice

Lemon posset is probably the world's simplest dessert. This is a little twist on it, using bergamot, which is the citrus fruit that gives Earl Grey tea its perfumed taste. If you can't get your hands on them, use lemons or Amalfi lemons, instead. As for the crystallised thyme, I often crystallise herbs and flowers to decorate desserts (see page 292).

1 To make the bergamot posset, put the cream and sugar together in a saucepan over a medium heat and bring to the boil for 3 minutes. Remove from the heat and allow to cool. Once cool, add the zest and juice from the bergamots and whisk. Pour into glasses or ramekins and chill for 3 hours.

2 For the lavender shortbread, preheat the oven to 170°C (325°F), Gas Mark 3. If using an Aga, prepare the baking oven with the bottom shelf positioned. Sift the icing sugar, flour and cornflour together into a bowl, then stir in the ground almonds. Transfer to a food processor and add the cubes of butter. Also add some purple food colouring or violet liqueur if you want the shortbread to be a mauve colour. Pulse to incorporate the butter. (Alternatively, you can rub in the butter with your fingertips, but try to do this quickly to avoid melting the butter.) Add the lavender sugar and pulse (or mix). Remove the mixture, form it into a smooth ball of dough and roll out on a lightly floured work surface until the dough is 2cm (¾in) thick.

3 Use a cutter (of whatever shape you want) to cut the dough into biscuits. Lay the shapes on a baking sheet or in an ovenproof dish and bake in the oven for 8–12 minutes until just turning golden. Remove and allow to cool. Don't handle the biscuits while warm, or they will break. Dust with icing sugar.

4 To crystallise the thyme, paint each sprig with a little egg white, then dip, front and back, in a bowl of caster sugar. Leave the thyme to dry on a silicone sheet or piece of baking parchment.

5 Serve the ramekins of bergamot posset each decorated with two crystallised thyme sprigs and accompanied by some of the lavender shortbread.

Saffron Kulfi with Almond & Cardamom Tuile Biscuits

INGREDIENTS

Serves 10

Kulfi

1 tsp saffron strands

Pinch of sugar

1 x 397ml tin of condensed milk

1 x 410ml tin of evaporated milk

600ml (1 pint) double cream

600ml (1 pint) whipping cream, whipped

Tuile Biscuits

100g (3½oz) plain flour

100g (3½oz) icing sugar

3 egg whites, at room temperature

100g (3½oz) butter, melted

20g (¾oz) ground almonds

4–5 cardamom pods, shelled and ground to a powder

Equipment

Mortar and pestle

10 ramekins

Silicon mat or baking parchment

Rolling pin, for shaping tuiles

Kulfi is an Indian ice cream that is not churned and is therefore very easy to make without an ice-cream maker. This recipe is lighter than the Kulfi you may have been served at Indian restaurants, where desserts can be too sweet and heavy for many Westerners. This has become one of my standby desserts, one that I know will always go down well with guests. The recipe might make way more than you need, but the extra can be kept in the freezer and eaten another time.

1 For the kulfi, grind together the saffron and the sugar in a mortar and pestle. Mix with all the other ingredients in a large bowl and pour into ramekins. Freeze for 6 hours.

2 To make the tuile biscuits, preheat the oven to 180°C (350°F), Gas Mark 4. If using an Aga, prepare the baking oven.

3 Sift the flour and icing sugar together into a large bowl. Add the egg whites and beat in, then gradually add the melted butter, beating after each addition to create a smooth paste. Beat in the ground almonds and the cardamom powder.

4 Use the back of a metal spoon to spread extremely thin circles of mixture onto a silicon mat. Or use a paper stencil to spread them into a shape. This can take practice; the first few might come out looking a bit crap, but they will still taste good. Bake in the oven for about 5 minutes, keeping a close eye because they burn easily.

5 When the biscuits emerge from the oven they are soft, so immediately curl them over a rolling pin. They soon harden up in that curved shape.

6 You can serve the kulfi in the ramekins or loosen them by dipping the bottom of each ramekin in hot water and turning out onto a plate. Serve each one with a tuile biscuit. You could also scatter the kulfi with crystallised rose petals (see page 292) or a little gold leaf.

Giant Pavlova

My favourite dessert of all time is pavlova. I make giant ones, enormous icebergs of meringue that fill a whole baking tin. I like mountains of pavlova with gooey insides, creamy peaks, salted caramel and passion fruit. I normally make one per table, hand everyone a large spoon and let them demolish it! Pavlova also makes a great birthday cake. For that, I might shake some edible white glitter over it.

Serves 8

½ lemon

8 egg whites

400g (14oz) caster sugar

600ml (1 pint) double or whipping cream

150ml (5½fl oz) salted caramel (see recipe overleaf)

4 passion fruit

150g (5½oz) blueberries, or other fruit of your choice

1 Preheat the oven to its lowest setting. If using an Aga, prepare the simmering oven.

2 For making the meringue, use a copper bowl if you have one, or use a Nigella trick: first wipe the inside of your bowl with a lemon half. Any grease will make it hard to get the egg whites stiff. Also be careful not to get any yolk into the bowl of egg whites, as this causes the same problem. I normally mix the whites in my Kitchen Aid or with an electric whisk. I've done it with a hand whisk, but you'll probably have to take turns with someone else before your arm falls off. Whisk the egg whites in the clean bowl until they're frothy.

3 Slowly add the sugar and continue whisking until the mixture becomes stiff and glossy, and forms peaks, but don't go too far, or it will split into weird bobbly bits. Now grab a silicone sheet or piece of baking parchment and use it to line a baking tray. Dollop the meringue onto it. Bake the meringue in the oven for about 1½ hours. Once the cooking time is finished, turn off the heat and leave the meringue to cool still inside the oven with the door slightly open.

4 In the Aga, I often just leave the meringue for about 4 hours, walking around the house with a timer round my neck and checking on it every so often to see that it's not burning or browning too quickly. If you need to go to bed or something, take it out and rest the tray on the silver lids of the Aga where the meringue will gradually dry out. To be honest, I don't think you can beat Aga meringues. They go a lovely golden colour and retain the sticky centre. Yum.

5 When the meringues have cooled, whip the cream until it's thick and fluffy, then pile it onto the meringue. Drip salted caramel all over it and scatter with the fruit. If using passion fruit, use wrinkled ones, cut them in half and spill the luscious sour, sweet seeds across the pavlova. This is not a neat dessert. It's controlled chaos.

Salted Caramel

Make loads of this: it keeps for a long time – a month or more – in a jar and I use it for everything, on ice creams or Eton mess, mixed with frosting for cupcakes or just spooned out of the jar when you are crying on the sofa or in bed because you've just had a horrible date, for instance.

INGREDIENTS

Makes 500ml (18fl oz)

125ml (4½fl oz) cold water

330g (11½oz) caster sugar (use processed not natural, to avoid crystallisation)

250ml (9fl oz) double cream

Big pinch of good-quality sea salt

1 Combine the sugar and water in a medium-sized saucepan and heat gently until the sugar has dissolved. Turn up the heat to medium and bring the mixture to the boil, without stirring but giving it an occasional swirl, until it turns a deep amber colour. This takes 15–20 minutes. (Everybody likes their caramel a different shade, but too dark and it will develop a bitter note.) Now and then, brush down the sides of the pan with a brush dipped in water, to prevent crystallisation happening. Once the caramel has reached your desired shade of brown, remove from the heat and carefully whisk in the cream.

2 When the caramel has cooled down (hot sugar can really burn your mouth), add salt to taste and pour into jars.

Clafoutis

A nineteenth-century French dessert from Limoges that is not only good for pudding but also a great as a cold brunch the next morning. I love the way the tart redness of the cherries slightly bleeds into the batter. Make sure you have plenty of ripe fruit – you could even roast the cherries for 10 minutes with a little sugar and lemon juice to ensure maximum juiciness. Traditionally, you leave the pits in the cherries to impart that extra Kirsch flavour. When made with other fruits, it's called a Flognarde.

INGREDIENTS

Serves 4–6

500g (1lb 2oz) cherries (preferably a sour variety such as Montmorency or Morello), stalks removed, or 10 large ripe plums, stoned and halved

20g (¾oz) butter, for greasing

4 eggs

100g (3½oz) caster sugar

50g (1¾oz) plain flour

600ml (1 pint) double cream

Kirsch, for brushing (optional)

Equipment

25cm (10in) square, ovenproof dish

1 Preheat the oven to 180ºC (350ºF), Gas Mark 4. If using an Aga, prepare either the bottom shelf of the roasting oven, or the top shelf of the baking oven. Grease the ovenproof dish with butter and lay the fruit in the bottom in an even layer.

2 Whisk the eggs in a large bowl, then add the sugar. Once thoroughly mixed, slowly sift the flour into the bowl, stirring the batter all the time. Lastly, add the cream and whisk.

3 Pour the batter over the fruit.

4 Bake in the oven for 30 minutes or until the batter has set. The fruit will be poking through. If you want, brush the clafoutis with Kirsch when it leaves the oven. Then allow it to rest for 30 minutes before serving still slightly warm.

Easy Apple Strudel

I made this in half an hour, just before going to a supper club called Latitudinal Cuisine, where you bring your own dish. Every week, guests cook dishes from a different latitude or longitude around the globe. The week I went, this included Cameroon, Northern Scandinavia, South Africa and Graz in Austria, amongst other locations. It's a really funny supper club because it doesn't cost any money, and everyone sits in a circle at the beginning and says something about the dish they have made. I chose to do an apple strudel. Real strudel pastry is a skill in itself, rolling pastry so thin that it stretches across a table. Filo pastry is a good cheat. One of my fellow guests was Austrian. He gave this strudel the Austrian seal of approval. The schnapps-soaked raisins are not authentic but add a nice boozy note.

Serves 4–6

750g (1lb 10oz) eating apples, peeled, cored and diced

90g (3oz) caster sugar

1 tbsp ground cinnamon

2 tbsp pine nuts

40g (1½oz) raisins, soaked in schnapps and left for a few hours

Juice of ½ lemon

6 sheets of filo pastry

50g (1¾oz) butter, melted

2 tbsp semolina

Icing sugar, for dusting

1 Preheat the oven to 190°C (375°F), Gas Mark 5. If using an Aga, prepare the roasting oven.

2 Mix the apples, sugar, cinnamon, pine nuts and raisins together. Squeeze the lemon juice over the mixture to prevent the apples discolouring.

3 Lay out a sheet of filo pastry and brush it with melted butter, then take another and lay it alongside, with the longest edge overlapping the corresponding edge of the first sheet by 1cm (½in) or so. Together, the two sheets have become one very large sheet of filo. Brush with more melted butter.

4 Lay another two filo sheets on top, brush with melted butter, then add the final two sheets, so that you have built up a large rectangle with three layers. Sprinkle with semolina, leaving the long edge nearest to you uncovered, then spread the apple mixture evenly all over the filo pastry.

5 Turn up the bare long edge nearest to you, folding it over the filling just a small distance. Then lift the long edge furthest from you and begin to roll it down towards you. Keep rolling until it finally meets the edge that you have already folded up. Use some melted butter to stick these two long edges together. You now have a sort of filo Swiss roll.

6 If your 'sausage' is very long, then bend it round into the traditional crescent shape. Brush it all with melted butter. Bake in the oven for 30 minutes until crisp. Dust with icing sugar and serve immediately with cream.

Chav's White Chocolate Trifle with Malibu

I liked the idea of a white trifle and served it at one of my dinners. I blogged about it and an anonymous commenter (a rival chef, I think) sneered. This made me laugh. I suppose certain puddings could be deemed as 'common', but if it's delicious who cares?

Is cream, sugar and meringue a class issue or is it the Malibu liqueur that really brings it down. If I called it tiramisu, would it be posher or even more déclassé? The only colour here is the vanilla tasting 'fraises des bois' wild strawberries which I happen to have growing in my garden like weeds! But if you want it ALL white, then use pale fruit like white grapes, white currants or banana slices.

The amount of ingredients here depends on the size of your bowl and the shape. I do think trifle should be served in a pretty glass bowl ideally.

INGREDIENTS

Serves 6–8

350ml Bottle of Malibu

15–20 Savoiardi biscuits (Italian sponge fingers)

500g (1lb 2oz) mascarpone

2 eggs

90g (3oz) caster sugar

3–4 white meringues

200g (7oz) wild strawberries, destemmed

20–30g (¾–1oz) good white chocolate, grated, kept refridgerated

1 Pour out some of the Malibu into a shallow bowl. You may need to top it up with Malibu, depending on how much the biscuits soak up. Dip the Savoiardi biscuits into the Malibu and layer the bottom and sides of a pretty glass bowl, breaking them in half if necessary.

2 Beat the mascarpone, eggs and sugar together.

3 Add a layer of the mascarpone mixture onto the Savoiardi biscuits.

4 Crumble a layer of meringue onto the mascarpone

5 Add a layer of the wild strawberries (which are very small).

6 Alternate the Malibu-soaked biscuits, mascarpone, meringue and strawberry, making sure you finish with a layer of mascarpone. Pour in the rest of the Malibu used for soaking the biscuits.

7 Grate the white chocolate on top.

8 Put in fridge for a few hours or even a day until all the flavours have matured.

9 Serve in portions or...this is what I did for the supper club: give a large bowl of trifle to each table, a big spoon and let them help themselves!

Candied Oranges, Lemons & Limes

This recipe is quite simple but rather time-consuming. You also need enough room to dry out all the peel. I don't like shop-bought candied peel, but home-made is very good. You can put the peel into bags for Christmas gifts, decorate desserts with it, use in cakes or serve to eat with coffee.

INGREDIENTS

Makes 200–250g
(7–9oz)

1 orange
1 thick-skinned lemon
1 lime
300g (10½oz) granulated sugar, plus extra for rolling
600ml (1 pint) water

1 Cut off the top and bottom of each fruit. Take the remainder of the fruit and score the skin vertically in quarters. Peel off the skin. Cut into 1cm (½in) wide strips.

2 Put the peel in a saucepan of water and bring to the boil. Boil for 5–10 minutes, then drain in a colander and rinse with cold water. Do this three times, adding fresh water to the saucepan each time. This process removes the bitterness.

3 Then put the sugar and 600ml (1 pint) water back in the saucepan. Bring to the boil and add the peel. Simmer until the peel has absorbed most of the syrup.

4 Line the bottom of a clean grill pan with a rack. Set out a dish of the extra granulated sugar. Use tongs to roll the peel, piece by piece, in the sugar. Then put each piece to dry on the grill rack, leaving them for at least 24 hours and up to 3 days, depending on how dry the atmosphere is. Turn the peel every so often to make sure all sides are drying.

5 Once dry, the candied peel can be kept in jars – I've had mine for 18 months so far.

Cheese
Course

*A*t The Underground Restaurant I generally serve a glorious cheeseboard. There is a debate as to whether one should serve cheese in the style of the French, before dessert, or like the British, after dessert. The advantage of the latter is that you can linger for hours at the end of the meal, carving off a little sliver of cheese from time to time, nibbling on nuts, crackers, a cognac or a port with the coffee. The French thinking on this is that cheese goes with the savouries and you move onto sweet things afterwards.

I'm passionate about cheese, buying from good cheese suppliers such as Neal's Yard, who specialise in British cheeses (now rivalling the French with 1,200 different types) and Mons, who import cheeses from France. I will, when appropriate to the meal, search out Italian or Spanish cheeses, or the kind of cheese that perhaps eighteenth-century seamen might eat (Edam, Epoisses) or even, for my comedy dining night, cheese strings. For the *Midsummer Night's Dream* forest menu, I served cheeses that were wrapped in leaves. You can do this yourself, too. I've used wild garlic leaves, vine leaves, chestnut leaves, walnut leaves, cedar fronds, sycamore leaves, nettles or dock leaves to wrap fresh cheese and have rolled curds in leek ash (made by cooking leeks until they become charcoal, then crumbling the ash), herbs or finely ground nuts. It makes them look posh and expensive as well as adding flavour. Supermarkets such as Waitrose do an excellent cheese range. I find the addition of a cheeseboard makes the occasion feel like a feast rather than an ordinary dinner. The French serve bread with cheese, but I serve a mixture of sourdough bread, oatcakes and crispbreads. I usually serve 3–5 types of cheese, with a few nuts, a chutney, a compote or a quince membrillo.

Rye Crispbread

Here is a recipe for crispbread if you'd like to make your own.

Vegetarian
Makes 12 crispbreads,
each the size of a side plate

———————————

*175ml (6fl oz)
lukewarm water*

*1 x 7g sachet of
fast-action dried yeast*

Pinch of sugar

200g (7oz) rye flour

1 tsp fine sea salt

20g (¾oz) pumpkin seeds

*50g (1¾oz) Emmental or
any hard cheese (such as
Wensleydale or Cheddar)*

1 Put the lukewarm water, yeast and sugar in a jug and leave for 5–10 minutes until frothy.

2 Combine the flour and salt in a large bowl. Pour in the frothy yeast mixture, then add the pumpkin seeds and cheese. Mix well for 10 minutes until the mixture becomes a dough. Leave to rest for 1 hour, covered, in a warm place.

3 Preheat the oven to 180°C (350°F), Gas Mark 4. If using the Aga, prepare the baking oven.

4 Line a baking tray with baking parchment or a silicon mat. Roll out a walnut-sized piece of dough directly onto the paper/silicon sheet, as thinly as you can (to just a couple of millimetres thick). If you like buying kitchen equipment, and I do, I've found a slim chapatti rolling pin is ideal for rolling dough out thinly. Repeat with the rest of the dough and prick the dough pieces all over with a fork so that they look like home-made Ryvita. They will be rough edged, which is fine.

5 Bake in the oven for 15 minutes until crispy. Allow the crispbreads to cool and serve with cheese or butter or as a canapé with nice toppings (for instance, fresh horseradish grated into cream cheese).

Fig Compote

I made this by laying the figs and walnuts in a baking tray, pouring over the wine, drizzling with honey, sprinkling with the star anise powder, then baking them in the Aga for three days. Why three days? Because I forgot about them. But it just made them taste even nicer. However, the conventional method is below. Guests really appreciate little hand-made touches like this, which help to distinguish your home restaurant.

Vegetarian
Makes 1 large jar

500g (1lb 2oz) dried figs
100g (3½oz) shelled walnuts
½ bottle of leftover red wine
1 star anise, finely ground
Drizzle of honey

1 Put your figs in a saucepan with all the other ingredients and simmer over a low heat for 1 hour or so until the mixture starts to thicken. Transfer to a clean jar and seal. The compote will keep for months.

Themed Menus

When I think about it, I've always done themed events: when my daughter was small I'd be the über-mum who did the extraordinary children's parties – for instance, a Hawaiian swimming-pool party for which I spent days and all my income making 'leis' from sweets and flowers, constructing tiny grass skirts for the vegetarian sausages and devising mini non-alcoholic cocktails complete with fruit trimmings for all the tots. Another party was at Easter in a city farm: all the food was egg-shaped or chick-shaped, the decorations were yellow and white, and baby lambs were brought in for the children to feed with bottles. It's a shame I've never been married, not for romantic reasons, although that would have been nice, but for the real thrill of planning the event. I've visualised myself getting married in a flamenco dress, with tapas-style food and an army of slim-hipped smouldering gypsy guitarists carrying me down the aisle. Actually, I think I've channelled Carlos Saura's *Carmen* for the wedding; the only problem is the complete absence of any suitor.

At The Underground Restaurant, in the summer months, when gardens and vegetable boxes are bulging with inspiring produce, I tend to cook using seasonal ingredients. But during winter, not being the kind of swotty cook who is happy to experiment with turnips for months, I'll often theme menus around characters, fictional or real, or colours, or books or films. These have been some of my most popular dinners; they sell out very quickly. It also gives me a chance to 'play' with food, to have a go at making legendary dishes I have only ever heard about, not actually experienced. Devising menus is for me one of the most fun parts of running an underground restaurant.

Here are a few ideas and menus; either copy them or use them as a springboard for your own themes!

Elvis Night

My first record was an Elvis single. Yes, I'm old enough to have bought vinyl, or 'big black CDs', as my teen called them when she was little. I lost my virginity to an Elvis lookalike in the back of my mum's Honda. I was a punk and he was a 'Ted'. At this time, the punks and the Teds were at war on high streets all over Britain. I was one of the first punks to go out with a Ted, we were even in the *News of the World*. This quiffed boyfriend sewed himself into tight drainpipe jeans every night, smelt of Paco Rabanne and hairspray, and under no circumstances was I allowed to touch 'the barnet'.

When Elvis's 75th birthday came up in January 2010, I decided this was the moment to go Deep South. This would, of course, entail a deep-frying spree! I'd never eaten a fried peanut butter, banana and processed cheese sandwich before and the idea gripped me. When developing an Elvis menu, you have to remember that this is a guy who died when his distended and blocked intestine split open inside of him whilst on the toilet. I think the official inquest called it 'strain'. Elvis lived on a diet of fat, sugar, salt and pills. I informed guests that they would have to provide their own prescription medicines. He took quaaludes, Valium, Valmid, Demerol, Amytal, Nembutal, Elavil, Aventyle, Codeine and Sinutab, all of which fatally clogged up his system. I just had to hope that no one would die on the loo during the meal.

Researching the recipes meant that I had to interpret American cooking terms such as broiling (grilling) and scallop, which is to bake food in a casserole dish with sauce, and of course drinks are 'beverages' and measurement are in pounds, cups or sticks. Many American recipes include instant food. For instance, you'll often see this: 'To make a cake, take a packet of Betty Crocker cake mix, then add an egg.'

Elvis's food was Southern 'comfort' food, basics like corn and squash that derive from Native American cuisine and culture. Corn is important to American cuisine: it's used for liquor (Bourbon), syrup (corn syrup), bread, as a vegetable, as a porridge (grits) and was sometimes treated with lime to make it easier to digest. Southern cooking is a shared heritage between both blacks and whites despite their other differences: white Southerners living in other parts of the USA would often go to black restaurants to eat the cooking of their childhood.

Elvis grew up in poverty, but at Graceland he had a cook. Despite possessing a grand dining room, he usually ate in the 'jungle room', which was furnished with Kon Tiki chairs, rabbit-fur throw pillows, fake-fur lampshades and a waterfall. He also frequently dined in bed. We would have been perfect together. Graceland dining meant towels rather than napkins (so that Elvis could wipe down his sweaty brow between courses?), gold-plated glasses, a TV permanently on, and all the food cut up into bite-sized pieces. He preferred his food over-cooked. As David Adler writes in *Eating the Elvis Presley Way*:

Coincidentally, Elvis's favorite word of endorsement was 'burnt'. *'That's burnt, man,'* he would say, which could indicate either a good steak or a good performance.

Adler also points out that many of the Elvis sightings after he died were in 'food related circumstances – grocery stores or fast food restaurants.'

In 1950s America, pre-packaged food was considered modern, more cutting-edge, than traditional, cooked-from-scratch Southern fare. Many recipes came from the back of packets. The Atomic bomb was also influential: radioactive colours, oversized food, ingredients that were processed so as to look plastic. Elvis was called 'The nation's first Atomic-powered singer'. The attitude of the American public towards nuclear bombs was not yet coloured by the environmental activism of the '60s; they were convinced by the authorities that this technology had hastened the end of the Second World War.

At the beginning of my meals, I always try to do a little talk about it, especially if it's a theme. On this occasion it was refreshing to be able announce at the beginning:

'Don't expect to like all your food tonight. In fact, scrap that – don't expect to like any of your food tonight.'

MENU

- BOTTLE OF BUD -

- DEEP-FRIED PEANUT BUTTER AND BANANA SANDWICHES -
- DEEP-FRIED DILL PICKLES -

- GLASS OF MILK OR BUTTERMILK -

- SHUNA'S CORNBREAD -
- CANDIED YAMS -
- CORN-ON-THE-COB -
- CHEESE 'N' GRITS -
- COLLARD GREENS -
- BLACKENED CATFISH -
- TWO TYPES OF FRIES -
- BROKEBACK BAKED BEANS -
- 7UP SALAD -
- KETCHUP (CLASSED AS A VEGETABLE FOR THESE PURPOSES) -
- RELISH (QUITE HEALTHY IN COMPARISON) -

- PECAN PIE -

- COCA COLA AND ROOT BEER -
(IN ORIGINAL GLASS COCA COLA BOTTLES)

uests loved the teensy, deep-fried peanut butter, processed cheese and banana sandwiches. I decided to fry them in tempura batter so that they wouldn't soak up as much oil. A woman wrote to me saying she was on a low-fat diet. I replied, '*You are so coming to the wrong dinner, love.*'

Unbelievably, one table devoured all their 7UP salads and wanted seconds. A guest remarked upon the sweetness of my Brokeback baked beans. I explained that sodas are used as a marinade in Southern cuisine, and that encasing salads in Jello is not only acceptable but desirable.

The catfish looked prehistoric. One guest looked askance as it was served... '*Is this even edible?*'

Dessert was a simple pecan pie. I served this along with Elvis's last meal (according to the contents of his stomach at the inquest) of peaches and chocolate chip cookies.

The cornbread was quite sandy in texture. Left to rest for a few hours and then warmed up again later, it became softer. I served it with butter whipped with maple syrup, something typically Southern.

In my drive towards authenticity, I served glasses of milk and buttermilk: Elvis drank at least four glasses a day. I served two shapes of fries; Elvis liked round fries and regular fries. I laid the tables with authentic glass Heinz ketchup bottles, American mustard and classic glass bottles of coke.

The baked Cheese 'n' grits was quite tasty, flavoured with a large tub of Dairylea. (My teen was thrilled with the shopping I did for this menu, a fridge full of junk food!)

Everything in this meal was historically and medically researched. No random decisions here, people!

The highlight of the evening was the fainting lady who staggered out to the hallway and, clutching her stomach, collapsed. Fortunately it was a friend. Shame she didn't do it on the loo for added authenticity.

ELVIS NIGHT

ELVIS NIGHT

Deep-fried Peanut Butter Sandwiches

INGREDIENTS

Vegetarian
Serves 4

1 batch of tempura batter
(see recipe on page 118), save
any extra for the dill pickles

8 slices of processed white
bread, crusts removed

Jar of peanut butter

4–8 slices of processed cheese,
depending on the size
of your bread

1 banana, thinly sliced

750ml (1 pint 6fl oz) corn oil or
groundnut oil (or, to be really
authentic, use shortening,
such as Crisco or Cookeen),
for deep-frying

Equipment
Deep-fat fryer, or a deep
heavy-based saucepan with
a chip pan

1 Make the batter following the recipe on page 118.

2 Lay out four slices of the bread and spread with peanut butter. Lay the slices of processed cheese on top of the peanut butter, then cover the cheese with thin slices of banana.

3 Close the sandwiches with the other slices of bread and cut each sandwich into quarters.

4 Dip the small quarters into the tempura batter.

5 Put the oil or melt the shortening in a deep-fat fryer and heat to 190ºC (375ºF). If you don't have a deep-fat fryer, you can use a deep, heavy-based saucepan with a chip basket and measure the oil temperature with a thermometer. (See page 83 for more advice about deep-frying.) Deep-fry the sandwiches until golden.

6 Serve with the deep-fried dill pickles.

Deep-fried Dill Pickles

INGREDIENTS

Vegetarian
Serves 4

1 batch of tempura batter
(see page 118), or use leftover
batter from the peanut
butter sandwiches

1 jar of sweet dill cucumbers

750ml (1 pint 6fl oz) corn oil or
groundnut oil (or to be really
authentic, use shortening,
such as Crisco or Cookeen),
for deep-frying

Wing sauce or chilli sauce,
to serve

Equipment
Deep-fat fryer, or a deep
heavy-based saucepan
with a chip pan

Sweet dill pickles are available from most supermarkets. Try the kosher section or have a look in a Polish food store. Mrs Elswood and Meli are brands I like.

1 Make the batter following the recipe on page 118. Dip the dill pickles in the batter.

2 Put the oil or melt the shortening in a deep-fat fryer and heat to 190ºC (375ºF). If you don't have a deep-fat fryer, you can use a deep, heavy-based saucepan with a chip basket and measure the oil temperature with a thermometer. (See page 83 for more advice about deep-frying.) Deep-fry the pickles until golden.

3 Serve with the peanut butter and banana sandwiches and a dish of wing sauce.

Shuna's Cornbread

★ INGREDIENTS ★
Vegetarian
Makes 1 loaf

100g (3½oz) plain flour
175g (6oz) cornmeal
(or finely ground polenta)
1 tsp sea salt
1 tsp baking soda, sifted
50g (1¾oz) brown sugar
175ml (6fl oz) buttermilk
1 egg
45g (1½oz) unsalted butter,
melted, plus extra for greasing

Equipment
450g (1lb) loaf tin or a 20cm
(8in) cast-iron skillet

This recipe is courtesy of my American pastry-chef friend Shuna Fish Lydon. You can make this bread in a loaf tin, but the most authentic way is actually to make it in a black cast-iron skillet. The cornbread is delicious eaten toasted with honey-butter, pan-sautéed with stewed greens, crumbled into soup, or dunked in cold buttermilk.

1 Preheat the oven to 180ºC (350ºF), Gas Mark 4. If using an Aga, prepare the baking oven. Generously grease the loaf tin or skillet.

2 Mix all the dry ingredients in a large bowl and create a well in the centre.

3 In a separate bowl, whisk together the buttermilk and egg. Pour this mixture into the well in the dry ingredients. Mix this with a spatula or wooden spoon until the liquid is incorporated. Then, continuing to mix gently, gradually add the melted butter until the batter is uniform.

4 Pour the cornbread batter into the greased loaf tin or skillet and bake for 30–40 minutes until a skewer or small sharp knife inserted into the middle comes out clean and the sides of the bread have pulled inwards away from the metal. It will probably take a bit longer to cook in a loaf tin than it will in a skillet.

5 When baked, put the tin or skillet on a cooling rack for 5 minutes, then turn the cornbread out and allow to cool completely on the rack before slicing it up. Fabulous with butter whipped with maple syrup.

6 The cornbread will keep for about 4 days in a bread bin or sealed container.

ELVIS WIGHT

Vegetarian
Serves 4

*4 medium-sized
sweet potatoes,
peeled and quartered*
100g (3½oz) unsalted butter
75g (2½oz) dark brown sugar
75ml (2½fl oz) lemonade
Pinch of sea salt

Candied Yams

What they call a yam in the USA is what we know as a sweet potato.

1 Boil the potatoes in a saucepan of water for 15–20 minutes until a fork goes in easily. Drain.

2 Combine the butter, sugar and lemonade in a large frying pan. Heat slowly over a low heat until caramelised, then add the potatoes and turn them until they are nicely covered and have absorbed all the syrup.

3 If you have an Aga, you can also cook the potatoes in a baking tin in the roasting oven until they are caramelised and the syrup has all been absorbed.

4 Season to taste, then serve with other dishes from the Elvis Night menu.

Vegetarian
Serves 4

*4 fresh or frozen
corn-on-the-cob*
75g (2½oz) sugar
Sea salt, to taste
Maple syrup, to drizzle
Pinch of paprika (optional)
Butter, to serve

Corn-on-the-Cob

I do these Caribbean-style: I first boil them in a sugar solution, before roasting them on the barbecue.

1 Bring a saucepan of water to the boil, add the sugar, then add the corn cobs and boil for 15 minutes or until the corn is soft enough to eat. You can test this with a fork.

2 Next, place the cobs on a barbecue, under a grill, or on top of an Aga roasting plate until the edges are nicely blackened.

3 Season with salt, drizzle with maple syrup, sprinkle with paprika, if using, and serve with mounds of butter. Finger-licking good!

INGREDIENTS

Vegetarian
Serves 4

600ml (1 pint) water, salted

150g (5½oz) grits

90g (3oz) margarine (though I can't bring myself to be that trashy, so I use butter)

1 x 200g tub of Dairylea cheese (or any soft processed cheese)

2 eggs, lightly beaten

50ml (1¾fl oz) evaporated milk

Freshly ground white pepper

Cheese 'n' Grits

You could say grits are like Southern porridge, a staple in that region of the USA. White corn grits are more natural, more flavoursome, and authentically Native American, whereas yellow ones are more common. In the UK I can find only instant grits in mini packets, but you can find out a lot more and order grits online from Anson Mills (www.ansonmills.com). You could also try using polenta.

1 Preheat the oven to 200°C (400°F), Gas Mark 6. If using an Aga, prepare the roasting oven.

2 Put the salted water in a heavy-based saucepan and boil your grits over a low heat, stirring until thickened. With instant grits this took me 5 minutes, but for different types check the packet instructions.

3 When thickened, add the margarine (or butter) and the processed cheese. Mix the lightly beaten eggs in a bowl with the evaporated milk and fold the egg mixture into the grits.

4 Pour the grits into an ovenproof dish and bake in the oven for 15 minutes or until golden. Season with lots and lots of white pepper, to give the dish a really contrasting taste.

INGREDIENTS

Vegetarian
Serves 4

1 x 500g packet of spring greens

Hot pepper sauce, to serve

Collard Greens

In the UK we call these spring greens. As a modern, urban vegetarian, my instinct is to just steam them lightly. But for Southern cooking you'd boil them into submission, in almost traditional English style, just how my nan cooked. Meat-eaters could boil them with some bacon fat ('fatback').

1 Take the spring greens and separate the leaves. Rinse each leaf individually under cold running water. Layer several leaves on top of each other and roll them together. This is to speed up the chopping process. Slice the roll into thin strips using a large knife on a cutting board.

2 Steam lightly in a saucepan of water until tender, then serve with hot pepper sauce.

4 catfish steaks or
2 whole catfish, gutted

25g (1oz) butter, melted

4 tbsp blackened seasoning
(Old Bay, or follow
recipe below)

Corn oil or groundnut oil,
for cooking (if using steaks)

Blackened Seasoning

2 tsp sea salt

1½ tsp cayenne pepper

1 tsp each of celery seeds,
paprika, sugar, onion powder,
garlic powder and freshly
ground black pepper

½ tsp thyme

½ tsp oregano

Blackened Catfish

I must admit that the catfish is an odd-looking creature: half reptile, half fish, it looks like a baby alligator. It is an ocean-bottom feeder, so some people think it tastes like mud. To get hold of them in London can be rather difficult, though I finally found whole catfish at an Asian supermarket, as they are often used in Vietnamese cooking. However, this recipe works better with catfish steaks than whole fish. Catfish steak is a typically Southern ingredient in the USA, where they often 'blacken' fish and prawns. The whole idea of blackening and barbecuing is very Southern and very Elvis: whether it was about food or a new song, 'That's burnt' would be a typical Elvis compliment. Blackened seasoning is a complex spice mix; you can buy it from shops that sell American foods or you can grind your own!

1 Mix together all the ingredients for the blackened seasoning in a food processor or pestle and mortar and grind finely.

2 If using whole catfish, slash them down each side and preheat the oven to 220ºC (425ºF), Gas Mark 7. If using an Aga, prepare the roasting oven. (If using steaks, you can pan-fry them.)

3 Brush the whole catfish or the steaks with melted butter, then rub the Blackened Seasoning all over them, pushing it into the slashes of the whole fish. The whole fish should be put in an ovenproof dish and roasted for 30 minutes in the oven, while the catfish steaks should be fried in a little oil in a cast-iron frying pan. Cook over a medium heat for 3–10 minutes, until the flesh is opaque but not dry. You may need to cut into the steak slightly with a sharp knife to see the colour of the fish underneath the blackened surface.

4 Serve with cheese 'n' grits, candied yams, collard greens, ketchup, hot sauce and cold Coca Cola!

Two Types of Fries

Serves 4

4 medium potatoes, peeled and cut into your two desired shapes

750ml (1 pint 6fl oz) vegetable or groundnut oil (or to be really authentic, use shortening, such as Crisco or Cookeen), for deep-frying

Equipment

Deep-fat fryer, or a deep heavy-based saucepan with a chip pan

1 Deep-fry the different-shaped potatoes in the fryer or heavy-based saucepan at 145°C (290°F) until translucent. (See page 83 for more advice about deep-frying.)

2 Remove from the oil, lay the chips on kitchen paper and sprinkle lightly with salt.

3 Leave for 15 minutes, then re-fry at 190°C (375°F) until golden. Serve.

Vegetarian
Serves 4–6

Vegetable or groundnut oil (or, to be really authentic, use shortening, such as Crisco or Cookeen), for cooking

1 onion, peeled and chopped

2 x 400g tins of haricot beans

2 tbsp brown sugar

175g (6oz) molasses

50ml (1¾fl oz) cider vinegar, plus extra to taste

175g (6oz) ketchup

2 tbsp mustard (ideally American burger mustard, such as Frenches)

Splash of chipotle sauce (store-bought or see page 91), optional

Sea salt and freshly ground black pepper

Brokeback Baked Beans

1 Heat some oil or shortening in a saucepan over a low–medium heat and fry the onion until soft and translucent. Add the beans and cook for 5–10 minutes until warmed through. Then add the sugar, molasses, vinegar, ketchup and mustard and mix together. Simmer for 1 hour.

2 Halfway through the cooking, remove some of the beans to a bowl, crush them up with a pestle or fork, then put them back in the pan.

3 Taste the beans from time to time and add chilli sauce, if using, and salt and pepper to taste. Serve with other recipes from the Elvis menu.

INGREDIENTS

Vegetarian
if jelly contains
vegetarian gelatine
Serves 4

750ml (1 pint 6fl oz) 7UP

1 x 135g box of lime jelly cubes

1 x 135g box of lemon jelly cubes

1 x 250g tub of cottage cheese

1 x 330ml can of pineapple crush

7UP Salad

Heat the 7UP in a bowl in the microwave or pour into a saucepan and heat gently over a low flame. Break both flavours of jelly into pieces and drop into the hot 7UP. Allow the jelly to melt, then remove from the heat, pour into a bowl and allow to cool.

When cool, mix the cottage cheese and pineapple crush into the 7UP jelly. Put in the fridge and allow to set for 2–4 hours.

Serve the 7UP salad family-style in a glass bowl in the middle of the table, so that your guests can share it and also appreciate its aesthetic beauty!

INGREDIENTS

Vegetarian
Serves 8-10

Pastry

175g (6oz) plain flour, plus
extra for dusting

½ tsp salt

½ tsp sugar

90g (3oz) unsalted butter,
chilled and cut into small
pieces, plus extra for greasing

40 –75ml (1½–2½ fl oz)
ice-cold water

Filling

3 eggs

150ml (5½ fl oz) pure maple
syrup

75g (2½ oz) light brown sugar

30g (1oz) butter, melted

1 tsp vanilla extract

175g (6oz) pecan halves

Maple Whipped Cream

300ml (10½ fl oz)
whipping cream

250ml (9fl oz) pure
maple syrup

Equipment

Food processor

25cm (10in) pie dish
or flan tin

Pecan Pie

1 In the bowl of a food processor, combine the flour, salt and sugar. Add the butter and process until the mixture resembles coarse meal or breadcrumbs. With the machine running, add the ice-cold water in a slow, steady stream. Pulse until the dough holds together without being wet or sticky. To test, squeeze a small amount together with your fingers: if it is crumbly, add more water, just 1 tablespoon at a time. Bring the dough together into a ball, flatten into a disc and wrap in cling film. Put in the fridge to chill for at least 1 hour.

2 When the dough is well chilled, preheat the oven to 180°C (350°F), Gas Mark 4. If using an Aga, prepare the baking oven with a shelf in the lowest position. Grease the pie dish and dust with flour.

3 Roll out the pastry into a 30–33cm (12–13in) circle, starting from the centre and giving it a quarter-turn after each roll. Press the dough into the buttered, floured pie dish. Crimp the edges of the pastry using your fingers and trim the pastry edges .

4 To blind bake the base, prick the bottom of the pastry several times with a fork. Cover with a circle of foil and pour baking beans into it. Bake in the oven for 10 minutes, then remove from the oven and remove the beans and foil. Leave the oven turned on.

5 Meanwhile, beat the eggs for the filling in a large bowl. Add the maple syrup, brown sugar, melted butter and vanilla. Pour into the prepared pie base and lay the pecan halves in a concentric pattern, flat-side down, around the pie, like a mosaic. Bake in the oven for 35–40 minutes, or until golden brown and the filling is set. Place on a wire rack to cool.

6 Whisk together the cream and the remaining maple syrup and serve with slices of the cooled pecan pie.

Menu

Black Russian cocktail

Black olive tapenade
Black cod's roe on black bread

Black sesame salmon balls with an avocado oil
and black vinegar dipping sauce

Nori handrolls stuffed with black rice, black kale,
black carrot and aubergine

Beluga lentils with goat's cheese

Squid-ink tortelloni stuffed with goat's cheese and lemon
zest with a death trumpet mushroom cream sauce
Black Himalayan salt and black pepper

Ash-covered cheese with charcoal biscuits
(see page 243)

Marmite chocolate cupcakes

Espresso with dark chocolates
Black Russian Cocktail

Midnight Feast: The Black Album

I went for a drink with a guy I met on Twitter. He was the night manager for a hotel where celebrities often stayed. He'd see them in their most vulnerable state: drunk or ill; he'd see who they took up to their room, what they ordered from room service. Sometimes he had to undress major stars (no names) and put them to bed.

He told me the worst thing about London is the lack of late-night places to eat. Maybe I should try a late-night event? So this meal began at midnight, which led to me making all the food black. Black food is very healthy, containing minerals, isoflavones and antioxidants. It was fun searching out all the black ingredients such as black carrots (£5 a kilo from Fortnum & Masons!). Carrots were originally purple or cream; legend has it that the Dutch bred them to honour William of Orange.

To fill the Nori handrolls (see page 268), I used Black Imperial rice, which, in Ancient China, only emperors had the right to eat. The hardest thing was making fresh squid-ink tortellini for 30 people. My arm ached from cranking that pasta machine, spewing out tongues of pasta like inner tyres.

I added details like black salt (available from WholeFoods) and made a playlist of songs with the word 'black' in the title (the Rolling Stones' 'Paint It Black', for instance. Unfortunately many of these songs are heavy metal.)

The meal began at midnight; guests arrived wearing pyjamas, nightdresses and hair rollers, some clutching teddy bears. At the end of the night we found one guest asleep at the table.

Black Russian Cocktail

INGREDIENTS

Serves 1

135ml (5fl oz)/
3 shots of vodka

90ml (3fl oz)/
2 shots of Kahlua

1 black cherry, to garnish

Crushed ice

Put some crushed ice in a martini glass. Pour the vodka over the ice, then add the Kahlua. Garnish with a black cherry and serve.

Black Olive Tapenade

INGREDIENTS

**Vegetarian
if anchovies are omitted
Serves 4
(Makes 200g/7oz)**

125g (4½oz) black olives
(black for the Midnight
menu but you can use green
olives for other, less dark,
occasions), pitted

1 clove of garlic, peeled

3 anchovy fillets in oil
(if vegetarian, you can
replace this with pine
nuts or walnuts)

1 tbsp capers

1 tbsp olive oil

1 lemon, half juiced,
the other half sliced and
cut into segments

Black bread (such as rye
bread or German bread),
to serve

Equipment
Food processor

This is a classic Provençale aperitif. Use good-quality olives such as Kalamata or Niçoise, nothing tinned or cheapo.

Put the pitted olives, garlic clove, anchovies, capers, oil and the juice of half the lemon together in a food processor and pulse until they become a thick paste.

To serve, thinly slice the black bread and spread with the tapenade. Put a tiny section (a segment slice) of lemon on the top of each.

Any remaining tapenade can be kept in a sealed jar in the fridge for a couple of weeks.

Black Cod's Roe on Black Bread

INGREDIENTS

Serves 4

Loaf of black bread (such as rye bread or German bread), thinly sliced

Good-quality butter

1 x 100g jar of black cod's roe or herring roe, or if your budget stretches, caviar

1 lemon, thinly sliced and cut into segments

A very quick, simple and impressive black canapé. Use rye bread or German bread, or try Polish food stores for similar types.

Spread the black bread slices with the butter, then spread the roe or caviar lightly on top. Cut each slice into small rectangles. Place a small segment of lemon in the middle of each rectangle and serve.

Black Sesame Salmon Balls with an Avocado Oil and Black Vinegar Dipping Sauce

INGREDIENTS

Serves 4

600g (1lb 5oz) sashimi grade salmon fillet, without skin, cut into 2cm (¾in) cubes

30g (1oz) water chestnuts

1 large egg white

2 tbsp cornflour

1 tsp wasabi powder

4 small spring onions, white and light green parts only, thinly sliced

2½ tsp finely grated root ginger

Sea salt and freshly ground pepper

100g (3½oz) black sesame seeds

Dipping Sauce

Black Chinese vinegar

Soy sauce

Avocado oil (or groundnut oil if you prefer)

Equipment

Food processor

Avocado oil has a lovely subtle taste, but can be costly, so if you want an alternative, try using groundnut oil (not olive oil, as it's too strong and will overpower the salmon). If you can't find black Chinese vinegar, you can use rice wine vinegar instead, although it won't make the sauce as dark, so stick to black vinegar if you want a fully midnight menu.

Spread out the salmon cubes on a plate and put in the freezer for 15 minutes. Then transfer to a food processor and add the water chestnuts, egg white, cornflour, wasabi powder, three-quarters of the sliced spring onion, 1½ teaspoons of the ginger, 2 teaspoons of sea salt and a pinch of pepper. Pulse 4–5 times, until the salmon is chopped and the mixture just comes together. Transfer to a bowl.

Spread the black sesame seeds on a plate. Scoop the salmon mixture into 24 mounds of 1–2 tablespoons each and roll into balls. Roll the balls in the seeds. Place the balls in a large steamer or in a colander sat over a saucepan of boiling water. Steam the salmon balls batch by batch until firm – about 6 minutes.

Meanwhile, in a bowl, combine the vinegar, soy sauce and avocado oil with the remaining spring onions and ginger. Serve the salmon balls with the dipping sauce.

INGREDIENTS

**Vegetarian
Serves 4**

---

*100g (3½oz) short-grain
black imperial rice*

1 tbsp white sugar

1 tsp sea salt

*1 tbsp unseasoned
rice vinegar*

*4 sheets of nori
(seaweed), cut in half*

4 tsp wasabi paste

*1 small aubergine,
thinly sliced, salted and
drained, then grilled*

*8 small kale leaves,
stemmed and blanched*

*3 black carrots,
peeled and sliced
lengthways into fine strips*

*4 spring onions,
halved lengthways*

*1 x 50g packet of pickled
ginger (optional)*

Dipping Sauce

Soy sauce

Sesame oil

2 tbsp rice vinegar

Nori Handrolls

Stuffed with Black Rice, Black Kale, Black Carrot and Aubergine

I managed to find black carrots in Fortnum & Mason. Be warned, they weren't cheap! I'm sure some ethnic stores will sell them too. If you want to try a different dipping sauce for the handrolls, you can use Ponzu. It's a rather expensive but very addictive citrussy soy sauce. A home-made alternative is regular soy sauce with some lemon juice squeezed in.

Cook the rice according to the packet instructions, until tender. Transfer to a wide bowl and fluff with a fork.

In a small saucepan, heat the sugar and salt with a couple of tablespoons of water until the sugar has dissolved. Stir in 1 tablespoon of the rice vinegar. Sprinkle the mixture over the warm rice and stir well. Allow the rice to cool.

Lay a piece of nori on a work surface. Spread a couple of tablespoons of the rice over half of it and spread ½ teaspoon of wasabi paste over the rice. Top with a slice of grilled aubergine, a blanched kale leaf, a couple of slivers of black carrot and half a spring onion. I also add a little pickled ginger. Fold the uncovered part of the nori over to form a cone or roll. Set on a platter and repeat with the remaining nori sheets and fillings to make 8 rolls. This can be done 2–3 hours in advance, if you wish.

To prepare the dipping sauce, stir together the soy sauce and sesame oil with the rice vinegar. Alternatively, use Ponzu. Serve the rolls with the dipping sauce.

Vegetarian
Serves 4

Olive oil, for cooking

1 onion, peeled and very finely chopped

1 celery stick, very finely chopped

1 chunk of fennel, very finely chopped

150g (5½oz) beluga lentils (Puy lentils will do instead. Any others won't)

Freshly ground black pepper

About 300ml (10½fl oz) hot vegetable stock (from a cube is fine, or see page 137)

3–4 fresh bay leaves

Sea salt, to taste

Handful of chopped flat-leaf parsley

2 small round goat's cheeses, cut in half horizontally and lightly grilled, or 1 x 200g packet of feta cheese, cubed

Drizzle of balsamic glaze

Beluga Lentils
with Goat's Cheese

I got this recipe from the astrologer Neil Spencer and we used it for the astrology-themed meal that I did once, based on the positions of the planets at the time of the meal. This dish is black, which is the colour astrologers associate with Pluto, and the goat's cheese in the recipe signifies Capricorn, the sign represented by a goat. I repeated this dish for the midnight feast: the black lentils are unusual, savoury and hearty.

Heat the olive oil in a saucepan over a low–medium heat and cook the onion, celery and fennel until soft and translucent, to create a good base for the lentils. Add the lentils and stir. It's important that they fry a little and absorb some of the oil. Season with pepper.

Pour in the hot vegetable stock, roughly twice as much liquid as lentils, though you can fine-tune this as you go. Stir until the bubbling calms down to a simmer.

Add three or four bay leaves, more than you would expect. Season with salt, though not too much because the stock is usually quite salty. Cover the saucepan and simmer the lentils on a very low heat for 20–25 minutes. Taste the lentils to check if they are done – they should be firm, but still soft. Crunchy doesn't do it. If necessary, add a little more hot water and cook for longer.

To finish, stir in a handful of well-chopped parsley. Top with the grilled goat's cheese or cubes of feta and drizzle with balsamic glaze.

Squid-ink Tortelloni

Stuffed with Goat's Cheese & Lemon Zest with a Death Trumpet Mushroom Cream Sauce

1 portion of fresh pasta (see pages 178–9, but add squid ink as per method below)

1–2 sachets squid ink (ask your fishmonger)

300g (10½oz) fresh goat's cheese

Zest of 1 lemon

1 egg white, lightly whisked

Semolina, to scatter

300ml (10½fl oz) fresh single cream

50g (1¾oz) trompettes de la mort mushrooms (small, black, trumpet-shaped chanterelles) or dried porcini mushrooms

On the day of my midnight-feast dinner, my friend Alyssia and I had to make 300 of these (to feed 30 people). At the end we felt like we never wanted to look at pasta again. Our arms ached, our focus was blurred, we became irritable and snappy. We suddenly understood why fresh hand-made pasta is so expensive. But for four people you should be ok, it's not too tortuous. Squid ink is available from most fishmongers, sold in sachets. Unopened, it will keep in the fridge for some weeks.

Make the pasta according to the recipe on pages 178–9, adding the squid ink to the dough at the same time as mixing in the beaten eggs. Follow the rest of the pasta recipe, running the dough through the machine as directed and finally cutting the strip into 5cm (2in) squares.

Mix together the goat's cheese and lemon zest. Put 1 teaspoon of the cheese and lemon mixture into one corner of a pasta square (not too close to the edges). Fold the pasta over on the diagonal to enclose the filling inside a triangle, sealing the edges with a brush dipped in egg white.

Lift the two base corners of your triangle and bring them together in the middle, overlapping slightly. Press them gently to seal, then tuck the top corner down towards them, so the pasta looks a like a little bishop's hat. Put on a baking tray and sprinkle a little semolina over the top. Repeat with the remaining pasta squares and filling. At this point, the pasta can be frozen if you want, though it is best to use it as soon as possible.

For the mushroom sauce, heat the cream gently in a saucepan over a low heat. Do not allow to boil. Put the trompettes de la mort mushrooms in the cream to soak and warm through while you cook the pasta.

To cook the tortelloni, plunge into boiling, salted water for about 7–10 minutes until cooked – they should float when done. Drain and serve immediately with the mushroom cream.

Vegetarian
Makes 12

60ml (2fl oz) fresh filter coffee (or if you want to go hardcore, 60ml (2fl oz) hot water with Marmite added to taste)

40g (1½oz) cocoa powder

60ml (2fl oz) cold water

60g (2oz) unsalted butter, at room temperature

140g (5oz) caster sugar

1 egg, beaten

125g (4½oz) plain flour

½ tsp baking powder

½ tsp bicarbonate of soda

Pinch of sea salt

Whipped Marmite Ganache
180ml (6½fl oz) double cream
Marmite, to taste

Frosting
70g (2½oz) cream cheese
250g (9oz) icing sugar
40g (1½oz) unsalted butter
Handful of edible glitter, to decorate (optional, should be available from specialist cake stores)

Equipment
Food processor (optional)
Muffin tin and
12 muffin cases

Marmite Chocolate Cupcakes

First make the ganache. Whip up the double cream until thick and whisk in as much Marmite as you dare. Set aside until needed.

Make some fresh filter coffee. You probably need a little break after all your hard work whipping cream, and you will also need it for your cupcake sponge. Or, for true believers (fanatics, dare I say...), make a hot Marmite drink. Put 60ml (2fl oz) of the coffee or Marmite drink into a bowl and devour the rest. Whisk the cocoa powder into the bowl of coffee or Marmite drink. When smooth, add the cold water and set aside.

To make the cake batter, put the butter and sugar together in a large bowl or food processor and beat together or pulse for at least 10 minutes (if using a food processor, do this on a high speed). Keep pausing to scrape down the sides. Add the egg slowly, very slowly, to make sure the mixture doesn't curdle.

In a separate bowl, sift together the flour, baking powder, bicarbonate of soda and salt.

Fold a third of this mixture into the cake batter, then fold in a third of the cocoa/coffee/Marmite liquid. Then fold in another third of the flour mixture, followed by another third of the cocoa mixture. Finally, fold in the remaining flour, then the remaining cocoa liquid. It's important to do it like this, a third at a time, otherwise the cake batter will become too stiff and won't take the liquid.

Preheat the oven to 160°C (325°F), Gas Mark 3. If using an Aga, prepare the baking oven – I found the cakes rose better without the cool shelf. Line a muffin tin with strong muffin cases. (You need 'em sturdy so that the cakes have a strong, sharp edge that you can later frost 'against'.)

Divide the cake batter between the cases, doing this equally by setting the muffin tin on a digital scale and checking that you are adding 45g (1½oz) each time. Bake the cakes in the oven for 20–22 minutes, until they are risen and spring back when touched. (In the Aga mine needed just 20 minutes.) Remove the cakes from the tin, being careful not to loosen the paper cases, and put on a cooling rack.

When cool, take a small knife and cut out a cone-shaped wedge from the centre of each cake to leave a hole. Set aside a small amount of the Marmite ganache and use the rest to fill the holes in the cakes. Replace the cones of sponge so that they sit on the ganache like little hats.

To make the frosting, mix the cream cheese with a third of the icing sugar in a food processor, pulsing until all lumps have gone, but being careful not to overbeat at this or any other point. With the food processor on a very low speed, add the remaining icing sugar and mix until just combined – the mixture will be quite dry and crumbly at this point. Give the sides of the bowl a scrape down.

Meanwhile, melt the butter in a saucepan or the microwave. With the food processor running, pour the melted butter onto the cream cheese mixture and beat slowly until the frosting is smooth. Mix in the reserved Marmite chocolate ganache. Be careful not to add too much, or the frosting won't be stiff enough to ice your cakes.

Use a palette knife to frost the chocolate cupcakes with the Marmite chocolate frosting. If you want, you can sprinkle a little edible glitter on top – I used gold.

Flower Menu

Wild flowers have been used in cooking for centuries, but a new generation of chefs has rediscovered them. Restaurants like Noma in Copenhagen are pioneering the use of unusual fruits, nuts, berries, herbs and flowers. Of course, Noma goes further, refusing to use any produce that cannot be grown in Northern climes, thus avoiding olive oil and basil. I'm afraid my Italian heritage is too strong for that, but I've always loved the idea of plundering the garden and the hedgerow for ingredients. My own garden has pears, elderflowers, fraises des bois (wild strawberries) and mint, alongside edible flowers such as geraniums, violets, roses and borage.

I've done two flower-based menus at The Underground Restaurant: the first coincided with the Chelsea Flower Show, but with an Indian influence; the second was based on Shakespeare's *A Midsummer Night's Dream*, all Arthur Rackham drawings, fairy-gauze wings and sweet herbs. To heighten the floral atmosphere, set vases containing posies on the tables and spray your tablecloths and napkins with rose and lavender water when ironing them.

Menu

Cava with sweet yellow rocket flowers
Elderflower champagne and ginger beer

Elderflower fritters
Courgette flowers stuffed with goat's cheese
Marigold bread

Asparagus mimosa

Vine leaf-wrapped fish

Mint and white chocolate ice cream served in a flower
ice bowl and sprinkled with crystallised rose petals

Leaf-wrapped cheeses and fig compote
(see pages 243–5)

Mint tea with pine nuts

Cava with Sweet Yellow Rocket Flowers or Hibiscus Flowers

INGREDIENTS

Serves 1

About 15ml (1/2fl oz)
elderberry syrup

125ml (41/2fl oz) Cava
or champagne, chilled

Handful of sweet
yellow rocket flowers
or Hibiscus flowers
in syrup

Rocket flowers have a lovely vanilla taste. If you can't get hold of these, you can easily buy hibiscus flowers in syrup from the supermarket – as shown in the pictures.

Put the elderberry syrup in the bottom of a champagne flute, then pour in your chilled fizz of choice. Add the rocket flowers or hibiscus flowers to the glass.

8 large courgette flowers,
with or without courgettes
attached (but make sure any
courgette parts are very small,
or they take ages to fry)

100g (3½oz) soft
goat's cheese

750ml (1 pint 6fl oz)
vegetable oil, for deep-frying

Flaked sea salt

Batter

1 egg, beaten

200g (7oz) plain flour, sifted

20g (¾oz) cornflour

30g (1oz) Pecorino or
Parmesan cheese,
freshly grated

180ml (6½fl oz) soda
or sparkling water, chilled

Sea salt, to taste

Equipment

Deep-fat fryer, or a deep
heavy-based saucepan with
a chip pan

Courgette Flowers
Stuffed with Goat's Cheese

The first time I had courgette flowers was in Los Angeles, where we ate them served with squid-ink pasta. The dish was so pretty and I couldn't believe I was eating flowers! The problem is that they are very expensive when you buy them at posh supermarkets, so either grow your own, or ask around your local allotments or a local fruit and veg stall.

The flowers on the end of baby courgettes are 'girls'. There is an almost gynaecological pleasure in teasing open the petals of the flower and inserting little goodies into it. It's lesbian cookery! The 'boy' flowers are larger and grow directly on the plant stem; these are the ones used in Italian cookery. Both types are good stuffed with cheese and fried in a batter mixed with Pecorino, though the 'boy' flowers, without the courgettes, are quicker and more straightforward to cook.

1 Mix all the batter ingredients together in a bowl and add salt to taste. Whisk the batter a little, but not too much or it will get tough.

2 Stuff the flowers not long before frying, or they will go soggy. Fill each flower with the goat's cheese and twist the ends of the petals together to prevent the cheese leaking out.

3 Heat the oil in a deep-fat fryer, or deep, heavy-based saucepan to 190°C (375°F). (For more advice on deep-frying, see page 83). Dip the flowers into the batter and deep-fry until golden. Drain on kitchen paper, then scatter with some flaked sea salt and serve immediately.

Elderflower Champagne

Makes 4 litres (7 pints)

3.5 litres (6 pints) boiling water, plus 500ml (18fl oz) cold water

1kg (2lb 3oz) sugar (any type)

20 elderflower heads (pick the ones with the strongest scent)

1 tbsp white wine vinegar

Zest (grated) and juice of 4 unwaxed lemons

Pinch of fast-action dried yeast

Equipment

Large, clean bucket or saucepan

Clean tea towel (or lid) to cover the container

Sterilised bottles (see intro, above)

Strainer or fine sieve

Funnel

Elder trees grow like weeds in London and the flowers are in bloom everywhere during June and July. So why not use them to make delicate elderflower 'champagne'? Use either plastic bottles that once contained fizzy drinks or, for something prettier, order swing-top glass bottles online (such as www.jamjarshop.com). But do not put into sealed glass bottles! Swing tops will automatically lift off if the champagne is fermenting too fast, but other glass bottles may break. I filled approximately 16 x 250ml (9fl oz) bottles, and served one between every two guests. You could also make pretty labels for them.

1 Pour the boiling water into your bucket or saucepan, add the sugar and wait until it has dissolved. Once dissolved, add the cold water and mix in the elderflower heads, vinegar and lemon zest and juice. Stir well and leave the mixture to cool.

2 Once cooled, add the yeast and cover the whole thing with a tea towel or lid. Put the container in a cool place to ferment for 2–4 days. When the champagne tastes fizzy, it is done. (In hot weather I find mine is ready in just 2–3 days. In fact, I keep it in the fridge to slow down the fermentation. In cooler weather it will take a little longer.)

3 Sterilise the bottles by cleaning them in hot soapy water. Rinse and set aside.

4 Strain the champagne into a fresh container, then pour it through a funnel into the sterilised bottles. Leave a 5cm (2in) gap at the top to allow for the build-up of gases. Do keep an eye out if using plastic bottles, in case they start to bulge. If so, loosen the caps to let the gas escape.

5 The champagne is best served cold. It apparently lasts for up to 1 year, but I generally drink it all pretty quickly!

Ginger Beer

*Whole root of ginger,
peeled and finely chopped*

1 unwaxed lemon, sliced

*250g (9oz) golden
caster sugar*

½ tsp cream of tartar

*2.5 litres (4½ pints)
cold water*

*½ tbsp fast-action
dried yeast*

Equipment

Large, clean saucepan

Clean tea towel
(or lid) to cover saucepan

Sterilised bottles
(see page 279)

Strainer or fine sieve

Funnel

I love ginger beer. It's great for a hangover, and generally good for your health. This recipe is quite spicy, Jamaican-style! I include a whole root of fresh ginger because I like my ginger beer peppery!

1 Put the ginger, lemon slices, sugar, cream of tartar and half a litre (18fl oz) of the water into a large saucepan over a medium heat. Bring to the boil, stirring to dissolve the sugar. Simmer for 5 minutes then remove from the heat.

2 Add the rest of the cold water and sprinkle over the yeast. Cover with a tea towel or lid and set aside in a cool place overnight.

3 Sterilise the bottles by cleaning them in hot soapy water. Rinse and set aside.

4 Strain the ginger beer into another container and then, using a funnel, divide between the bottles. Leave a gap at the top for the gas. Check every so often to make sure the gases aren't building up too much; if so, loosen the caps to let it escape.

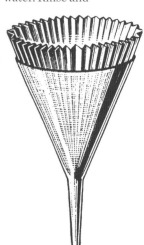

5 It will take 2–3 days for the ginger beer to become fizzy. In hot weather it might be slightly quicker, in cooler weather it will take longer.

6 Drink the ginger beer within 10 days.

Elderflower Fritters

8–12 elderflower heads, main stalk removed

750ml (1 pint 6fl oz) vegetable, groundnut or rapeseed oil, for deep-frying

Flaked sea salt

Batter

1 egg, beaten

200g (7oz) plain flour, sifted

20g (¾oz) cornflour

180ml (6½fl oz) soda or sparkling water, chilled

Sea salt, to taste

Equipment

Deep-fat fryer, or a deep heavy-based saucepan with a chip pan

Elderflowers are white, lacy flowers that are in bloom in June and July. Pick them in the morning (later in the day they smell a bit like cat's piss). They can be made into cordial, champagne or simply fried in batter. A lovely, delicate, unusual starter.

1 Mix all the batter ingredients together in a bowl and add salt to taste. Whisk the batter a little, but not too much or it will get tough.

2 Heat the oil in a deep-fat fryer, or deep, heavy-based saucepan to 190°C (375°F). (For more advice on deep-frying, see page 83.) Dip the elderflowers lightly in the batter, then deep-fry until golden. Sprinkle with flakes of sea salt and serve immediately.

Vegetarian
Makes 15–20 rolls

2 x 7g sachets of fast-action dried yeast

320ml (11fl oz) lukewarm water

1 tsp honey

500g (1lb 2oz) strong white flour (I use organic), plus extra for dusting

20g (¾oz) semolina

10g (⅓oz) sea salt

50ml (1¾fl oz) olive oil

70g (2½oz) sunflower seeds

Handful of marigold petals

Olive oil, for brushing

Handful of sesame seeds

Marigold Bread

These rolls are turned inside out to turn them into a flower shape. I also include seeds and marigold petals in the dough.

1 To make the dough, mix together the yeast, water and honey in a bowl. Leave for 10 minutes until frothing.

2 Mix the flour, semolina and salt together in another bowl, then add the oil, sunflower seeds and marigold petals. Pour in the frothy yeast mixture, mix to a dough and knead in the bowl for at least 10 minutes. (For more advice on kneading bread, see page 102.) When well-kneaded, cover the bowl and leave to rise for 1 hour or so in a warm place.

3 Tip the dough carefully onto a floured work surface and gently divide it into balls of 40g (1½oz) in weight, using a digital scale to measure this. Slightly flatten each ball with the palm of your hand.

4 Use a pair of scissors to snip the balls of dough in a criss-cross fashion across the top. Turn the balls upside-down so the cuts are underneath and pull each section out to form a rough petal. Once finished, each ball should look like a little flower. (Alternatively, leave as round rolls.)

5 Put the dough flowers, spaced apart, on an oiled baking tray, Brush with olive oil and sprinkle with sesame seeds. Cover and leave for 20 minutes in a warm place. Preheat the oven to 220°C (425°F), Gas Mark 7. If using an Aga, prepare the roasting oven.

6 Bake the marigold bread in the oven for 8–10 minutes or until lightly golden. The rolls are nice served warm or can be frozen until needed.

1 x 250g punnet of the sweetest baby plum or cherry tomatoes you can find

Handful of nasturtium leaves

Handful of marigold petals, pulled from the centre of the flowers

Dressing
1 tbsp raspberry vinegar
4 tbsp groundnut oil
1 tsp smoked salt

Nasturtium Leaf Salad

with Marigold petals & plum tomatoes

This salad was part of my Chelsea flower show menu, where I introduced my guests to edible flowers as an accompaniment to Indian food (see pages 170–1). The bright, eye-popping yellow of marigold petals, combined with the red of plum tomatoes and green of nasturtium leaves, edged with orange, reflected the deep exotic colours of Asia. It's an unusual salad and will stun your guests.

Cut the tomatoes in half and place in a large serving bowl. Scatter the nasturtium leaves and marigold petals around the tomatoes. Whisk together the ingredients for the dressing and adjust the seasoning to taste. Chill the salad and the dressing in the fridge, then drizzle the dressing over the salad just before serving.

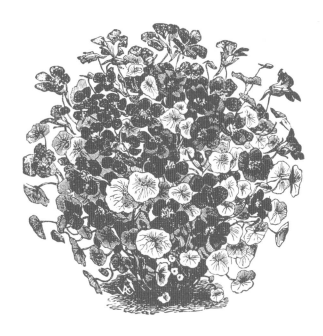

Vegetarian
Serves 4

500g (1lb 2oz) asparagus,
woody ends trimmed off
and discarded

4 eggs

125g (4½oz) garlic butter
(store-bought, or for
home-made see page 107)

Salted butter, for cooking

Half a dozen flowers
(eg violas) or handful of
chives or chive flowers,
to garnish

Sea salt and freshly ground
white pepper

Asparagus Mimosa

This is a great dish to have around Easter, when asparagus is in season in Britain. It's light, fragrant and sets up a nice appetite for the mains. A Mimosa is a yellow flower, but is also a term used to describe sieved egg, as in this recipe. This recipe is garnished with flowers – I use violas, as the purple makes a lovely colour contrast with the green of the asparagus and the yellow of the egg. But you can use chives instead, if you wish.

1 Put your asparagus in a deep frying pan and pour boiling water from the kettle over them to cover. Lightly steam over a low heat for just 5 minutes. Drain.

2 Hard-boil the eggs in a saucepan of boiling water for about 8 minutes. Remove from the water and allow the eggs to cool enough to handle, then peel them. While they're still warm, push the eggs through a sieve into a bowl so that they have a fine crumbly texture. Mix the garlic butter into the warm egg mixture.

3 Just before serving, pan-fry your asparagus very gently in the salted butter, over a low heat and just enough to melt the butter and warm the spears.

4 Lay out the cooked asparagus on a plate and sprinkle the egg mixture over it. Garnish with the flowers or chives. Serve warm.

Mint & White Chocolate Ice Cream

250ml (9fl oz) whole milk

150g (5½oz) white caster sugar

Pinch of sea salt

600ml (1 pint) double cream

2–3 large handfuls of mint leaves

5 egg yolks

100g (3½oz) good-quality white chocolate, melted (see page 224)

Equipment

Ice-cream maker

This ice cream has a subtle pastel colour and a clean, unusual flavour. When you think of mint ice cream, you probably think of the classic mint/choc chip. Using fresh mint transforms it. A revelation, even.

1 Warm the milk, sugar, salt and half of the cream in a saucepan over a low heat, until the sugar has dissolved. Take the pan off the heat and add the mint leaves, leaving them to steep for at least 1 hour.

2 Put the egg yolks in a large bowl. Pour the milk mixture through a sieve into another saucepan, straining out the mint leaves and discarding them. Add the rest of the cream to the mixture and heat slowly on a low heat, then pour this newly warmed mixture into the bowl of egg yolks. (It's important to do it this way, rather than putting the yolks straight in the pan, or they might scramble.)

3 Return the mixture, now including the egg yolks, to the saucepan, whisking all the time. Warm gently again for about 10 minutes until it starts to become like a custard (coating the back of a wooden spoon), then strain into a bowl. Leave to cool.

4 To make ice cream, I use a Kitchen Aid ice-cream attachment. I find that if I chill my mixture too much, the paddles keep getting stuck. So I let it cool down but I don't refrigerate it. Once cool, pour the mixture into your ice-cream maker and leave to churn for at least 30 minutes. You will see the mixture start to thicken.

5 Take a small jug of melted white chocolate and pour it into the churning mixture, trying not to get it on the paddles. The chocolate should form little iced flakes within the ice cream. Once churned, pour the ice cream into a plastic container and freeze.

6 To serve, decorate the ice cream with crystallised flowers (see page 292). It's beautiful presented in a flower ice bowl (see overleaf).

Flower Ice Bowl

This is a beautiful way to present ice cream. You will need 2 glass bowls (don't use ceramic, I ruined two good mixing bowls when they split in the freezer), one of which fits into the other, leaving a gap of about 2–3cm (1–1¼in) all round. Collect some flowers; I use pink and white geraniums and roses, and some herb sprigs with distinctive leaves, like rosemary. I put the roses at the bottom of the larger glass bowl, with some ice cubes to separate the flowers from each other and also to create a large enough gap at the bottom so that the resulting ice bowl will be strong. I then arrange the rest of the flowers and herbs artfully up the sides of the larger glass bowl. To keep the flowers in position, I brush some egg white onto the flower before sticking it down.

I then place the second, slighter smaller, bowl into the large one with the flowers, weighing it down if necessary. I fill the space left between the two bowls three-quarters full with boiled and cooled mineral water. (This process is to remove calcium from the water for a clear, glasslike look.)

Place the bowls carefully in the freezer. In fact, I'd pour in the water next to the freezer so that you don't have far to go and risk spilling it. After a few hours, top up the water around the rim, adding more flowers if necessary. Continue to freeze.

Remove the bowls from the freezer and turn them, both together, upside down in the sink. Run some hot water over the base, and they will come apart easily, releasing the ice flower bowl from the space between them. Don't let the hot water run for too long, just enough to loosen, or your whole ice bowl will melt!

To use ice bowls at the table, you will need a large shallow bowl sat underneath to catch the water as it melts. The bowls last at least a couple of hours, depending on the temperature of the room.

How to Crystallise Herbs & Flowers

This is so simple, but the flowers add a thrill and finish to your dishes out of all proportion to the effort spent on doing it! I often crystallise thyme sprigs and rose petals. For rose petals, snip off the white heel of the flower, as that part is quite bitter. Dip the petal or sprig in egg white, then dip it lightly in fine caster sugar. Leave to dry for a few hours on a silicone mat or sheet of baking parchment.

INGREDIENTS

Serves 1

Handful of fresh mint leaves
Hot water
Sugar, to taste
Sprinkling of pine nuts

Mint Tea with Pine Nuts

I used to drink this when I lived in Paris, near Belleville, which is a fairly poor Arabic area. In the boulevard cafés of that area, one could hang out all day with a tall glass of sweet mint tea. They would often sprinkle a few pine nuts on top.

Put the mint leaves in a pot or glass. Cover with hot water and allow to steep. Add sugar to taste and sprinkle with pine nuts.

Directory

J've put in a few guiding comments when I've visited or have knowledge of the supper clubs.

This is obviously an ever-changing list; people move, things change, stuff happens, especially in such an ephemeral and clandestine area! It is as accurate as possible before publication.

For an up-to-date directory, do check my supper club group:

supperclubfangroup.ning.com

UNITED KINGDOM & EUROPE

BASINGSTOKE

Mr H goes Gorilla
facebook.com/people/Paul-Henry/100001718412381

BOGNOR REGIS

Hery's Supper Club
facebook.com/group.php?gid=154278026201

BRIGHTON

Loco Dining
locodining.com

Love Poppy
lovepoppy.blogspot.com

Open House Dining
prettyclever.co.uk/open-house-dining

The Bay Supper Club
thebaysupperclub.blogspot.com

BRISTOL

Secret Service Supper Club
facebook.com/TheSecretServiceSupperClub

Bishopston Supper Club
restingchef.wordpress.com/about

The Montpelier Basement
supperclubfangroup.ning.com/profile/
TheMontpelierBasement

CAMBRIDGESHIRE

The Outlawed Epicurean
facebook.com/group.php?gid=134857601316

The Secluded Tea Party
thesecludedteapartyshhh.blogspot.com

CANTERBURY

Kao's Underground Restaurant
supperclubfangroup.ning.com/profile/
kaosundergroundrestaurant?xg_source=activity

CHELTENHAM

Chocolate Poppy Supper Club
supperclubfangroup.ning.com/profile/Ann?xg_
source=activity

DORSET

Yee Tak Hampton
supperclubfangroup.ning.com/profile/Yee
TakHampton
Asian specialities.

KENT

Hari Covert
haricovertundergroundrestaurant.wordpress.com
Gastronome and chef cooking from home.

BROMLEY

Annie's Supper Club
supperclubfangroup.ning.com/profile/
AnniesSupperClub
Gluten-free.

LONDON

Chefs London
facebook.com/chefslondon

Floating Diners
floatingdiners.co.uk

Pistachio & Pickle
pistachioandpickle.com/supperclub

Potentino
potentino.blogspot.com

VARIOUS LOCATIONS

Latitudinal Cuisine – Alex Haw
facebook.com/group.php?v=wall&gid=
103347851342
Pot-luck dinners all over London, creative, arty guests.

ALL OVER

Pips Dinners
pipsdish.co.uk

E2

Comida Divertida
eatmynels.blogspot.com/2010/06/
comida-divertida-2.html
*Charlie has done a stage at The Fat Duck
but cooks hearty peasant cuisine, ranging
from Mexican to pizza.*

BARNET

Pash Friend
facebook.com/PashandFriend?v=app_2344061033#
Suburban dining, sometimes in the garden.

BLACKHEATH VILLAGE

Friday Food Club
fridayfoodclub.com
Often have famous guest chefs.

BLACKHEATH

Savoy Truffle Club
savoytrufflesupperclub.com
*Professional restaurant style food in
nice flat, but far from transport links.*

BRIXTON

Crumbs and Dirty Dishes
crumbsanddirtydishes.blogspot.com

The Saltoun Supper Club
eatwithyoureyes.net
Excellent food in an artistic flat.

The Last Supper Club
facebook.com/pages/The-Last-
Supper-Club/126835904272?ref=mf
This cook is gluten-free friendly.

Salad Club
saladclub.wordpress.com
*Homely suppers from their allotment,
pretty waitresses.*

BROCKLEY

Eat Meet Supper Club
eatmeetsupperclub.blogspot.com

CAMDEN

The Rambling Restaurant
facebook.com/ramblingrestaurant
Food Rambler roams with fresh home cooked food.

Francesca's Secret Kitchen
francescassecretkitchen.wordpress.com

CLAPTON
Sugarloaf Supper Club
sugarloafsupperclub.com

CRICKLEWOOD
Mama Lan Supper Club
mamalan.co.uk/index.php
Chinese home cooking.

CROYDON
The Decadent Tea Party
undergroundteaparty.blogspot.com

DALSTON
Number 68 Project
number68.com
Molecular cuisine, good company.

Parkholme Road Supper Club
parkholmesupperclub.co.uk

The Pale Blue Door
tonyhornecker.wordpress.com

Shacklewell Nights
shacklewellnights.com

The Loft Project
theloftproject.co.uk/about
*Cutting edge gastronomy, the latest
in food trends, at a price.*

EAST LONDON
The Curious Kitchen
thecuriouskitchenlondontown.blogspot.com

Tete à Tea
facebook.com/group.php?gid=112544302106117

FINSBURY PARK
Clandestino's
clandestinos.co.uk/index.html
Brazilian cooking from a friendly couple.

FULHAM
Cucina Cinzia Supper Club
cucinacinzia.com
Authentic Italian food in London.

Love a Locavore
facebook.com/group.php?gid=85605693559

GREENWICH
The Meridian Supper Club
meetup.com/meridiansupperclub

HACKNEY
Fernandez & Leluu
fernandezandleluu.co.uk
Spanish/Vietnamese couple. Great pho.

The Bruncheon Club
thebruncheonclub.blogspot.com
Brunches, with great Bloody Mary's.

The Claptonian Arts Club
theclaptonianartsclub.blogspot.com
Brunches.

Snackney Downs
facebook.com/people/Snackney-Downs/
100001465442135

HARINGEY
The N15 Tea Party
then15teaparty.blogspot.com

HENDON NW4
Superb Suppers
superbsuppers.blogspot.com

HIGHBURY
Single Suppers
singlesuppers.webs.com

HOLLAND PARK
Nomad Chef
supperclubfangroup.ning.com/profile/NomadChef
SecretRestaurant?xg_source=profiles_memberList

HOLLOWAY
The Secret Larder Supper Club
facebook.com/group.php?gid=301190367870
*Beautifully decorated flat with hearty student
food from food blogger James Ramsden.*

ISLINGTON
Eat Me
supperclubfangroup.ning.com/profile/
AlexandraAntonioni

Lex Eat
lexeat.co.uk/2009/12/lex-cook-you-eat.html

The Old Hat
oldhatclub.com
Beautiful space and Sunday roast lunch.

KILBURN
**MsMarmiteLover's
The Underground Restaurant**
marmitelover.blogspot.com

KINGSTON UPON THAMES
Jay Kay's Supper Club
jaykays-supperclub.com
Very popular supper club.

LEWISHAM
Stocks and Hares Supper Club
supperclubfangroup.ning.com/profiles/profile/
show?id=stocksandhares&xg_source=activity

LONDON FIELDS
Ben Greeno
bengreeno.wordpress.com
*Noma-trained chef and forager,
fine dining at a reasonable price.*

MUSWELL HILL
The Sunday Pie Making Club
ooh.com/uk/food-drink/cooking/london/london/
sunday-pie-making-club-3_2812.html

NEWINGTON GREEN
The Secret Ingredient
facebook.com/pages/City-of-London-United-
Kingdom/The-Secret-Ingredient/114200085161
*Musician Horton Jupiter's take on Japanese
cuisine in an East-End council flat.*

The Shed
theshedlikesfood.blogspot.com
Hearty food, no profit meals in a wooden shed. Lovely.

The Civet Cat Club
thecivetcatclub.wordpress.com
Nice house, nice art, good food.

NOTTING HILL
Stolen
stolen.it
*Interesting menus deliberately
ripped off or a homage to top chefs.*

The Sunday Lunch Club
supperclubfangroup.ning.com/profile/Whirlybird

OLD STREET
The Hidden Tea Room
hiddentearoom.com
Superlative baking from American cook.

OSTERLY
Chakula's Secret Dining Club
facebook.com/pages/Chakulas-Secret-
Dining-Club/372135957711

PUTNEY
The First Bite Is
thefirstbiteis.blogspot.com

SHEEN
Sheen Suppers
sheensuppers.wordpress.com
*Tasty home cooked food by a lady with
a pink kitchen. Even her knives are pink!*

SHEPHERDS BUSH
Le Secret Supper Club
supperclubfangroup.ning.com/profile/MiaWallace

SHOREDITCH
Bootleg Banquet
bootlegbanquet.com
*Professional chefs turn their catering unit
into a supper club in the evening.*

Full House
ilovefullhouse.com
Workshops and conceptual meals.

Greek Food Lover's Supper Club
facebook.com/GreekCookery

White Room Supper Club
whiteroomsupperclub.blogspot.com

SOUTH KENSINGTON
David Clasen's First Weekend
firstweekend.co.uk

STOKE NEWINGTON

Stokey Secret Supper

facebook.com/Stokey.Secret.Supper?v=wall

TOOTING

Broadway Lofts Supper Club

facebook.com/pages/London-United-Kingdom/Broadway-Lofts-Supper-Club/113955838635705?v=wall

TOWER BRIDGE

Good Stock

supperclubfangroup.ning.com/profile/GoodStock?xg_source=activity

TUFNELL PARK

Joginder's Supper Club

jogindersupperclub.wordpress.com
Home-cooked food by an Indian mum.

WIMBLEDON

Frangipani Supper Club

supperclubfangroup.ning.com/profile/StephanieBiden

MANCHESTER

The Spice Club

spicediary.com/thespiceclub

NORFOLK

NORWICH

The Unthank Supper Club

unthanksupperclub.blogspot.com
Varied menus, open once a month.

NORTH EAST

The Next Big Event

thenextbigevent.net/#/welcome/4536312519

NOTTINGHAMSHIRE

Clarkies Supper Club

supperclubfangroup.ning.com/profile/LibbyClark

OXFORDSHIRE

The Secret Supper Society

thesecretsuppersociety.co.uk

POOLE

Tansy's Kitchen

tansyskitchen.blogspot.com/2010/11/pop-up-south-american-restaurant.html

READING

Friday Dinner Secrets

facebook.com/pages/Reading-United-Kingdom/Friday-Dinner-Secrets/110398075687528

WARWICKSHIRE

Secret Squisito Supper Club
squisito-deli.co.uk/default.aspx

YORKSHIRE

DONCASTER

The Gourmet Kitchen
the-gourmet-kitchen.co.uk

HUDDERSFIELD

Cafe Nouveau
supperclubfangroup.ning.com/profile/
CafeNouveauatHome?xg_source=activity

LEEDS

The Secret Tea Room
bakelady.wordpress.com

SCOTLAND

EDINBURGH

Charlie & Evelyn's Table
charlieandevelynstable.blogspot.com

Queen of Tarts
facebook.com/QueenofTartsEdinburgh

WALES

BANGOR

Moelfaban Supper Club
moelfabansecretsupperclub.wordpress.com
Welsh family farmhouse using great Welsh produce.

CARDIFF AND BRIDGEND

Calonygegin
calonygegin.co.uk

IRELAND

BELFAST

Plot 15 Supper Club
plot15supperclub.com

AUSTRIA

VIENNA

The Dining Room
theflyingapple.typepad.com/thediningroom/
2008/01/welcome-to-thed.html

DENMARK

COPENHAGEN

Silver Spoon
silverspooncph.ning.com
A group for guerilla diners, not a supper club.

FRANCE

COTE D' AZUR

Radish Supper Club

redradishsupperclub.blogspot.com

PARIS

Jim Haynes Every Sunday

jim-haynes.com

Been going for 30 years. Not a sit-down dinner, more of a buffet.

The Hidden Kitchen

hkmenus.com

Fine cuisine from American chefs.

Rachel Khoo

rachelkhoo.com

Food creative who also does events in London and in Australia.

Aux Chiens Lunatiques

chienlunatique.monsite-orange.fr

So far, the French scene seems to be restricted to Anglo chefs. This has to change! Allons, les français!

GERMANY

BERLIN

Fisk & Gröönsaken

groonsaken.wordpress.com

The supper club scene is certainly taking off in Germany after my forlorn visit back in November 2009, when proper restaurants were calling themselves supper clubs.

Metti Una Sera a Cena Supper Club

mettiunaseraacena.wordpress.com

The Shy Chef

theshychef.wordpress.com

Travels with my Fork

twmfsupperclub.moonfruit.com

Loteria Supper Club

loteriasupperclub.blogspot.com/p/about-loteria-supper-club.html

Zagreus

zagreus.net/programm.php

Thyme Supper Club

thyme-supperclub.com/about-thyme-supperclub

GREECE

ATHENS

The Secret Supper

thesecretsupper.wordpress.com

HOLLAND

tafelvantwaalf.nl/01-pagsHKR/02-Allerestaurants. html

Site with list of huiskamer (living room) restaurants. It's in Dutch, which isn't easy, but I'm sure the hosts speak English.

ITALY

FLORENCE

Cucina Cinzia Supper Club
cucinacinzia.com/supperclub

BOLOGNA & ELSEWHERE

homefood.it

Home Food Italy: 'Cesarine' Italian housewives host dinners in their homes, authentic home cooking. Book with association, paperwork slightly arduous, which is also very Italian.

POLAND

WARSAW

Leniwe Raz
leniweraz.wordpress.com

Uczta Babette
ucztababette.blog.com

SPAIN

BARCELONA

Tintoria Dontell
tintoreriadontell.com

GRANADA

Jardin de la Alpujarra
supperclubfangroup.ning.com/profile/
JardindelaAlpujarra?xg_source=activity

PORTUGAL

LISBON

Hush-hush Garden
hush-hushgarden.blogspot.com

INDONESIA

JAKARTA

Azanaya
azanaya.com/#/up-date-news/4536841104

YOGYAKARTA

Sawah
thesawah.com

SINGAPORE

Khana Commune
khanacommune.wordpress.com

NORTH AMERICA – US

GEORGIA

ATLANTA
Rogue Apron
rogueapron.com/events

CALIFORNIA

LOS ANGELES
Orgasmo de la Boca
orgasmodelaboca.wordpress.com

Sent by Joe Supper Club
facebook.com/group.php?gid=95483117154

Taste of Pace Supper Club
tasteofpace.blogspot.com

OAKLAND
Canvas Underground
canvasunderground.wordpress.com/about

Ghetto Gourmet
theghet.com

Paladar Temescal
paladartemescal.blogspot.com

SAN FRANCISCO
Forage SF
foragesf.com/blog

Graff Eats
graffeats.com

Shaw's Supper Club
shawssupperclubsf.com

Spice Supper Club
spicesupperclubsf.wordpress.com

Sub Culture Dining
thescdsf.com

Radio Africa and Kitchen
radioafricakitchen.com/about.html

SANTA CRUZ
Outstanding in the Field
outstandinginthefield.com

CHICAGO
Clandestino
clandestinodining.org

X-marx
xmarxchicago.com

Yo Soy
yosoy.squarespace.com

COLORADO

DENVER
Noble Swine Supper Club
nobleswinesupperclub.wordpress.com

Hush Denver
hushdenver.com

FLORIDA

MIAMI
Cobaya Gourmet Guinea Pigs
cobayamiami.blogspot.com

MICHIGAN

ANN ARBOR
Bona Sera Supper Club
bonaserasupperclub.com

MISSOURI

ST LOUIS
The Clandestine Chef
entreunderground.com

MONTANA

Hush Bozeman
hushbozeman.com/index.html

NEW YORK

WOODSTOCK
Woodstock's Hidden Kitchen
woodstockhiddenkitchen.com/index.html

NEW YORK CITY
Chinatown Cake Club
chinatowncakeclub.com

Reel Tasty Brooklyn
forkingtasty.com/category/events

Brooklyn Edible Social Club
bkediblesocial.blogspot.com

Thursdays at Worth Street
thursdaysatworthstreet.blogspot.com

Guerilla Culinary Brigade
thepopuprestaurant.com

Four Course Vegan
4coursevegan.com

The Highlands Dinner Club
highlandsdinnerclub.tumblr.com

Studio Feast
studiofeast.com

City Grit
sarahmcsimmons.com/city-grit

Forking Tasty
forkingtasty.com

Tchoup Shop
theghet.com/profile/TchoupShop

The Sunday Night Dinner at the Astoria
oneasskitchen.blogspot.com

Supper Funk
theghet.com/events/supper-funk

Whisk & Ladle
thewhiskandladle.com

NORTH CAROLINA

GREENSBORO
The Next Supper
thenextsupper.com

OREGON

PORTLAND
Plate & Pitchfork
plateandpitchfork.com

SOUTH CAROLINA

CHARLESTON
Guerrilla Cuisine
guerrillacuisine.com

L.I.M.E.
limeincharleston.com

TENNESSEE

The Poetry Reading
poetryreading.info

Voodoo Kitchen
sites.google.com/site/vkhospitality/restaurants/
the-voodoo-kitchen-supperclub/bacon-dinner---
june-17th

TEXAS

AUSTIN
Dai Due
daidueaustin.net/supper-club

Supper Underground
supperunderground.com

DALLAS
Lightbulb Oven
lightbulboven.com/lightbulboven.com/about_
me.html

WASHINGTON

The Wandering Table
thewanderingtable.com

SPOKANE
Ghetto Gourmand
ghetto-gourmand.com/index.html

WASHINGTON D.C.
Hush Supper Club
hushsupperclub.net

CANADA

TORONTO
Hidden Lounge
hiddenlounge.ca/index.html

VANCOUVER
Vegan Secret Supper
vegansecretsupper.com/main.html

Swallow Tail Supper Club
swallowtailsupperclub.blogspot.com

SOUTH AMERICA

ARGENTINA

BUENOS AIRES
Casa SaltShaker Dan Perlman
casasaltshaker.com

Cocina Sunae
cocinasunae.blogspot.com

Casa Felix Diego Felix
diegofelix.com/nuestras_cenas.html

La Cocina Discreta
lacocinadiscreta.com/blog

Comer con Amigos
comerconamigos.blogspot.com

Mis Raices
restaurantmisraices.com.ar/index.htm

Noches Grimod
nochesgrimod.blogspot.com

Tipo Casa
tipo-casa.com.ar

Trentesillas
treintasillas.com

Xochitl
xochitl-resto.blogspot.com

MENDOZA

Los Chocos
loschocosweb.blogspot.com

CHILE

SANTIAGO

Oty's Family Dinners
chile-travel.com/family-dinners/index.html

PERU

AYACUCHO

Hilda Maurina Mamani Caceres
kiva.org/lend/22137

AUSTRALIA

ZingaraCucina
zingaracucina.com

SYDNEY

Bite Club
biteclubsydney.blogspot.com

Secret Supper Society
secretsuppersociety.org

Table for 20
tablefor20.blogspot.com

Table Nosh
tablenosh.blogspot.com

MELBOURNE

Global Gobbler
globalgobbler.blogspot.com

NEW ZEALAND

AUCKLAND

Plum Kitchen Supper Club
plum-kitchen.blogspot.com

WELLINGTON

The French House
thefrenchhousenz.blogspot.com

ASIA

CHINA

HONG KONG

Chowchung Restaurant
Flat B, on Fifth Floor, Kin Tye Lung Building,
27-29 Bonham Strand West, Sheung Wan,
(852) 2805-1116, fax (852) 2805-1117

Mum Chau's Sichuan Kitchen

5B, Winner Building, 37 D'Aguilar Street, LanKwai
Fong, Central, (852) 8108-8550.
Hours: noon to 2 p.m. and 6 to 11 p.m.
Lunch is $10, and dinner is $46 for two,
with a minimum of four people required.

AFRICA

SOUTH AFRICA

PRETORIA

Red Tomato Bistro @ Home
facebook.com/group.php?gid=132459610773

GENERAL SITES TO CHECK OUT ON UNDERGROUND DINING

Ghetto Gourmet
theghet.com

Underground Dining Scene
saltshaker.net/underground-dining-scene

Bibliography

Dona Flor and Her Two Husbands

by Jorge Amado

Avon

Magical realism from Brazil with recipes and voodoo.

Dough

by Richard Bertinet

Kyle Cathie

A brilliant book on bread making, get it.

Eating the Elvis Presley Way

by David Adler

Blake Publishing

Amusing and informative book on how Elvis Presley ate.

Fit for a King, The Elvis Presley Cookbook

by Elizabeth McKeon, Ralph Gevirtz and Julie Bandy

Rutledge Hill Press

Ham on Rye

by Charles Bukowski

Rebel Inc.

Great writing and not much about sandwiches.

Heartburn

by Nora Ephron

Virago

Fiction combined with recipes and humour.

Lobscouse and Spotted Dog

by Anne Grossman and Lisa Grossman Thomas

W.W. Norton & Co

These ladies are huge fans of Patrick O'Brian, who wrote Master and Commander. *They've researched and developed recipes for all of the 18th-century recipes that were used in the shipboard meals.*

Serendip
by Peter Kuruvita

Murdoch

Beautiful photographs and intriguing and tasty recipes from a Sri Lankan but Australian-based chef.

Sauces
by Michel Roux

Quadrille

Clearly illustrated and written explanation of how to make all the classic sauces.

The Invention of the Restaurant
by Rebecca L Spang

Harvard University Press

This book is fascinating although rather academic on the history of the restaurant.

The Little House Cookbook
by Barbara M. Walker

HarperCollins Publishers

One of my favourite cookbooks, full of Little House on the Prairie pioneer homesteaders cooking.

The Mish-Mash Dictionary of Marmite, an Anecdotal A-Z of 'Tar-in-a-Jar'
by Maggie Hall

Revel Barker

I'm in this book under 'Underground'. Great loo book.

Wild fermentation
by Sandor Ellix Katz

Chelsea Green publishing co

This guy is a pioneer in the United States for DIY underground food movements. He lives in a 'fairy' commune.

Index

Acknowledgements

I have so many people to thank not just for this book but for the help I've received with The Underground Restaurant.

My gratitude to volunteers who've helped out at The Underground Restaurant: above all, Alissia Durbridge for her enthusiasm and optimism and Lenny Gibbons for her unflustered professionalism, as well as EvaDestruction and Jessicakaka.

My sister Imogen, Angie Ma, Audrey Khoo, Catherine Phipps, Olly Farsi, Signe Johansen, Emma Reynolds, Taka, Michelle Eskeri, Charlie Nelson, Hattie Mauleverer, Ali Stanger-Leathes, Claire Roberson, Yinka Openeye, Craig Clark, Anna and Tony, Adam Pinder, Alex Watts, Helen Lewis, Claire Everett, Food Urchin, Joanna Tubbs, Sarah Drinkwater, Aida Wilson, Carla Spuri, Bethan Hughes, Nicola Swift, Maggie Spicer, Kitchen Jezebel, Hollow Legs, Beth Everard, Mary Bowman and sons, Olivia, Martine, Saskia and Ali, Bethea Jenner (psychic in the shed), James Benson of Cotswold Food Year, Petra Barran, Mat Follas, Patrick Carpenter, Jane Milton, Blanch & Shock, Rachel McCormack, Helen Yuet Ling Pang, Susan Foynes, John Kerr, Jo Kehagias, Margherita Burns, Sandrine, Seb Thomas, Roberto Cortez, Brooke Procida, Hardeep Singh Kholi, Shuna Fish Lydon, Wakana and Hiro from Akashi Tai, Marcus Berkmann, Michelle Newell, Calum Walker, Les Wong (Bellaphon), Clare Wrixon, Phoebe and Lorna for their breastmilk, Eleanor Seabird, Tinderflint, Neil Rankin, Keiko Yamamoto, Atiha Sen Gupta, Ariana Mouyiaris, Eva Wong, Zoe Wilson and everybody else that helped make it a success!

I am also grateful to my volunteer recipe testers: Gary Hills, Joy Pitts, Karen Hench, Florian Rodgers, Aunty Marianne, Barbara Hill, Irene Bell and Beggs.

I'd also like to thank Paul Jardine from Riverford Organics, am Bompas of Bompas & Parr and Simon and Sam of Ten Green Bottles, Curd Nerd, Neal's Yard and John Thrupp and Suzanne of Mons.

Thanks to the Underground Farmers' Market helpers for their help, including Scarlett Cannon, Maria Grist, Ali of Bristol Vintage, Brie O'Keefe, Joanna Anastasiou-Milne of The Deli Station and Hiromi Stone: much gratitude for helping with these mammoth events.

Thanks to Lynn Hill for her help with the ning supperclub site.

I'd like to thank my neighbours for their tolerance.

I'd like to thank Jenny Heller for believing in me and Laura James of Aga for introducing me to her.

Thanks to Camilla Goslett and Melissa Pimentel for holding my hand.

With regards to this book I'd like to give thanks to Helen Hawksfield, Ione Walder, the designer Lucinda Lowe and Lee Motley for the cover. Thanks also to Jason Lowe, Louisa Carter and team for the wonderful pictures.

Of course, I must thank my mum and dad, who gave me a great and varied food education.

And most of all I must thank my gorgeous daughter Sienna Poppy Carmela Rodgers, also known as The Teen: without you putting up with having strangers in the living room every week, nothing would be possible. You've also become a brilliant assistant in every way! I love you so much.

First published in 2011 by Collins

HarperCollins Publishers
77-85 Fulham Palace Road
London W6 8JB

www.harpercollins.co.uk

13 12 11
9 8 7 6 5 4 3 2 1

Publishing Director: Jenny Heller
Senior Project Editor: Helen Hawksfield
Designer: Lucinda Lowe
Food Stylist: Louisa Carter
Prop Stylist: Liz Hippisley

ISBN: 978-0-00-738299-6

Printed and bound in China by South China Printing.

Picture Credits
Photographs © Jason Lowe with the exception of p. 46, 52, 65, 76, 77, 160, 199, 236,
260, 279 ©Kerstin Rodgers; p.76 © Elisabeth Blanchet; p.77 © Gavin Rodgers.
Illustrations; p4, 33, 309 © Margaret Rodgers.